E-RETAILERS' EXPANSION TO SOCIAL MEDIA PLATFORMS:

ROLE OF BUSINESS MODEL ALIGNMENT

By Erik Ernesto Vázquez Hernández

Abstract

Expansion to social media platforms is common in business-to-consumer markets, but e-retailers expanding to social media platforms experience market success with substantial heterogeneity. Successful expansions bring questions about the best way to align parameters of business models of e-retailers and social media platforms. Transactional content alignment between e-retailers and social media platforms determines e-retailers' market success in terms of perceived quality, online purchase intent, and intention to recommend online. Using concepts of the search-experience-credence classification of goods, tie strength, social presence, and information richness, this study proposes a theoretical framework. It is tested with primary data obtained from online experiments with e-retail shoppers in the United States. The results show the role of transactional content alignment between search goods and tie strength, experience goods and social presence, and credence goods and information richness. Greater market success for e-retailer with search goods (e.g. computer-electronics and appliances) using a social media platform with weak ties (e.g. Twitter) than using a social media platform with strong ties (e.g. Facebook). Similar market success for e-retailer with experience goods (e.g. apparel and accessories) using a social media platform with high social presence (e.g. Facebook) or using a social media platform with low social presence (e.g. Twitter). Greater market success for e-retailer with credence goods (e.g. nutritional supplements) using a social media platform with high information richness (e.g. YouTube) than using a social media platform with low information richness (e.g. Twitter). Additional findings arise from a complementary analysis of narratives provided by participants. Implications include extending the applicability of an existing business model parameter known as transaction content and communication theories with a guide to align e-businesses of retail and media to improve returns on channel expansions.

Keywords: E-Business, Channel Strategy, Online Experiments, E-Commerce, Consumer Behaviour, Transaction Content, Amazon Mechanical Turk, Marketing and Advertising Communications

To my beloved mother who takes care of me from heaven. My father, my sister, and my brother that always support me and encourage me to do my best.

"Have patience with all things, But, first of all with yourself" Francis de Sales

Acknowledgments

Dr Chirag Patel and Dr Joanna Berry were always providing support and inspiration to work in this research. I thank them for sharing with me their valuable time and their research talent. I also want to thank the administration team: Dr Dimitris Assimakopoulos, Dr Robert Willison, Dr Mark Smith, Dr Dimo Dimov, Stella Lishman, and Susanne Laidler who helped me to cope with all paperwork and regulatory standards.

All feedback and support from Dr Reto Felix, Dr Carlos Basurto, Dr Ghassan Kahwati, Dr Arnaud Chevallier, Dr José Vallejo, Dr Pablo Collazzo, Dr Ulrike Gretzel, Dr Oliver Trendel, Dr Valerie Sabatier, Dr Klaus Schoefer, Dr Miguel Ángel Montoya, Dr Andrew Parker, Dr Diogo Hidebrand, Dr Savvas Papagiannidis, and Dr Asensio Carrion who helped me during this research journey.

It would be impossible to write down the names of all the people that gave me their support, to all of them: THANK YOU!

I am grateful to the organisations that provided financial support: the Mexican National Council of Science and Technology (i.e. CONACYT), University of Monterrey (i.e. UDEM), the Institute of Technology Innovation and Transference (i.e. I2T2), and the support of the French Government Institutions for students. Finally, I am also thankful for other organisations that helped me to learn: Coursera.org, World Economic Forum, American Marketing Association, Harvard Business Publishing, IMC University of Applied Sciences Krems, and Caterpillar Inc.

Table of contents

Abstract i

Acknowledgments iii

Table of contents v

    Figures vii

    Tables vii

Chapter 1 Introduction 1

    1.1 Background 1

    1.2 Problem 4

    1.3 Justification 5

Chapter 2 Literature review 9

    2.1 Foundations of communication theories 9

    2.2 Theoretical perspectives underpinning the business model and strategy concepts 29

    2.3 Overview of e-retailers' expansion to social media platforms 49

    2.4 Marketing and advertising objectives of e-retailers' expansion 52

Chapter 3 Conceptual framework 59

    3.1 Definitions 59

        3.1.1 E-retailer and typology 59

        3.1.2 Social media platform and typology 60

        3.1.3 Business model and transaction content 63

    3.2 The Stimulus-Organism-Response paradigm 67

    3.3 Alignment of e-retailer and social media platform 70

        3.3.1 H1: Alignment of search goods and tie strength 71

        3.3.2 H2: Alignment of experience goods and social presence 72

        3.3.3 H3: Alignment of credence goods and information richness 73

Chapter 4 Methodology 75

    4.1 Research design 75

    4.1.1 Selection of empirical context 75

    4.1.2 Measures 77

    4.1.3 Pilot study 82

4.2 Research procedure 87

    4.2.1 Data collection 87

    4.2.2 Sample 90

    4.2.3 Data analysis 91

Chapter 5 Results 93

5.1 Hypothesis testing 93

    5.1.1 H1: Alignment of search goods and tie strength 97

    5.1.2 H2: Alignment of experience goods and social presence 98

    5.1.3 H3: Alignment of credence goods and information richness 99

5.2 Complementary qualitative and explorative analysis 100

Chapter 6 Conclusions 107

6.1 Concluding remarks 107

6.2 Research implications 107

    6.2.1 Theoretical and methodological implications 107

    6.2.2 Managerial implications 110

6.3 Limitations and further research 112

References 115

Figures

Figure 1 S-O-R paradigm 68

Figure 2 Influence of social media platforms on consumers of e-retailers' products 69

Figure 3 Research hypotheses 74

Figure 4 Three product categories represent the search-experience-credence classification .. 83

Figure 5 Histogram – Total time of pilot study 86

Figure 6 Screenshot of Experimental Treatment for Group 1 89

Figure 7 Screenshot of Experimental Treatment for Group 2 89

Figure 8 Geographic distribution of the sample 93

Figure 9 Tie strength affects e-retailer with search goods 98

Figure 10 Social presence not affects e-retailer with experience goods 99

Figure 11 Information richness affects e-retailer with credence goods 100

Tables

Table 1 Examples of e-retailers and typologies 60

Table 2 Definitions of social media 60

Table 3 Types of social media platforms 61

Table 4 Examples of social media platforms and typologies 63

Table 5 Definitions of a business model 64

Table 6 Adapted scales to brand familiarity 77

Table 7 Adapted scales to measure perceived quality 78

Table 8 Adapted scales to measure intent to purchase online 79

Table 9 Adapted scales to measure intent to recommend online 79

Table 10 Item-correlation matrix 85

Table 11 Exploratory factor analysis 85

Table 12 Estimation of monetary awards of participants 86

Table 13 Treatment groups of the experiment 90

Table 14 Estimated geographic location of participants 94

Table 15 Sample description 95

Table 16 Treatment groups 96

Table 17 Equivalency of treatment groups 96

Table 18 Reliability of scales measuring dependent variables 97

Chapter 1 Introduction

1.1 Background

The research firm Forrester Inc. (2015) forecasts revenue from e-commerce will grow from $334 billion United States Dollars (USDs) to $480 billion USDs during 2015 and 2019 in the United States. It also forecasts 10% of average annual growth rate. Only between 2011 and 2014, online purchase intention rates have doubled for more than half of e-retail's product categories (Nielsen 2014a). The global share of e-retail revenue from total retail sales will represent 10% in 2017 (Forrester Inc. 2011). According to Rigby (2011), e- retailing could represent 20% of total retail sales worldwide, though the proportion will vary considerably by industry and region. Additionally, Gartner Inc. (2014) explains the importance of retail expansion with digital technologies (e.g. customers across shopping processes). It reports multi-channel retailing (e.g. interaction between the customer contact points, cross-channel shopping, and personalisation of offers to customers) is a key retail trend.

Integrating cross-channel strategies and social media could improve customer satisfaction and drive sales in consumption markets (e.g. Chatterjee 2010; Stephen and Galak 2012; Taylor et al. 2011). New communication channels can provide competitive advantages for first-movers by improving promotion, loyalty, customer satisfaction, and market intelligence. These channel expansions affect market acceptance positively despite their inherent risks (Geyskens et al. 2002; Kim and Park 2005; Lee and Kim 2008; Patel 2013). *"In a multichannel, multimedia retail marketing environment, marketers must design and implement an integrated channel and communications strategy that maximizes short-run sales and long-run brand equity" (Keller 2010 p. 67)*. Thus, expansion to new communication channels, such as social media platforms, could provide market advantages to e-retailers' competitive marketing and communication strategies.

Channel expansions in knowledge economies are crucial to capture and to secure value for e-businesses (Amit and Zott 2001; Carlson and Zmud 1999; Geyskens et al. 2002). Consider, for example, people in United States use near to four digital devices and spend near to sixty hours per week consuming content from social media platforms (Nielsen 2014b). In fact, the use of multiple social media channels has become a norm for large companies as Burson-Marsteller (2012) reports. On average, Fortune 500 companies in the retail sector have adopted two social media platforms (Culnan et al. 2010). As the transaction medium of e-retailers is also their market (Frey et al. 2011; Hoffman and Novak 1997; Wang et al. 2002), adopting social media platforms comes naturally to them. According to Internet Retailer Magazine (2012), more than 90% of the top 500 e-retailers in the United States adopted Facebook, Twitter, or YouTube. Although most managers remain unconvinced about the impact of social media platforms (Lipsman et al. 2012) because it is difficult to measure (Fisher 2009; Murdough 2009), social media platforms impact on e-retail. For instance, by increasing awareness of obscure products through social media platforms it is possible to increase their sales (Oestreicher-Singer and Sundararajan 2012). Some social media platforms are better than others to communicate certain messages (Kaplan and Haenlein 2010), consequently, focusing on the right ones is central to improve the return on marketing and advertising investments. This is crucial for e-businesses in knowledge economies where marketing and consumers closely converge in diverse Internet communication channels. Therefore, studying the alignment of e-retailers and social media platforms is important for e-retailers' marketing and channel strategy.

Expanding to social media platforms exposes companies to higher levels of interactivity and transparency with their consumers (Aula 2010; Champoux et al. 2012; Jones et al. 2009; Kaplan and Haenlein 2010). In the e-retail sector, user-centred communications allow electronic word-of-mouth to enhance open interactions among consumers that use social media (Berthon et al. 2012; Jansen et al. 2009; Kietzmann et al. 2011). This has become a game changer for the marketing communication strategy of e-retail companies. Nielsen (2012) reports that social media impact is rising worldwide because 46% of e-retailers' customers used social media platforms to make their buying decisions. Similarly, across other sectors of society—media, politics, and entertainment—new communication channels provide substantial changes to Internet strategies (Amit and Zott 2001; Hoffman and Novak 1997; Porter 2001; Wind and Mahajan 2002). For example, promotion of offline and online products and services with user-generated content (e.g. Oestreicher-Singer and Sundararajan 2012; Ye et al. 2011) produces competitive advantages and value through that content (e.g. Hagel and Armstrong 1997; Lumpkin and Dess 2004). As higher levels of interactivity and transparency add sociability to media with social media platforms, the use of these platforms becomes an important element of e-retailers' expansion strategy.

However, according to data obtained from Internet Retailer Magazine (2012), e-retailers expanding to social media platforms experience substantial heterogeneity regarding how their consumers respond. For example, by the end of 2011, J&R Electronics Inc. and Radio Shack Corp. had 12,933 and 422,133 'likes' on Facebook respectively. As this example shows, substantial heterogeneity marks the outcomes of e-retailers expansion to social media platforms. More important, the ratio of Twitter 'followers' to Facebook 'likes' might unveil an alignment between product categories and social media platforms. For instance, J&R Electronics and Radio Shack Corp. have very different ratios, whereas J&R Electronics has a ratio of 7 to 9, Radio Shack Corp. has a ratio of 1 to 9. Both retail chains sell online and offline computers and electronics in the same market with a single online shop, however, their online sales significantly differ. During 2011, J&R Electronics sold $168M USDs whereas Radio Shack Corp. sold $50M

USDs. Does this indicate that Twitter is a better communication channel than Facebook to promote and to sell online computers and electronics? Conversely, Nordstrom Inc. has a ratio of 1 to 8 whereas Lululemon Athletica Inc. has a ratio of 1 to 3. Both retail chains sell online and offline apparel and accessories in the same market with a single online shop, however, their online sales significantly differ. During 2011, Nordstrom Inc. sold $917M USDs whereas Lululemon Athletica Inc. sold $106M USDs. Does this indicate that Facebook is a better communication channel than Twitter to promote and to sell apparel and accessories? The winning strategy when expanding to new communication channels depends on selecting and concentrating in the most relevant ones. This suggests the emphasis on a social media platform could affect e-retailer market success according to their product category. Thus, the alignment between e-retailers and social media platforms plays an important role in e-retailers' successful channel expansion.

To succeed in this expansion to social media platforms, e-retailers should align them to their own characteristics. In doing so, an e-retailer needs to identify these characteristics from their own core business and concentrate on the social media platforms with characteristics that facilitate its promotion of products. On one hand, studies classify e-retailers by their competitive strategies as prestigious, discount, and pure play or by their product offerings as search, experience, credence, offline, and online goods (e.g. Francis 2007, 2009; Korgaonkar et al. 2006). On the other hand, studies classify social media platforms as social networking sites (Benkler 2006; Borgatti and Halgin 2011), microblogs, and content communities (Hoffman and Fodor 2010); or by their network (Dwyer 2007; Frey et al. 2011; Newman 2003) and content (Smith et al. 2012). E-retailers appear to find complementarities through social media platforms in successful expansions, therefore, exploring e-business models and aligning their transactional content for e-retailers and social media platforms is crucial for e-retailers' market success.

E-business models conceptualise systems in terms of content and its structure (Zott and Amit 2010). Transactional content is a consumer-side parameter of e-business model, it represents information and goods being exchanged and capabilities or resources required to enable these exchanges for e-businesses (Amit and Zott 2001). Content allows firms to create new value in social media platforms (Laroche et al. 2012; Schau et al. 2009) since they can build capacities that improve e-retailing through new transaction content (Amit and Zott 2001; Zott et al. 2000). Content in social media platforms affect loyalty and promotion for e-retailers (e.g. Kietzmann et al. 2011; Laroche et al. 2013). It also impacts consumer behaviour according to product offerings (Franke et al. 2004; Nelson 1970; Obal et al. 2011). Indeed, new content does complement e-business models and their competitive strategy (Amit and Zott 2001; Lumpkin and Dess 2004) in the degree it influences e-retailers' customers to make transactions.

Alignment between content from e-retailers (e.g. tangible products and intangible services) and content of social media platforms (e.g. user-generated content) is crucial for e-retailers' competitive strategy. However, the literature does not study this alignment, it mainly studies the effects of word-of-mouth communication as a new promotion channel (e.g. Bollen et al. 2011; Brown et al. 2007; Colliander and Dahlen 2011; Jansen et al. 2009; Kumar and Mirchandani 2012; Oestreicher-Singer and Sundararajan 2012; Paek et al. 2011; Steyn et al. 2010). Thus, the present study aims to complement the literature by considering the alignment of two e-businesses: E-retailer and social media platform.

1.2 Problem

Studies in social media platforms arise from two domains: information systems and marketing. Literature in information systems looks to develop predictive models by measuring and characterising content (e.g. Bollen et al. 2011; Heidemann et al. 2010; Kwak et al. 2010; Tumasjan et al. 2010). In the marketing literature, two streams stand out. The first one focuses on advertising where empirical studies aim to understand attitudes, motivations, and consumers' responses to content (e.g. Hung and Li 2007; Strutton et al. 2011; Taylor et al. 2011; Teixeira 2012). The second one concentrates on branding in which relationship marketing guides studies of content in virtual communities and consumers' involvement with the brand (e.g. Felix 2012; Kornberger 2011; Laroche et al. 2012; Sung et al. 2010). This thesis focuses on virtual communities in social media platforms as a channel expansion for e-retailers' marketing communications; it studies how consumers respond to these communities, considering them as ongoing advertisements.

Studies have explored the effects of firms' virtual communities in social media platforms. Their findings explain how electronic word-of-mouth influences the promotion strategy and competitiveness of businesses. For instance, word-of-mouth affects sales paths of e-retailers' product offerings (e.g. Dellarocas et al. 2007; Oestreicher-Singer and Sundararajan 2012). Positive word-of-mouth adds long-term value to firms (e.g. Dwyer 2007; Villanueva 2008) and it is related to good business performance (Stephen and Galak 2012; Trusov, Bucklin, et al. 2009). Further, word-of-mouth communication influences brand performance through consumers' involvement (e.g. Christodoulides et al. 2012; Park and Lee 2008) and awareness in social networking sites (Lipsman et al. 2012). Hsu et al. (2012) and Laroche et al. (2013) explain how the content in social media platforms affects consumers' trust and loyalty. Social media platforms can influence potential customers and give feedback to businesses through the revolving content within them impacting the business performance (e.g. Giamanco and Gregoire 2012; Kozinets et al. 2010;

Laroche et al. 2013; Schau et al. 2009; Ties and Benkler 2006). Therefore, most research concentrates on how social media platforms influence potential customers.

However, studies do not consider how influence differs across diverse e-retailers and social media platforms. This is the main problem. Which social media platforms are better to promote certain e-retail products? There is a lack of studies that compare the impact of diverse social media platforms between e-retailers with diverse product categories although e-retailers' offers vary in the ease to evaluate their quality (e.g. De Figueiredo 2000; Obal et al. 2011) and content of virtual communities in social media platforms differ (Laroche et al. 2013; Smith et al. 2012). Therefore, few studies address the implications of alignment between e-retailers' content (e.g. tangible products) and content of social media platforms (e.g. user-generated content).

By investigating alignment between e-retailers and social media platforms, this thesis addresses calls to study the effects of user-generated content (e.g. Christodoulides et al. 2012; Lee and Youn 2009) according to product categories (e.g. De Maeyer 2012; Nakayama et al. 2010). In a business-to-consumer setting, this study answers the following research questions:

How does the alignment between transaction content of e-retailer and transaction content of social media platform affect e-retailer market success? Why?

To answer these questions this research builds upon typologies of e-retailers and social media platforms to propose a bridge with the business model theory by focusing in transaction content, which is a consumer-side parameter of e-business models. The literature review starts taking a step back to contextualise relevant theories underpinning the theoretical framework and the topic of e-business. It continues describing an overview of e-retailers' objectives when expanding their communication channels to social media platforms. In doing so, the influence of social media platforms on e-retailers' customers has also been investigated. Particularly, this study concentrates on how social media platforms influence e-retailer's market success in terms of perceived quality, purchase intent, and intention to recommend for diverse e-retailers.

1.3 Justification

By addressing the research questions, the study offers two contributions to the academic literature. This study links the business model literature with competitive marketing and communication strategies in the context of e-businesses using the framework from Amit and Zott (2001). It does so by focusing only in a parameter of e-business model called transaction content. *"The links between relevant business model parameters and competitive advantage is less well understood" (Amit 2014).* It investigates how transactional content alignment between e-retailers' product categories and user-generated content of social media platforms leads to market advantages. In contrast, recent studies focus on testing new methods for data analysis (e.g. Asur and Huberman 2010; Bollen et al. 2011; Heidemann et al. 2010) and on creating theoretical definitions for the social media phenomena as a whole (e.g. Kaplan and Haenlein 2010; Kietzmann et al. 2011). Existing literature concentrates on specific products or single product categories and single platforms neglecting differences between social media platforms (Christodoulides et al. 2012; Lee and Youn 2009; Smith et al. 2012). In addition, only few studies consider how people react to electronic word-of-mouth about distinct product categories, such as hedonic versus utilitarian or search versus experience versus credence product categories (De Maeyer 2012). Therefore, the literature omits studies that classify content of social media platforms and its effects on diverse e-retailers' product categories. This thesis studies these differences through the lens of alignment of transaction content between e-business models from e-retailers and social media platforms.

To investigate alignment between e-retailers and social media platforms, this research explores diverse e-retailers' product categories and virtual communities of e-retailers in diverse social media platforms. This approach aims to discover how e-retailers could gain a competitive advantage by choosing social media platforms according to their product categories. The study uses economist classifications of goods and communication theories to propose research hypotheses. In doing so, this study investigates market success as positive changes on perceived quality through diverse virtual communities. The research compares the level of these changes as a proxy for business competitiveness. Only few studies like the one from Kumar & Mirchandani (2012), Bollen et al. (2011) and Asur & Huberman (2010) link content from social media platforms with business competitiveness. However, each study only concentrates on a specific business type or on a specific product (e.g. ice cream retailer, movie theatres, and financial markets). This reinforces the need for studies focusing on how virtual communities affect the competitiveness of e-retailers with diverse product categories as inferred from Christodoulides (2012), Lee and Youn (2009), and Smith et al. (2012). Additionally, empirical research does not attempt to generalise their findings to e-retailers with diverse product categories and current social media platforms as this study does. This research therefore aims to fill this gap by considering changes on perceptions and attitudes towards diverse product categories after exposure to diverse social media platforms. The effect of social media platform's type and the type of e-retailer's product category is an academic gap. Although empirical research in business-to-consumer marketing shows the importance of consumer relationships with products and social media platforms to improve consumers' loyalty and trust (e.g. Laroche et al. 2012, 2013; Muñiz and Schau 2011; Schau et al. 2009), previous research does not focus on both relationships. Most present studies consider specific products and do not consider product categories; furthermore, current research does not consider the largest social media platforms. Therefore, existing literature does not compare the effect of diverse actual social media platforms on the performance of e-retailers with diverse product categories.

Content from social media platforms serves as a vehicle of social exchange in the form of conversations, identity (Kietzmann et al. 2011), presence, and disclosure (Kaplan and Haenlein 2010) which are the origins of social media platforms (Brown et al. 2007; Dwyer 2007; Trusov, Bodapati, et al. 2009) and key ingredients for any economic transaction. This study builds on the theoretical perspective of transaction content as a source of value from Amit and Zott (2001). The authors noted that content novelty could be a source of value for e-businesses because it relates with other sources of value, such as lock-in, efficiency, and complementarities. E-retailers could turn virtual communities based on social media platforms into sources of new transaction content in the degree their user-generated content influences consumers' behaviour towards purchasing their products. This thesis argues that alignment between e-retailer and social media platform affects e-retailers' market success because both transaction content could be complementary to each other at the transaction content level. It is important to know how to determine which type of social media platform fits better e-retailers' product categories. This research therefore concentrates on how transactional content alignment of e-retailer's products and social media platform affects e-retailer market success; Chapter 2 introduces relevant theories for the conceptual framework.

Chapter 2 Literature review

2.1 Foundations of communication theories

This section describes general communication theory pertaining to this research. It describes communication theories and concentrates on information theory as it is inexorably tied to communication. It also describes some communication theories and models including social and psychological perspectives relevant for human interactions over the Internet.

Information theory and communication

Communication is essentially information transference. It involves at least two entities exchanging information and gathering some meaning. According to its etymology, the word communication means to share, to impart, to inform, and to make common (Harper 2015). Communication therefore implies information flowing, sharing information, transferring information, getting information, and information in common by definition.

Information theory is the basis to understand communication theories. It has strong foundations as philosophers and academics carried out several studies about electronically mediated information. For example, a book called 'The mode of information: Poststructuralism and social context' by Poster (1990) depicts how social contexts and information interact. More than twenty-five years ago, it predicted the implications of information on society and its future trends. It was an early look into the information age. Another book: 'Holding onto Reality: The Nature of Information at the Turn of the Millennium' by the philosopher Borgmann (1999) has produced a resonance in the academic world. For instance, Higgs and Sahay (2000) reviewed Borgmann's work and explained the power of electronically mediated information to influence human behaviour. Long before them, Shannon and Weaver (1949) worked on improving communication channels based on studying information in a systematic, objective, and precise way. They did so by following a deterministic approach for telecommunications, but also proposed to analyse information in terms of the influential problems about the effectiveness of information on human behaviour. They thought the former analysis has equal importance as analysing: (1) Technical problems about measuring information and (2) Semantic problems relating to meaning and truth. The latter falls more into an interpretative approach with subjective connotation that was not fully explored by Shannon and Weaver in their first papers about information theory and telecommunications. However, recent research discuss the relevance of interpretation for information theory from a cultural and philosophical perspective (e.g. Adams 2003; Ess 2008; Floridi 2004, 2010; Spink and Cole 2004; Zemanek 1990). This brought also non deterministic approaches in the field of information theory. Thus, the multidisciplinary relevance of information theory is the first step to understand communication; after all, communication is a flow of information (Craig 1999).

The word 'information', however, carries with multiple meanings making this word ambiguous. In the words of Shannon (1993 p. 180) *"it is hardly to be expected that a single concept of information would satisfactorily account for the numerous possible applications of this general field"*. The seminal work known as 'The mathematical theory in communications' of Shannon and Weaver (1949), contains two essential and practical principles to understand and analyse communication channels: Entropy and channel capacity described below.

Entropy

Entropy is a term used to quantify the uncertainty resulting from a message according to Shannon (1950) and Shannon and Weaver (1949). Entropy is directly related with the work from Kaplan and Haenlein (2010). They explain that one objective of communication is resolving ambiguity and reducing uncertainty. How many interpretations do messages in social media have? This logical and deterministic standpoint that follows the term entropy is frequently used in communication theories related with telecommunications. For example, information richness theory depicts how a medium differs by its number of cues (e.g. Carlson and Zmud 1999; Daft and Lengel 1986; Dennis and Kinney 1998; Lengel and Daft 1988). One simple and practical example in business comes from comparing communication over the phone (i.e. audio content) and by teleconferences (i.e. audio and visual content). Another example shows that social presence theory considers social disclosure and closeness as drivers of effective communication (e.g. Tu and McIsaac 2002; Wrench and Punyanunt-Carter 2007; Yoo and Alavi 2001). In both examples these theories share their foundations in information theory and also include developed notions proposed by Shannon and Weaver (1949).

Studying communication channels under the lens of entropy definitely portrays a more realistic view of digital mediated communication. The literature suggests that communication in social media is positively biased. For instance, one empirical study from Archak et al. (2011) shows that many frequent phrases used by consumers are generally positive when reviewing products online. To arrive to this conclusion, the authors used a machine-learning model to classify messages in social media. In line with them, another empirical study from Smith et al. (2012) shows descriptive statistics about the positive direction of messages in social media. In this case, the authors worked with independent human coders to classify messages from social media. The results are also conclusive. Most messages in Facebook, Twitter, and YouTube are generally positive (41-56%). In contrast, negative messages (6-15%) and unclear messages (7%) are few; even both of them do not represent together half of the total positive messages. However, a large portion of messages (31-37%) were neutral. Although the direction of a particular message is uncertain and its effects may portray high entropy, empirical studies suggest that the direction of communications is largely positive in social media.

Channel capacity

Channel capacity refers to the velocity with which information travels, it is also known as transmission rate. This concept has been used to study communication channels since the origins of information theory particularly in the domain of telecommunications. How much communication can be achieved through a channel? Perhaps the theorem proposed by Shannon and Hartley helps to answer this question to some extent. Shannon–Hartley theorem serves to compute the maximum transmission rate at which information flows over a communication channel with noise (Hartley 1928; Shannon 1949). It does so by assuming Gaussian noise for digital data conditions, these data are also known as information bits. The theorem establishes the capacity of the channel to deliver digital communications without error. Consider the implications of this reasoning about communication channel on messages flowing through the Internet. On one hand, communication in social media is prone to errors as it allows anybody to participate and misinterpret others' messages also influencing others into a misinterpretation of a message. This creates noise. On the other hand, how many communication channels exist? One can get easily lost with the plethora of social media options available within the Internet. For example in social media, Twitter, Pinterest, and YouTube offer distinct Internet communication channels. The question for companies' communication strategies naturally appears: Which communication channel or channels would generate the greater positive impact for them? To answer this question it is important to take a step back and understand more about communication and how Internet channels become the information link between two entities.

Communication models

One of the earliest major communication models used to explain the communication process was the one conceived by Shannon and Weaver (1949). They built a communication model to reflect how radio and telephone work. It was used to improve telecommunications during the Second World War. Their model has at least three main components: (1) Source or sender, (2) Channel, and (3) Receiver. The sender is an information source, which produces a message; the channel where the message is encoded and transmitted; and the receiver, which decodes the message and interprets its meaning. In this communication model, the communication flows linearly. This is also referred as the standard communication view or the transmission model of communication. Berlo (1960) later extended Shannon and Weaver's linear model of communication by separating it in four main components: source, message, channel, and receiver. His communication model is also known as the Source-Message-Channel-Receiver model or the SMCR model. It involves the unique set of communication skills, attitudes, knowledge, and culture of each individual participating in a communication process. These characteristics of individuals affect the encoding process of the message carried out by the source and the decoding process of the message carried out by the receiver. The channel is simply the conduit in which the message travels between source and receiver. However, not all communication models are lineal and not all of them follow this sequential approach from source or sender to receiver as these two models propose. Communication is also a social interaction.

Communication as a social interaction

Communication is a social interaction; as such it involves two entities communicating at the same time and without a sequential order. Communication also has semiotic rules as Schramm (1954) explains. He classifies rules of information transmission in the following: (1) Syntactic, that focuses on the formal properties of signs and symbols, (2) Pragmatic, which concerns about the relations between signs or expressions and their users, and (3) Semantic, which studies relationships between signs and symbols and what they represent. As a social interaction, communication should engage the sender and the receiver simultaneously. These premises are included in the transactional model of communication proposed by Barnlund (1970). He contended for the reciprocal link between sender and receiver. He emphasised on how the way an individual communicates determines the interpretation of his or her messages. Information is separated from communication as communication is a channel by which information is transferred from one individual to another. Individuals are reciprocally linked! The sender and the receiver have personal and different filters when communicating. These filters may depend on their culture, status, gender, or traditions jeopardising the interpretation of messages. Consider a well-known example from Gladwell (2008) about the crash of Avianca 52 in the early-90s due to a lack of fuel near to Long Island, New York. He explains how communications between the Capitan, the co-pilot, and the air traffic controller contributed to the crash. According to Gladwell (2008), the co-pilot was not effective at communicating with the pilot and the air traffic controller, failing to avoid the tragic episode. First, the co-pilot was afraid to question the poor judgement of the Capitan who was very tired to think clearly in the moments before crashing. Second, the co-pilot was unable to transmit a sense of urgency to the controllers as the plane was running out of fuel. Scripts and recordings of the black box reported by the National Transportation Safety Board (1990) show that; Although the content of the message from the co-pilot to the controller was accurate, his tune of voice was not. He sounded too relaxed! Hence, the controller did not understand the urgency of the situation until it was too late to help them to land. Gladwell (2008) explains that the main reason of these misunderstandings was the power distance dimension of cultures acknowledged by several scholars (e.g. Gladwin and Hofstede 1981; Hofstede 1980, 1983). The Colombian cultural background of the co-pilot, the recordings, and transcripts show the high power distance characteristic of the Colombians' culture. The co-pilot was not able to stand up against his fatigued Capitan neither was the co-pilot able to strongly command the controller to free a landing strip in the airport for an urgent landing. To act rapidly, the controller with an American cultural background expected a direct and strong approach to an urgency of this kind. In contrast, he received passive and relaxed messages from the Colombian co-pilot. As this example indicates, the participants did not communicate effectively despite exchanging information. They were not reciprocally linked. In the transactional model of communication, communication is a social interaction that involves continual engagement from the sender and the receiver simultaneously. This model also considers how the message is delivered and the individuals' characteristics of those who participate in the communication process.

Web 2.0, a user-centred model of mass communication

Communication processes over the Internet have been accompanied by a user-centred model of communication, particularly, in the era of the Web 2.0. According to the American Marketing Association (2015), the Web 2.0 refers to a new generation of Internet-based services. These services involve collaborating and sharing information online; for example, in social media platforms. Berthon et al. (2012) describes three effects that arise from the Web 2.0. First, activities are moving from the traditional Personal Computer (PC) to the Web also known as the Cloud. Second, value production is moving from the firm to the consumer. The main reason is technologies based on Web 2.0 simplify the creation of content. Third, as a result, power is moving from the firm to the consumer. These effects are part of the user-centred model of mass communication where users are at the core of social media. Users do not want to be receivers and only listen to companies; on the contrary, they want companies to listen and respond to them appropriately (Kietzmann et al. 2011). Users are active participants in social media; they are at the centre of communications and not the firms. Communication in this sense becomes bi-directional and democratic. This non-hierarchical nature of communication comes together with the Web 2.0 and it is popularly known as the democratisation of the Internet. In contrast, previous mass communication models posit the firm as the main source of unidirectional and authoritative communication where the receiver has typically a passive role. In the Web 2.0, the receiver turns into the main source of communication as media becomes more interactive (Jansen et al. 2009).

The implications of the user-centred model of mass communication in social media are evident. According to Hennig-Thurau et al. (2010), these communications: (1) Avoid 'gate keepers' such as publishers in traditional media; (2) Are pro-active as consumers can review and co-create new products at any point in time; (3) Are visible as a third person may see the interactions of two people; (4) These communications happen in real time and have memory as they can be retrieved following time stamps usually common in social media; (5) These communications are based on networks, as such, it is crucial to build relationships with other users to share content; and (6) Communications in social media are ubiquitous as communications can be reached by many other devices connected to the Internet and not just by the traditional PC. For example, one can communicate at any time and from anywhere using a smartphone. The connectivity of users determines the value of social media (Gneiser et al. 2010), this is also in part due to the user-centred model of mass communication as interpersonal relationships are crucial to communicate effectively. Social relationships and interaction therefore improve and maintain the use of social media as empirically demonstrated by Dwyer (2007). This increases social media value. People identify some value as they are grouped together (Fernback and Thompson 1995; Rheingold 2000). Communication is social; however, individuals interpret messages differently. Thus, the user-centred model of communication in social media also includes individuals' psychology in their communication processes and online interactions.

Psychology of communication

In electronically mediated communication the psychology of communication affects online and offline behaviour. For example, the group identity and social influence interact to shape online communication behaviour. How individuals see themselves in a group influences their relative salience of personal and social identity (Handbooks in Communication and Media 2015). As a result, individual's personality may show diverse facets depending on his or her social media groups. This is only an example about how psychological theories emphasise elements of human communication. In psychological models of communication, the source is influenced by his or her own knowledge, communication skills, attitudes, and the socio-cultural system to which he or she belongs as Popescu (2012) explains. From this psychological perspective, the author mentions messages are structured and organised to safeguard the bond between emotional and intellectual elements of the personality of communicators. As psychology is important in effective communication to influence offline and online behaviour, companies apply it in their marketing and advertising communication to improve their market success. One principle guiding companies' marketing and advertising communication relies on a simple but useful model to promote their offers explained below.

The Attention-Interest-Desire-Action model

In a traditional way, the goal of marketing and advertising communication is to attract people's attention to later persuade them to take action by purchasing firms' offers. This principle is described by Rawal (2013 p. 37) in the following text: *"The mission of an advertisement is to attract a reader, so that he will look at the advertisement and start to read it; then to interest him, so that he will continue to read it; then to convince him, so that when he has read it he will believe it. If an advertisement contains these three qualities of success, it is a successful advertisement"*. First, companies look to capture the attention of an audience. Second, turn this attention into an interest. Third, evolve from this interest to a desire. Fourth, this desire will ultimately provoke an action. This model uses a linear approach to promote an action, which is often a purchase but can also be something else benefiting the firm. For example, positive electronic word-of-mouth as outlined by Anderson (2009). In his non-monetary digital economies the author explains how companies compete for attention. Firms therefore influence online behaviour while appealing for the psychology of individuals as the Attention-Interest-Desire-Action or AIDA model describes. According to Mcdonald and Scott (2007), for instance, town-criers made public announcements aloud capturing the attention of crowds in earlier societies. Merchants employed therefore town-criers to shout praises about their goods and services. This old scene depicts the essential goal of marketing and advertising communication is attracting people's attention, informing and reminding customers about merchants' offers, and persuading them to buy merchants' offers. The purchasing funnel is a metaphor traditionally used to illustrate the Attention-Interest-Desire-Action model and its outcome although more recently Edelman (2010) proposed the metaphor of the consumer decision journey. In both cases, as more potential customers become aware of a firm's offers, there are higher chances that they buy; consequently, a larger sales volume is expected. This rational is also present in the hierarchy of effects described by Barry (1987). This model explains why the performance of marketing and advertising communications has been largely viewed as the number of impacts associated with the amount of people's attention. When planning expenses for marketing and advertising communication, the number of impacts serves as the proxy of attention which is easier to predict than buying behaviour and actual sales. However, this does not account for individuals' differences towards information.

One of these major differences between individuals is their preferred information. As people respond differently to information, capturing their attention by diverse forms of information is the first objective of marketing. The role of marketing in a company is necessary, in its basic form is about communications, broadcasting, and promotion (Kotler 2012). The effect of preferred information beyond gathering attention is contemplated in the cognitive fit theory. Similarly, successful firms should consider individuals' preferred information for effectively promoting their offers through their marketing and advertising communications.

Cognitive fit and the empirical approach for media studies

By understanding individuals' preferred information, one can look into the cognitive psychology embedded in communication from an empirical perspective. This idea is not new. When communication technology became massively available with the PC, Vessey and Galletta (1991) advanced this field with the cognitive fit theory. They did so by evaluating differences about performance of information acquisition when equivalent data were presented in different ways. They made an empirical study comparing the mode of information presentation (e.g. tables and graphs) assessing its fit with two types of tasks (e.g. symbolic and spatial). A symbolic task which requires answering questions as the following: How many millilitres of beer were sold in January? How much did wood merchants earn in the year 1500? One spatial task that needs answering questions as the following: Between the years 1800 and 2000 whose earnings increased faster, those of wood, steel, or rice? The authors proposed that for symbolic tasks, data presented in a table is better than data presented in a graph. For spatial tasks, on the contrary, data presented in a graph is better than data presented in a table. They demonstrated this is true by using continuous measures for performance such as the amount of time required to resolve several information tasks. Their results showed performance is higher (1) For symbolic tasks resolved using tables than using graphs and (2) For spatial tasks resolved using graphs than using tables. Although preferred information differs between individuals, the authors showed with their research there is room to extend the cognitive fit theory and application. They did so by generalising the mode of information presentation according to the type of task. This experiment was done also in the context of information technology, which is appropriate for this thesis. The results of the experiment of Vessey and Galletta (1991) suggest that the cognition required in resolving a communication task can guide the optimal mode in which information is presented. Therefore, an individual resolving the subjective task of evaluating goods may prefer a particular mode of information presentation depending on the type of goods he or she evaluates.

One mode of information presentation pertaining to this research comes from social media. How social media present information differently? Do these differences significantly affect people's evaluation of goods? To get a perspective about how to address these questions a brief review on the literature of media studies in the context of Internet communication follows. Several studies investigate the appropriateness of media in this context. Rice (1993), for example, compared media in organisational communications. In his study he ranked media such as face-to-face, e-mail, and videoconferencing. In doing so, Rice (1993) showed a way of extending the empirical approach of cognitive fit explored by Vessey and Galletta (1991). This suggests that it is pertinent to investigate how media differ and which media are better to communicate. One way to do so relies on the intrinsic differences of social media. In computer-mediated communications where large-scale reach and networked environments are common, a new communication model is required to succeed in marketing (Novak and Hoffman 1996). Understanding specific differences within Internet media such as network, content, and reach can serve to understand social media differences for instance. Opposed to traditional media, social media represent an alternative way to carry on marketing activities that challenge the traditional paradigms behind businesses, particularly Internet based businesses as e-commerce (Hoffman and Novak 1997). Social media differ (Smith et al. 2012). Its diverse sociocultural characteristics affect how marketing and advertising communication works (Maclaran et al. 2011). Consider the far reaching implications of electronic word-of-mouth. In social media, one of the marketers' challenges is to identify influential individuals and to connect with them to encourage positive word-of-mouth about companies' offers (Smith et al. 2007). Constantinides et al. (2008) show how social media has provided retail customers with more information about goods, more control, and more power over retailers' marketing and distribution processes. At the same time, they identify the relevance of social media as a strategic marketing tool with the power to generate competitive advantages for retailers. The influence of social media and its relevance for the marketing strategy is obvious as explained by Hoffman and Novak (2012a; b). For marketing and advertising communication, the mode of information presentation matters as potential customers triangulate information to learn about goods.

Triangulation

One of the research strategies to increase the validity of research findings in the social sciences is called triangulation; it helps to combine multiple data sources to converge in a single construct (Yeasmin and Rahman 2012). This principle not only applies to academic research, it is also part of the cognitive psychology of individuals. When potential customers learn about the goods a firm offers, they combine information to evaluate them. People can improve the accuracy of their evaluations by gathering diverse kinds of data bearing on the same research object (Todd 1979). Triangulation is therefore embedded in the psychology of Internet communications.

Theories of Internet communications

This section describes fundamental theories for Internet communications. At the same time, it concentrates on social behaviour as Internet facilitates interactive communication with a variety of content. Internet communication theories arise from a mixture of sociology, psychology, and information theories. Internet communications happen in environments surrounded by networks

(Novak and Hoffman 1996); hence, network theory underpins the understanding of such communications. As human behaviour is behind every social communication over the Internet, these communications share principles found in long-lasting concepts pertaining to the social sciences. The seldom ordered nature of communication also explained earlier as 'entropy', permits the inclusion of information processing and contingency theories at the core of Internet communications. Thus, the next section describes essential theories to understand better Internet communications underpinning the conceptual framework of this research.

Network theory

Network theory is vital to understand Internet communications. Combs (2000) and Zimmermann (2000) explain information governs in the emergent-networked economy as it captures customers' data and complements production or usage. Internet communications and social connections between individuals can be modelled as networks (Newman 2003). Networks are one way to represent multiple relations in abstract terms. In social science, networks depend on the typologies of ties, which represent similarities, relations, interactions, or flows between elements (Borgatti et al. 2009). This form of representation is appropriate to show interconnected elements of a greater and usually complex system, such as many social or information systems together. For example, an information system may include the connections between PCs and Servers. It can also represent affiliations between users in social media. Consider 'subscribers' of YouTube channels, 'followers' of Twitter accounts, or 'friendships' in Facebook, which have virtual communities. In this context, the network term is almost a synonym of the term community. Two elements are basic in network theory: edges and vertexes. Edges can represent bidirectional relations between vertexes in their simplest form; these relations can also be presented as a matrix. It is known as adjacency matrix. It is symmetric and binary. In fact, the matrix's columns and rows are equal in number. Both columns and rows represent the same vertexes in and adjacency matrix. Firstly, it means the number of elements in the matrix is the result of the number of vertexes to the second power. Secondly, it means that its values represent only two possibilities: (1) no relation between vertexes by the number zero or (2) a bidirectional relation between vertexes by the number one. To compute the possible unique relations in a bidirectional network it is important to subtract the number of vertexes from the total number of elements and divide this result by two. The first operation eliminates to count edges between the same vertexes. The second operation eliminates to double count edges describing two directions of the same relation as in this example relations are bidirectional. This type of network with bidirectional relations is widely used to model social networks as it has been shown in studies with social media (e.g. Gneiser et al. 2010; Heidemann et al. 2010; Shriver et al. 2013).

Other studies look into unidirectional relations between elements to show communication flows (e.g. Ahmad and Teredesai 2006; Elias et al. 1956; Fiore-Silfvast 2012). Research in social media communications is linked to the diffusion of innovations mechanics (Füller et al. 2013). For example, Gibbons (2004) investigates how diffusion occurs through a network where social relations accompanied by social influence and adaptation shape its path. In fact, many academics study Internet communications through the community lens. For example, Archer-Brown et al. (2013), Brodie et al. (2013), Seraj (2012), and de Valck et al. (2009). In addition, virtual communities have a great power to reorder the relationship between customers and companies according to Hagel and Armstrong (1997). The authors explain this happens because companies use networks to empower customers in order to take control of their own value as potential customers of the company's goods and services. Questions arise about the influence of virtual social networks on the flow of communication. How social media affect the flow of communication over the Internet? Studies about social media use network theory to model virtual social networks and virtual communication networks. Therefore, network theory is essential to understand and analyse communications over the Internet.

Network theory provides tools to analyse Internet communications. This field is known as network analysis and moves from the theoretical and mathematical perspective of network theory to dig more into the methods to analyse networks. These methods commonly share a mixed approach: qualitative and quantitative. Consider the early thoughts on the field. Some of them are summarised by Borgatti et al. (2009). They explain the origins of the field with Comte's idea of social physics. In doing so, they also acknowledge Durkheim's argument describing a human society as a biological system in the sense it was made up of interconnected elements. They also describe early social network analysis by the sociometrist Moreno who explained girl's runaways in New York through their network position and diffusion of ideas. Moreno's work shows proof of the flow of social influence and ideas among girls. Borgatti et al. (2009) also mention that social network analysis helps to explain adoptions. Social network analysis is widely used to understand behaviour in marketing and economics (Wasserman and Faust 1994). In the domain of Internet communications, Watts et al. (2002) indicate identity and ties on social networks set the basis for searching on the Internet and information databases. They explain, for instance, that group membership and message transmission can be used to run decentralised and efficient searches. Analysing communications over the Internet is appropriate under the network perspective. Watts (2004) explains Internet communications belongs to typical scale-free networks and generally displays power law tails, also known as long-tails. He also mentions that real social networks can be represented as small-world networks characterised by social affiliation. A social media platform can be both as it uses the Internet and it is also based on social affiliation. Thus, considering these two types of networks (i.e. scale-free and small-world), social network analysis has become a popular methodological approach to analyse Internet communications in social media.

Interpersonal virtual ties, social capital, and the strength of weak ties theory

Interpersonal virtual ties bring social capital embedded in networks within social media. A social network is one of the types of complex networks studied by sociologists in which social capital rests (Newman 2003; Portes 1998). *"To possess social capital, a person must be related to others, and it is those others, not himself, who are the actual source of his or her advantage" (Portes, 1998 p. 7)*. Sociologic studies on the field of social networks have been growing exponentially between 1970 and 2000 whereas many of them look at structural social capital and contagion (Borgatti and Foster 2003).

One of the big theories in sociology is called the strength of weak ties which also has implications in economics. Granovetter (1973) explains the diffusion of new and redundant information through interpersonal ties. He proposed to evaluate interpersonal tie strength in social relations by the amount of time, intimacy, and intensity. This view is also shared by Krackhardt (1992) who explained that any kind of relationship needs at least interactions, affection, and time in his organisational study. While building his theory, Granovetter (1973) showed empirical evidence of information diffusion through diverse social structures in his seminal study about job searching. In his research, people found a job faster through acquaintances rather than through relatives. He showed that strong ties are more likely to provide redundant information and less likely to provide new information than weak ties. The potential benefits of weak ties involve optimising search efforts; however, weak ties tend to generate less return for non-specialised seekers than for specialised seekers (Granovetter 1983). According to Kavanaugh et al. (2005), communities with higher levels of social capital typically have weak ties across groups and strong ties within groups. The authors explain that while weak ties serve to bridge social capital across groups, strong ties serve to bond social capital within groups. This combination is the most effective for collective action. People with weak ties are more efficient to bridge social capital when using Internet communications such as social media. As the authors explain, these communications enhance their capability to educate and to organise the community. Therefore, the diffusion of information through interpersonal virtual ties is central to understand the social capital embedded within social media.

The social capital potential of virtual ties has been shown in Milgram's famous online experiment which depicts Internet's social network. His experiment suggests Internet users are only six degrees away from each other and it has been cited by many scholars who study social networks and marketing communication (e.g. Procter and Richards 2002; Watts and Strogatz 1998).

Marketing and advertising communication value is proportional to the attention it gathers. For instance, Facebook provides its users with the means to build up and maintain their social capital as Ellison et al. (2011, 2007) and Ahn (2012) suggest. It allows people to build or maintain social capital, communicate with others, keep up with other peoples' lives, and discover several types of social information such as rumours and gossips (Smith et al. 2012). However, virtual ties may not be as effective to acquire new social capital. Pénard and Poussing (2010) show an example where virtual ties are not directly associated with acquiring new social capital. However, they mention that virtual ties serve as a way to maintain social capital. As explained earlier, social media help to organise information which naturally facilitates keeping up and bridging social capital. According to Hung and Li (2007), social media is a source of social capital due to their potential to generate and disseminate electronic word-of-mouth. They demonstrated this effect empirically with computer-mediated data. Thus, the potential of virtual ties to improve social capital is evident as information travels through individuals connected in social media.

Information travels as flows in a social network; these networks are valuable because they set the basis to search for information within the Internet. Users may run decentralised and efficient searches by leveraging social affiliation and transferring messages (Watts 2004; Watts et al. 2002). The network structure governs the likelihood of information to flow bi-directionally (Rosvall and Bergstrom 2008). For instance, Borgatti and Halgin (2011) also explain that cooperation and contagion depend on the position in the network. As social networks model consumers' choices (Potts et al. 2008), they build up marketing and advertising value. The structure of a network is therefore important for reaching potential customers. Weak ties connecting groups which have different information add value to a network (Burt 2001). Search engines and social media do so because they have the potential to connect diverse groups with different information; groups that otherwise would not be connected! That is the strength of weak ties. Consider the study from Levin and Cross (2004). They proposed and empirically tested a two-party model for knowledge exchange where they demonstrated the structural benefit of weak ties as information conduits and information brokers. Their results are consistent with previous research that posits weak ties as major sources of non-redundant information in a network. In a related study, McFadyen et al. (2008) shows that the average tie strength and the network density are responsible, to some extent, of knowledge creation. These studies are only few examples of how the network perspective is useful to investigate communications in the social sciences. They also concentrate only in few of several network properties. Therefore, understanding virtual ties potential to unlock social capital is crucial for studying Internet communications within social media platforms.

Uncertainty reduction, social exchange, and symbolic interaction theories

Social communication over the Internet involves bi-directional flows of information between at least two individuals which is also known as interpersonal communication. Communication between two individuals is effective if the individuals participating in interpersonal communication convey similar meanings from the information exchanged. This includes both sides of the basic communication model: the source or sender and the receiver. As any other type of interpersonal communication, it is characterised by some degree of uncertainty, social exchange, and symbolic interaction.

The idea of uncertainty surrounding interpersonal communication coincides with the entropy notion explained earlier. Its foundation stems from the information theory and is a cornerstone to understand the origins of uncertainty reduction theory also known as initial interaction theory (West and Turner 2003). Berger and Calabrese (1975) suggested research priorities in their theoretical paper about the uncertainty embedded in interpersonal communication. They presented axioms for examining and predicting variables in the communication process of getting to know someone. This is why this theory is also known as initial interaction theory. Their axioms aim to relate the amount of uncertainty in interpersonal communication with key variables such as self-disclosure and similarity, normally present in this process of getting to know someone. Uncertainty reduction theory comes from a socio-psychological view. It deals with the fundamental process of acquiring knowledge about other people in interpersonal communication. At the same time, it assumes people have difficulties with uncertainty and people want to predict the behaviour of others while communicating (Berger and Calabrese 1975). Based on West and Turner (2003, 2010), these axioms are summarised as follows:

1. Verbal communication. The amount of uncertainty in interpersonal communication is negatively related with the amount of verbal communication. However, if the amount of verbal communication is too high and passes a threshold, it will lead to higher levels of uncertainty and information seeking behaviour.
2. Non-verbal warmth. The amount of uncertainty in interpersonal communication is negatively related with the amount of non-verbal warmth also known as non-verbal affiliate expressiveness.
3. Information seeking. The amount of uncertainty in interpersonal communication is positively related with the amount of information seeking behaviour.
4. Self-disclosure. The amount of uncertainty in interpersonal communication is negatively related with the amount of self-disclosure between individuals engaged in interpersonal communication.

5. Reciprocity. The amount of uncertainty in interpersonal communication is positively related with the amount of reciprocity between individuals engaged in interpersonal communication.
6. Similarity. The amount of uncertainty in interpersonal communication is negatively related with the amount of similarity between individuals engaged in interpersonal communication.
7. Liking. The amount of uncertainty in interpersonal communication is negatively related with the amount of liking between individuals engaged in interpersonal communication.
8. Shared communication networks. The amount of uncertainty in interpersonal communication is negatively related with the amount of shared communication networks accessible to individuals engaged in interpersonal communication.
9. Communication satisfaction. The amount of uncertainty in interpersonal communication is negatively related with the amount of satisfaction obtained through this communication.

Uncertainty reduction therefore is one of the premises of interpersonal communication during initial interactions. However, it is not the only one. One of the biggest theories in the social sciences is the social exchange theory. This theory is related with the disciplines of social psychology and sociology and it is also instrumental in the field of interpersonal communication. It defines social exchanges as the exchanges between at least two people involving tangible or intangible activities considering their costs and benefits (Emerson 1976; Homans 1961). Under this view, even interpersonal communication can be considered as an economic transaction. Social relationships therefore satisfy people's self-interest and entail interdependence (Cook et al. 2013; Cropanzano 2005; Homans 1961) as in any economic transaction. The challenge, however, is the subjective nature within interpersonal communication. To what extend it is possible to accurately measure economic transactions in interpersonal communication? The hardship involved to answer this question is evident. This is one of the reasons why many studies about interpersonal communication follow qualitative methods and remain descriptive. Particularly, studies following the symbolic interaction perspective.

As interpersonal communication is inexorably social, the symbolic interaction perspective leverages this component of communication. This social component is the major source of meaning which is transferred through symbols within interpersonal communication as previous studies suggest (e.g. Blumer 1980, 1994; Kanter and Blumer 1971). Consider, for example, the multiple meanings of words in a casual conversation. How easy it is to misinterpret words' meanings? Symbolic interaction is therefore a sociological perspective of communication. It relies on creating a common ground of shared meaning with others where people act based on the meaning they assign to events, things, and other people (Fischer 2008; Liebendorfer 1960). At the same time, symbolic interactionist research contends to demonstrate how people's reality is a social construct through qualitative methods such as participant observation. Symbolic interactionism is also important in studies about social media as these media are entwined with virtual communities and social networks. People within the community may meet or not outside the Internet (Rheingold 2000) and their communications depend on trust and expectations among them (Hsu et al. 2007). They also construct their social identity through communities in social media as previous research suggests (e.g. Dholakia et al. 2004; Ellison et al. 2010; Kietzmann et al. 2011). Thus, the social interaction of communication and its role to construct social realities and meanings is present in the interactions and exchanges Internet communications provide in social media.

Social presence theory

Social presence theory arises from a social psychological view of interpersonal communication and it serves to understand people's involvement within the communication process. This theory is widely used in the context of Internet communication (Cui et al. 2012). It has its origins in two main concepts that come from the late 60s: (1) Immediacy and (2) Intimacy. These initial notions are the origins of social presence theory even though Internet communications were not widely adopted back then. However, the concepts of immediacy and intimacy help to comprehend the general notion of social presence theory. Consider the book from Wiener and Mehrabian (1968). In their book, the authors defined immediacy as the behaviour that enhances closeness to nonverbal interaction while communicating. At the same time, they highlighted the importance of nonverbal cues (e.g. eye contact, facial gestures, and body movements) on the level of intensity and the immediacy of interactions. Back then there were not strong communication theories considering nonverbal communication effects on intensity and immediacy; only few studies were considering the nonverbal communication effects on interpersonal communication. One of them was concerned about intimacy. Argyle and Dean (1965) suggested intimacy is the result of mixing eye contact, intimacy topics, physical proximity, and smiling. According to their view, these components result in intimacy when they are at equilibrium. These two concepts of immediacy and intimacy were taken into account by Short et al. (1976) to develop the social presence theory. The general view of the social presence theory considers social cues embedded in interpersonal communication as ways to improve understanding and influence. Social presence enhances interpersonal involvement. As one promise of social media is to allow the possibility for online interpersonal involvement, social presence theory is important in the context of this type of Internet communications.

Interpersonal involvement arising from social presence is also related with information processing theory and the literature in online behaviour (e.g. Netemeyer and Haws 2011; Oh et al. 2013). Interpersonal involvement needs mutual awareness. Social presence theory therefore categorises communication media within a spectrum in which the level of social presence can be represented in a single dimension; this dimension is often considered the level of awareness people have of each other when they communicate (Sallnäs et al. 2001). Social presence theory has proved that educational environments with higher social presence are better for learning, the empirical research from Wei et al. (2012) demonstrated this. The authors showed the importance of user interface in online learning environments as they concluded it affects social presence and learning interaction, which contribute to enhance learning performance. Social presence theory has been widely used in communication studies about distance learning (e.g. Kehrwald 2008; Tu and McIsaac 2002). It is also used to understand organisational communication. For example, Yoo and Alavi (2001) used social presence theory to compare the differences between communication channels (e.g. audio conferencing and video conferencing) on decision making with an empirical study. Finally, social presence theory has served to understand how social media communication works (e.g. Kaplan and Haenlein 2010; Mennecke et al. 2011). Intimacy and immediacy provided by the medium influence on social media presence which increases the likelihood to make influential conversations (Kaplan and Haenlein 2010; Kietzmann et al. 2011). One empirical study from Oh et al. (2013) shows the immediacy of Twitter. It does so by exploring collective communication as an information processing mechanism. Their study considers online social reporting to address crisis problems and obtain community intelligence. The authors found that interpersonal involvement is a key factor to spread information about social crises in Twitter. Hence, social presence theory is important in the context of Internet communications where it also merges with information processing theory to understand the effects of interpersonal involvement.

Information processing and contingency theories

Internet communication requires processing and ordering information. This information view is widely used across the sciences and humanities and it is also known as information philosophy (Zemanek 1990). One of the essential theories in information science is information processing theory. It models the cognitive processes of individuals as computers. According to Gray (2010), individuals' minds comprise three elements: (1) Attention and perception mechanisms for bringing information in, (2) Working memory for actively manipulating information, and (3) Long-term memory for passively keeping information that can be retrieved in the future. Information processing requires several tasks. Heuristics about how people convey knowledge and belief is one of the major challenges in the field. For instance, early literature looked into the complex processes within people's mind while processing information and forming an inferential belief (e.g. Dover 1982). Another study from Phillips and Sternthal (1977) looked at differences between people regarding information processing. In their research, age differences result in a complex set of changes in people's susceptibility to social influence, ability to learn, and the use of sources of information. Their findings have direct implications for the theory and practice of marketing and advertising as information processing differences affect the effectiveness of communications. Therefore, viral marketing and advertising communications are studied under the lens of information processing.

Consider two recent studies. The first study from Eckler and Bolls (2011) uses information processing theory to explore the effect of emotions in viral video advertisements over the Internet. The study shows that emotional tones of pleasant and coactive nature elicit attitudes towards the advertisement and brand. Additionally, these emotional tones increase the likelihood to share the video advertisement. The results from the study by Eckler and Bolls (2011) contrast the popular belief that scaring and shocking online users motivate them to share content. The reason is that emotional tones of unpleasant nature result in the lowest likelihood to share the video advertisement in their study. Following information processing theory, the authors look to show the sequential nature of online viral video advertisements in three steps: (1) Individual's attitude towards the advertisement, (2) Individual's attitude towards the brand, and (3) Individual's intention to share the advertisement. Similarly, the second study from San José-Cabezudo and Camarero-Izquierdo (2012) uses the processing information theory to look into variables affecting viral messages over the Internet. However, this study merges a social capital approach with information processing theory in the context of business communication. The authors found that viral marketing through e-mail, also considered as a form of electronic word-of-mouth, depends on individuals' social capital. Someone who believes that opening and forwarding persuasive e-mails would increase his or her social capital will be prone to share e-mail viral messages. The results of this study have direct implications for the theory and practice of marketing and advertising as well. The reason is these results show that social capital and information processing affect the reach of viral marketing and advertising communications over the Internet. Social capital affects the viral dynamics. In that line, individuals' integration and relationship with the network and their attitudes towards viral messages are critical to the information processing of receiving and forwarding e-mails (Camarero-Izquierdo and San José-Cabezudo 2011). Information processing is a cornerstone of Internet communication and it requires ordering and organising information.

Contingency theory considers the lack of a perfect way to organise information and its uncertainty as the major challenges to overcome in communication. The best way to organise depends on the environment to which an organisation relates (Mills 1983; Scott and Gerald 2007). According to the interpretation of some studies (e.g. Deetz 1996; Jermier and Forbes 2011), contingency theory can be summarised by considering the following three assumptions. First, organisations are open systems balancing internal needs. At the same time, organisations adapt to environmental circumstances. Second, there is not a general best way for organising. It is only determined through in a case by case basis involving the environment in which an organisation competes and the type of activities an organisation carries out. Third, top managers aim to achieve good fits between the structure of their organisation and the different environments in which their organisation operates. As different types of organisations are needed according to different types of environments, the concept of congruence lies at the heart of contingency ideas as Tushman and Nadler (1978) explain. In their study, the authors also propose and integrated view by merging contingency and information processing approaches as these two approaches are used in organisational design and organisational structure. Similarly, contingency and information processing theories are often considered the two pillars of information richness theory which is essential to understand media studies and Internet communication.

Information richness theory

Information richness theory is also known as media richness theory, one of the major theories in research about media, communication, and advertising. This theory considers the uncertainty of interpersonal communications and the equivocality of information processing as acknowledged by Daft and Macintosh (1981). It brings a social perspective to the deterministic origins of telecommunication entropy first acknowledged in information theory. Information richness theory was formally conceived and integrated by Daft and Lengel (1986) who used information processing notions at the organisational level. In their paper, the authors aim to answer the question: Why do organisations process information? They do it by addressing two main information contingencies: uncertainty and equivocality. *"Uncertainty is a measure of the organization's ignorance of a value for a variable in the space. Equivocality is a measure of the organization's ignorance of whether a variable exists in the space"* (Daft and Lengel 1986 p. 557). Uncertainty is the known which is unknown; equivocality is the unknown which is unknown. Equivocality therefore entails more entropy than uncertainty. This rationale suggests that equivocality is less desirable than uncertainty in organisational communication. It is not a surprise that selecting communication media became a relevant skill for executives as more channels of communication are readily available in organisations. Lengel and Daft (1988) found that the most successful executives possess the skill for selecting appropriate media within the context of business organisational communications. They matched the routineness of messages with the richness of diverse media such as paper letters, face-to-face dialogues, telephone calls, and teleconferencing. In doing so, they propose a framework for effective managerial communications following the nature of messages. Lean media used for routinely messages is more effective to communicate than rich media because rich media provide data glut. Data glut is also known as information overload in recent studies and it is a recurrent issue in social media communications (e.g. Garg et al. 2009; Park and Lee 2008; Xu and Liu 2010). Information cues in excess may confuse the receivers resulting in communication failures. Contrariwise, Daft and Lengel (1986) also prevent communication failures related with data starvation in their framework. This happens when using lean media for non-routinely messages. Rich media therefore is more effective to communicate non-routinely messages than lean media. Multiple and conflicting interpretations of information are more likely to generate equivocality (Dennis and Valacich 1999; Dennis et al. 2008). Receiving a message with high equivocality, such as a non-routinely and complex message, will need more cues and data for its proper interpretation. The richness of a medium, however, relies not only on its ability to communicate messages with high equivocality but also on the skill of the sender and receiver.

Channel expansion theory

The importance of skills for using a medium as a determinant for effective communications over the Internet is exalted in a newer theory known as channel expansion theory (see Carlson and Zmud 1999; D'Urso and Rains 2008; Timmerman and Madhavapeddi 2008). Even when channel expansion theory concentrates on the subjective nature of skills with the medium, information richness is easier to apply as it concentrates on the objective differences of information richness and messages' equivocality. Particularly when comparing multiple media channels. Some examples of this come as follows: comparing face-to-face conversation and a conversation over telephone; comparing non-routinely messages with routinely messages; and comparing the number of words between two messages. Which message conveys more equivocality? Now think about comparing the skills of two people in multiple media channels. The particularities of individuals and media make studies less practical if the objective of a study is to compare media channels as in this thesis rather than exploring media adoption. Channel expansion theory, however, may be useful for studies which objectives are to explore media adoption, to discover critical skills, and to compare skills across cultures for a particular medium. However, several studies pertaining to social media consider information richness as a driver of recent frameworks (e.g. Aljukhadar et al. 2010; Kaplan and Haenlein 2010; Shaw et al. 2009). Thus, both information richness and channel expansion theories remain keystones for investigating communication channels for marketing and advertising purposes.

2.2 Theoretical perspectives underpinning the business model and strategy concepts

It is important to acknowledge that not a single strategic management theory can fully explain the value creation potential (Amit and Zott 2001). Therefore, this review describes selected perspectives underpinning the business model concept pertaining to this research in the following list:

- Digital markets and strategy theory
- Competitive advantage and corporate strategy
- The resource and knowledge based views of the firm
- Value chain and strategic networks
- Operational effectiveness and differentiation strategy
- Network effects and innovation
- Strategies of e-commerce companies
- Traditional business models adopting e-commerce

The expression 'business model' was used for the first time in a journal of operations research during the year 1957. The term was used in the design of a business game aimed for coaching business top managers (Bellman et al. 1957; Osterwalder et al. 2005). However, the business model concept started to become widely used until the 90s. This was a time where the use of Internet and computer software such as word processors and spreadsheets began to prevail in the business context. With a PC one can design businesses before implementing them; for instance, forecasting and simulating financial statements with spreadsheet software (Magretta 2002). It is during the 90s when the business model concept became part of the business language as it connoted the changing nature of these times due to the adoption of computers and the use of Internet. The documentary film from Heilemann (2008) describes this change when digital markets appeared in the early days of the information age. These were times of change. Internet communication touched American businesses in every way and disrupted several of their traditional management practices. The term business model became popular since then as it was used with the connotation of this change provided by the use of computer software and Internet (Osterwalder et al. 2005; Seddon et al. 2004). Business model came together with the changing nature of the new economy whereas theories in business strategy and digital markets proliferate.

The change caused by Internet technologies opened the highway for the information age. Economies based on labour for the production and manufacturing of goods were displaced or evolved. It was the starting of service based economies and the knowledge economy underpinning the information age. The industrial age was ending. At the same time, information and knowledge management rapidly became relevant ideas as technological changes and the globalisation represented new challenges for traditional businesses. Walters (2004) explained that managerial approaches relying on asset ownership and vertical organisational structures to control and to secure increasing profits were constantly challenged as the information age permeated the economy. At the same time, the importance to expand the managerial approach and include concepts of collaboration, flexibility, and co-operation in traditional business models became evident. Business strategy had to evolve. In the information age, traditional markets were disrupted by technological innovations shaping the new economy. For example, digital markets disrupted the economy of traditional book shops or traditional media for video content (e.g. business model of Amazon and YouTube). Therefore, business strategy is inexorably entangled with the business model concept, strategy theory, and digital markets rising during the information age as they shaped the new economy.

Digital markets and strategy theory

As digital markets conduct business transactions through open networks based on Internet infrastructure, these have unparalleled reach due to their lack of geographic limitations according to Amit and Zott (2001). The authors explain these markets put great emphasis on networks and information goods, provide high connectivity, and concentrate on transactions. In doing so, they highlight the richness of information and the ease of reach available in these markets. For instance, the detail and depth of information exchanged and accumulated by each player in this marketplace or the number of reachable products and people immediately at low cost. The authors also explain how digital markets portray few geographical boundaries and time-zone restrictions. In addition, they note how the richness of information reduces information asymmetry between customers and companies, facilitates product customisation, and increases transaction speed. Besides digital markets have richness of information and ease of reach, Amit and Zott (2002) added these markets have the characteristic of digital representation. It refers to how customers increase anonymity in some transactions, lack of human contact, and have greater control over spreading personal information in digital markets.

Digital markets have made companies rethink their strategies since the mechanisms of value creation practically evolved together with the growth of these markets. For example, business transactions are no longer only viewed as exchanges of money and goods because proprietary content becomes relevant in digital markets characterised by a fierce competition for attention (Anderson 2009; Lumpkin and Dess 2004; Porter 2001). In the context of e-commerce, Yen and Yao (2015) mention that the Internet of Things would amplify the depth and scope of business transactions over the Internet. They explain the Internet of Things as the incorporation of offline objects into digital markets with people and smart devices. The authors explain this will lead to an unprecedented growth of big data about product performance, customer behaviour, and customer experience, shaping the future of e-commerce and challenging its actual business model. Digital markets combined with large cost reductions for information processing allow radical changes in the way companies operate which opens opportunities and challenges traditional theories for value creation (Amit and Zott 2001). Thus, digital markets come as a natural expression when looking back to the origins and to the aims of the business model concept and strategy theory surrounding e-businesses.

Strategy theory is perhaps the most related field with the business model concept as it is concerned with organisational objectives and operations needed to achieve those objectives. Strategy comes together with war. It is widely accepted that strategy aims to anticipate enemy's movements in armed conflicts. All strategies are circumstantial and contextual by nature. As Rumelt (1979) explains, one's strategy is another's tactics, strategy depends upon where you sit. In organisational research for example, business strategy concentrates with internal and external change in which organisations operate. Strategy therefore sets the direction of an organisation (Rumelt 1979; Rumelt et al. 1994, 1995). It does so under competitive environments (Porter 1991; Zott and Amit 2008), one necessary condition embedded in the theory and practice of business strategy.

One of the definitions comes from Timmers (1998). He states a business model is: (1) An amalgamation of diverse business actors and their roles together with information, service, and product flows; (2) A description about value sources of businesses; and (3) A description of the potential benefits of diverse business actors. In an economic sense, a business model explains an organisation's logic and operations for generating money. These operations are guided by business strategy, which is part of the literature in economics and management. Some studies, however, contend for the distinction of business model and business strategy (e.g. Björkdahl 2009; Chesbrough and Rosenbloom 2002; Morris et al. 2005; Zott and Amit 2008). These studies suggest the literature about business model focuses on describing and conceptualising value creation mechanisms while the literature of business strategy aims to understand value through mergers and acquisitions. Although the concepts of business model and business strategy are very related, research about business model is not the same as research about business strategy according to Magretta (2002) and Seddon et al. (2004). They argue these two branches of research have distinct origins. However, the line that divides the literature of business model and strategy is often blurred as several studies show (e.g. Amit and Schoemaker 1993; Amit and Zott 2001; Amit 2014; Boulton and Libert 2000; Chung et al. 2004; Kauffman and Wang 2008; Mayo and Brown 1999; Yip 2004; Zott et al. 2000, 2011). It is therefore acceptable to explain business model and business strategy concepts together. These two streams of research also find common ground within the concepts of innovation and competitive advantage which will be discussed later (e.g. Chesbrough 2007; Lumpkin et al. 2002; Martins et al. 2015; Porter 1991).

Competitive advantage and corporate strategy

Theory about business model comes together with concepts of corporate strategy and competitive advantage. Ansoff (1965) developed the notions about vertical and horizontal integration together with concepts of market entry, product development, and diversification which were later incorporated in the business strategy and business model theory. By developing theoretical frameworks for large corporations, the author started the field of corporate strategy. This field was later advanced through the influence of Andrews (1987) who separated the concepts of business strategy and corporate strategy. On one hand, he explains that business strategy is about managers taking decisions about specific markets such as selection of product offerings, which also shape the competitive environment of the market. On the other hand, he explains that corporate strategy is about the whole business environment in which the firm operates. For instance, mergers and acquisitions as mentioned earlier. Specific studies about corporate strategy came after this separation was acknowledged (e.g. Fahey 1989; Moussetis 2011). Both corporate strategy and business strategy literatures contain notions directly used in research about business model.

The business model literature builds upon several ideas from studies. For example, Amit and Zott (2001) proposed a theoretical framework to describe business models for e-businesses. In doing so, they used the value chain and strategic positioning ideas proposed by Porter (1985), which are widely employed in the literature of business strategy. Additionally, the competitive advantage concept intersects with the literature about corporate strategy and business model. For example, Lumpkin and Dess (2004) simultaneously describe competitive advantages for e-businesses, corporate strategies, and business models. Similar to research in corporate strategy, Dyer and Singh (1998) explain how strategic alliances and cooperative strategies are linked to the business model concept. Therefore, a business model involves corporate strategies to gain competitive advantages that could be obtained through information technology used in organisations (Barney 1991, 2001; Mata et al. 1995).

The term competitive advantage was introduced together with the concepts of synergy and product-market scope of Ansoff (1965). Synergy is a recurrent concept within the business model literature and systems thinking which often portrays a competitive advantage. Consider, for example, the application of the synergy concept behind the sources of value creation defined as complementarities by Amit and Zott (2001 p. 504) *"Complementarities are present whenever having a bundle of goods together provides more value than the total value of having each of the goods separately"*. A synergy therefore is one of many sources to create value and therefore a competitive advantage in the business model framework for e-businesses of Amit and Zott (2001). The term competitive advantage is inspired in the resource based view and aims to create and to preserve value for companies as some studies suggest (e.g. Barney 1991, 2001; Mata et al. 1995). According to these studies, the main objective of top business managers is to bring together strategies to gain competitive advantages; these are adapted to the organisation's resources. Morris et al. (2005) associate the concept of business model with competitive advantage. They explain that business models are concise representations of a set of decision variables often related with several areas dealing with economics, strategy, and architecture. Under their view, these areas of businesses are interrelated and work together in coordination to create sustainable competitive advantages.

A competitive advantage may emerge as e-businesses manage economies of scale. Although technical barriers of entry are low for e-businesses, grouping many sellers and buyers provides a competitive advantage (Porter 2001). Company size increases its negotiation power. For instance, Amazon follows this approach through the 'get big fast' strategy explained in the documentary film from Heilemann (2008) depicting the history of e-commerce companies in the United States. However, competitive advantages based only on the novelty of using Internet may not be sustainable as it becomes more accessible to everybody (Lumpkin et al. 2002). Differentiation therefore becomes more relevant to build competitive advantages for e-businesses (Porter 2001). Firms differ quantitatively and qualitatively in creating value which is evident in their management strategy (Nelson 1991). One example for business models related with the Internet comes from Lumpkin and Dess (2004). They argue that content can be a source of a competitive advantage because it can aid on searching, evaluating, problem-solving, and trading. Content is unique what makes Internet business models based on commissions, advertising, production, referral subscriptions, and fee-for-service typical examples of how content can produce value for e-businesses. Value for e-businesses also comes from their strategic positioning and sustainable competitive advantages as inferred from previous research (e.g. Amit and Zott 2001; Porter and Millar 1985; Porter 1985, 1996, 2001). The concepts of competitive advantage and strategy are rooted in management studies. These concepts underpin business model research and are often related with value creation, the resource based view of the firm, and the literature of value chain.

The resource and knowledge based views of the firm

Business model and business strategy research are also inspired by the resource based view (Barney 1991, 2001; Mata et al. 1995; Nair et al. 2008; Penrose 1959). The reason is that strategy became a relevant concept under the resource based view proposed by Penrose (1959). In her book, she indirectly approached to the strategy concept while explaining the underlying mechanism of firm's growth. In doing so, she showed an image of the firm as interrelated components. The resources of a firm can be structured in these components describing investment capital, employees, and technology for example. The organisational structure clusters these resources in components. Chandler (1962) argues that organisational structures in businesses arise from the business strategy. The resource based view is therefore tied to business strategy. This view from Penrose (1959) introduced three ideas aiming to provide a common language when explaining how businesses grow: diversification, economies of scale, and entrepreneurship. Although her book did not refer explicitly to business strategy, her notions were influential in organisational research pertaining to business strategy. Her resource based vision of the firm paved the way in the following years of research about business model and business strategy.

The resource based view of the firm builds on the value creation notions of Schumpeter where firms differ on the control they exert over capabilities and resources according to Amit and Zott (2001). The authors explain how this difference coexists until some external change occurs. Hence, they note the resource based view posits a firm's unique bundle of capabilities and resources as the main driver of value creation. They also explain that the emergence of digital markets opens up new sources of value creation due to the new relational capabilities obtained by complementarities among firm's resources. In this line, Dyer and Singh (1998) showed how firms reduce their costs by developing relational capabilities.

Research also shows how developing dynamic capabilities for firms leads to organisational rents (e.g. Blyler and Coff 2003; Eisenhardt and Martin 2000; Teece et al. 1997). Value therefore is not created solely by resources, but rather by the organisation's actions, products, markets, and internal transactions as drawn from the dynamic capabilities approach (Di Gregorio 2013). Furthermore, the combination of digital and physical resources to create entirely new capabilities and sources of value is the big transformation taking place in today businesses (Rigby and Tager 2014). However, these digital markets also portray a challenge for the resource based view. Capabilities and resources based on information are more perishable than those based on tangible fixed assets because the high mobility of information jeopardises the sustainability of new competitive advantages (Amit and Zott 2001; Barney 1997). The resource based view takes a deeper emphasis on knowledge creation and transference when studying Internet based companies. The competitive advantages, the dynamic capabilities, and the resources of these companies are based on knowledge. Consequently, the resource based view contributes to developing the knowledge based view widely used by e-businesses.

The knowledge based view became popular with the book 'The Knowledge-Creating Company' (Nonaka 2007; Takeuchi' 2013). This view sees knowledge as the most important asset for businesses. In the same line, several studies posit knowledge as the main source of value for companies (e.g. Acedo et al. 2006; Amit and Schoemaker 1993; Nair et al. 2008; Pitelis 2004). The knowledge based view is at the intersection of the dynamic capabilities approach, the network perspective, and the resource based view of the firm (Acedo et al. 2006). Complementary resources, capabilities, and knowledge-sharing routines between firms are strategic for developing competitive advantages (Amit and Zott 2001; Dyer and Singh 1998). Consider, for example, strategic assets of firms driving organisational rents as outlined by Amit and Schoemaker (1993) in their article 'Strategic assets and organisational rent'. The authors explain how strategic assets arise from the combination of people and information such as intangible resources (e.g. knowledge). The firms' capacity to extract rents from environments in disequilibrium and the principles governing firms' growth are visible on mergers and acquisitions (Nair et al. 2008; Pitelis 2004). These assets are important in organisational and strategy theories because mergers and acquisitions could improve goodwill and market position based on intangible resources. Therefore, intangible resources such as knowledge are important sources of sustainable competitive advantages (Nair et al. 2008; Penrose 1959) for e-businesses.

Value chain and strategic networks

Research about organisational strategy concentrated on the notion of value chain. Porter and Millar (1985) looked at organisations' operations and focused on two questions according to Amit and Zott (2001). The first aims to discover possible actions that an organisation could carry out: which actions should be done by organisations and how? The second aims to prioritise and organise these actions to generate the maximum value in a competitive environment: which organisational structure is the best to create value while improving industry standards? The authors explain these questions provided the foundations of the classificatory framework for value chain analysis from Porter (1985) which involved the following: (1) Identifying strategic business entities, (2) Determining critical actions, (3) Identifying offers, and (4) Identifying potential benefits. Research about value chain aims to discover the main activities exerting an influence on the operations of value generation in organisations. These main activities are typically associated with producing and manufacturing tangible goods. Under the value chain literature, these activities are mainly related with logistics, supply chain management, and distribution operations (see Christopher 2011). Handfield et al. (1997) also explains that management strategies must be integrated into all phases of the value chain, which includes all processes from product distribution, logistics, packing, assembly, manufacturing, and procurement to design. At the same time, the extraordinary growth of the Internet have changed the value chain based on traditional logistics systems into one value chain based on electronic logistics systems (Büyüközkan et al. 2008). However, the value chain is not often a set of sequential processes. For instance, Hamel (2000) explains how creating and appropriating value can occur in a network including suppliers and distribution channels. Additionally, business models based on the Internet mainly create value through complex linkages and networks (Baden-Fuller and Mangematin 2013). Therefore, the notions of strategic networks are deeply related with the value chain.

Strategic networks in the value chain take the form of long-term supplier–buyer partnerships, strategic alliances, and joint ventures (Gulati et al. 2000; Jarillo 1988). According to Amit and Zott (2001), strategic networks are 'stable inter-organisational ties which are very important for the strategy of participating firms. They mention strategic networks theorists aim to answer the following questions: What is the collection of interfirm ties that lets firms to compete in the market? How and why strategic networks are formed among firms? How do different ties in the networks of the firms affect their performance? How does network position of the firm affects its performance? In this line, the authors explained how network theorists with backgrounds in sociology and organisational theory usually concentrate on the implications of the network structure for value creation. For example, research aims to look into how the network structure of an organisation in terms of centrality and density influence its performance (e.g. Freeman 1979; Hinterhuber and Levin 1994; Krackhardt 1992). More recently, an empirical study from Peng et al. (2015) demonstrates how the centrality of a firm within its strategic networks helps to improve its performance. The heterogeneity of ties and the size of the network influence on how information is available, bringing advantages such as referral, access, and timing benefits (Amit and Zott 2001; Burt 2004; Granovetter 1973). Strategic networks also offer the possibility to generate economies of scale and share risk by permitting access to information, to markets, and to technologies facilitating learning (Amit and Zott 2001; Dyer and Singh 1998; Gulati et al. 2000; Shapiro and Varian 1999). According to Amit and Zott (2001), strategic networks are important to understand value creation in e-businesses due to the relevance of partnerships in digital markets. The authors add that strategic networks may not capture completely the potential of e-businesses to create value but enable transactions in new and unique ways. They mention that the analysis of network parameters such as centrality and density together with strategic network theory partially explain value creation. In doing so, they bring the example of Priceline.com which has well-known and stable inter-organisational ties with airlines and credit card companies. They highlight that Priceline.com is essentially attached to its mechanism of transaction—namely, the introduction of reverse markets where sellers decide to accept or reject customers' proposed prices—by which airline tickets are sold over the Internet. According to the authors, this method differentiates Priceline.com from an ordinary travel agency and demonstrates how digital markets open innovative opportunities to create value by structuring transaction mechanisms. Therefore, value creation mechanisms go beyond the value created through the reconfiguration of the value chain or the formation of strategic networks (Zott et al. 2011).

Porter (1985) considers value as the amount of money purchasers would disburse for the firms' goods. In doing so, he makes clear value should be measured in terms of total returns as firms are profitable only if their total costs are below their total revenues. The value chain aims therefore to find mechanisms leading to the generation of value by improving operations and developing enhanced goods at lower costs. Consequently, the value chain analysis has been often used in the theory and practice of business strategy to create sustainable competitive advantages based on operational effectiveness.

Operational effectiveness and differentiation strategy

Operational effectiveness, however, is not a strategy; when an operative advantage is not sustainable, firms should also develop their competitiveness with a differentiation strategy (Porter 1996, 2001). The sources of product differentiation are generic strategies for organisations looking to sustain competitive advantages (Porter 1985). Information technology serves to generate value through the delivery and the reassurance of differentiation policies (Porter and Millar 1985). The integration of information technology and the value chain has intangible value for businesses. It has the power to contribute in product differentiation as Internet communications have shown. Consider, for example, how customisation options for Dell.com products served to differentiate Dell's product offerings (Shin 2001). Alternatively, the intangible value of a company's brand serves as a differentiation strategy (see Aaker 1995, 1996). As previous research suggest (e.g. Aaker et al. 1982; Keller and Aaker 1992), actions related with distribution, sales, marketing, communication, service, and advertising may contribute to improve company's value through its brand. The brand serves to differentiate products in the market. Its value is often capitalised by improving consumers' perception about a firm and its main products, which may include extending brand value to other secondary products or services (e.g. Boush and Loken 1991; Goh et al. 2013). As the supply and demand sides are often pieces of information readily visible and available in the Internet, the realised value chain and differentiation strategies are often visible in e-businesses. In the context of e-commerce, the value chain helps to understand information processing and distribution, which is behind every online transaction (Rayport and Sviokla 1995). It also aids to redesign mechanisms behind online transactions, to offer different goods and services, and to connect people in new ways making possible to enhance differentiation and value (Amit and Zott 2001; Shapiro and Varian 1999). Connecting people in new ways requires coordination of logistics and distribution operations pertaining to the value chain, doing so at large scale is a common differentiator of e-businesses. This makes the value chain of these businesses often looks like a network instead of a chain. The implications of this network are also known as network effects or network externalities. This is a reality in the business model literature pertaining to e-businesses. For example, complex tightly controlled network linkages are typical of business models used by search engines such as Google.com (Baden-Fuller and Mangematin 2013). Using network effects therefore is an innovative way to create and to protect value (Mizik and Jacobson 2003). At the same time, network effects can serve to increase operational effectiveness and articulate differentiation strategies for e-businesses.

Network effects and innovation

Network effects are typically related to the demand side of the value chain and economies of scale. *"The existence of network externalities requires increased coordination of consumer adoptions because, the technology's value depends on the total size of the adopter population"* (Sarvary et al. 2000 p. 48). This networked reality embedded in the value chain of e-businesses connecting people at large scale can be exemplified with Metcalfe's law. This law has been widely used to come up with a value for telecommunication networks (e.g. Madureira et al. 2013; Tongia and Wilson III 2011). Metcalfe's law states that the value of a network is directly proportional to the square of the total number of members within the network (Metcalfe 1995). Although this law is commonly used as reference to estimate the value of telecommunication networks, there are few studies that validate Metcalfe's law empirically such as the one from Madureira et al. (2013). Even though incremental costs of growing and maintaining a network are rarely accounted properly (Tongia and Wilson III 2011), Metcalfe's law is widely accepted as an indicator of network value. As e-businesses facilitate the formation of networks and exchanges between many people from several locations in real time, their network effects become relevant and convey value. Parker (2009) explained some of the implications of network effects for e-businesses at the Web 2.0 Summit. He mentioned network effects are the most powerful of all business externalities and that companies can take advantage of these if they control networks. He added this means two things: On one hand, connecting people is more valuable than collecting data; on the other hand, companies that understand how to build, to develop, and to manipulate networks will dominate the future of the Internet.

When a network effect is present, the value of a product or service is dependent on the number of others using it (Shapiro and Varian 1999; Zimmermann 2000). For example, building a virtual brand community depends on the number of customer to customer interactions through social media as these interactions are becoming an integral part of building and nurturing the brand (Noble et al. 2012). It is not a surprise virtual communities potentially enhance value of companies as these are online networks. Consider popular communities generated by marketers contributing to the demand side of the value chain, such as, Coca-Cola, Apple Students, Pringles, Vitoria's secret PINK, and Nike Shoes studied by Sung et al. (2010). Customers have learned to expect connections with businesses (Giamanco and Gregoire 2012). These communities can develop a sense of trust towards a business which is the basis to develop customer loyalty within these communities (Laroche et al. 2013). Networks within these communities could lead to a higher level of commitment (Lipsman et al. 2012) which is also essential for customer loyalty (Zhou et al. 2012). According to de Valck et al. (2009), there are two major perspectives about studying virtual communities: (1) To discover the true motives that lead individuals to participate in virtual communities and (2) To find how companies can exploit virtual communities to gather marketing insights in new ways.

However, another way to study communities is through the utilitarian view. How can virtual communities bring value to companies by switching costs? Switching marketing and advertising costs to social media users is, therefore, another way to study virtual communicates as a source of value, one conveying also network effects over the Internet. Switching costs to customers is an opportunity to gather value (Mizik and Jacobson 2003). The potential effects of networks portraying electronic word-of-mouth are important for the success of businesses. Particularly for business models based on the Internet, switching costs contributes to acquire and to protect value. This is consistent with the novelty and lock-in sources of value for e-businesses described in the business model framework of Amit and Zott (2001). In the case of social media, this happens when consumers' positively participate in the promotion process as suggested by Taylor et al. (2011) also pertaining to the network effects entwined with successful viral advertisements (Teixeira 2012).

The conquest of social media channels represents an opportunity to develop a competitive advantage due to their potential network effects. Consider, for instance, the threshold of critical mass that can be achieved through the creation and development of virtual communities in social media. Gladwell (2000) explains this concept through his 'tipping point' concept. He mentions ideas, behaviours, and products spread as viruses whereas successful adoptions of innovations depend on people's involvement. Social contagion and innovation come together as these are intrinsically part of any adoption process (see Burt 1987; Walker et al. 1997). It is not surprising therefore that managing virtual communities has benefits for customers and sellers as Amit and Zott (2002) explain. The authors mention customers can access to competing sellers and ideas, share their experiences, and interact with the content they receive. They contend for the idea that sellers can better allocate their offers to specific demographic groups which have segmented themselves. The authors conclude that communities are also means of leveraging the reach of the Internet to improve the flow of communication since users organise themselves according to their interests. Therefore, network effects underpin important value creation mechanisms for the strategy and business model of e-businesses aiming to build sustainable competitive advantages through innovation with social media.

The term innovation is often present in the literature of strategy and business model as it connotes change and value generation. This term became relevant in economics as Schumpeter (1934) explained his theory of economic development by incorporating the market disequilibrium caused by innovations. In doing so, he also identified some sources of innovation, such as, the discovery of new supply sources and new production methods, the introduction of new products or the creation of new markets, and the reorganisation of industries.

Understanding innovation in changing environments is key for business progress (Sood and Tellis 2005). This has special relevance for e-businesses that often deal with uncertain environments with radical and incremental innovations. Regardless of innovation typologies, such as radical or disruptive (e.g. Chandy and Prabhu 2011; Garcia and Calantone 2002), innovation conveys risk as it implies to be the first at doing something. However, being the first in the market provides advantages as this helps to fix customers' opinions (Kerin et al. 1992; Lieberman and Montgomery 1988, 1998). This is known as the first-mover advantage which is often seen as a motivator and major payback of successful innovations. Innovation therefore increases the firm's competitiveness by discovering new markets and creating new offers as explained by the 'creative destruction' idea and the 'blue ocean approach' from Schumpeter (1942) and Kim (2005) respectively.

Innovation implies the discovery and the development of new markets. One law of marketing states that it is necessary to innovate to be first in the market or create a new category in which one can be the first (see Kurts 1993). Integrating innovative distribution services into the value chain is one way to achieve innovation. For example, experimenting with drones to delivery retail products such as the Prime Air from Amazon (2013), which looks to innovate the e-commerce industry. Innovation does not necessarily depends on the size of the firm, it depends on knowledge (Minniti 2011). Innovations can only gather and secure long-term value if these are hard to imitate and commercially feasible (Teece 2010). The same logic applies to the design of an innovative business model as it must connect with the firm's strategy and protect its competitive advantages. Business model innovation is vital for the market success of e-businesses. As several studies suggest (e.g. Chandy and Tellis 1998; Chandy et al. 2003; Fischer and Henkel 2010; Gibbons 2004), investments on technological innovations generate advantages. An innovative business model results in operational efficiency and effectiveness which drive customer appropriation beyond product and process innovation (Sorescu et al. 2011). In the same line, Teece (2010) explains how innovation in business model designs and strategies with technology are necessary for their growth. Additionally, an effective innovation strategy needs knowledge based on external and internal sources (Prabhu et al. 2005) Therefore, innovation implicitly shapes the competitive strategy and the business model of e-businesses.

Strategies of e-commerce companies

E-businesses focusing only on growing their customers base must concentrate in making profits through a clear profitable strategy (Baden-Fuller and Mangematin 2013; Shin 2001). The value drivers of e-commerce business models depend on two main generic strategies proposed by an empirical analysis from Amit and Zott (2002). The first strategy aims to enhance transaction efficiency. The authors found e-commerce companies which increase transaction efficiency have the possibility to create value for all stakeholders involved by considering the next aspects: (1) Fortification of the supply chain by cost reduction and vertical integration; (2) Concentration of large selections of products and services; (3) Making transactions convenient for customers; (4) Saving customers' purchasing and searching time; and (5) Reduction of information asymmetry amongst stakeholders. In that line, Yen and Yao (2015) explain how in the current e-commerce scenario, competitive pricing, personalised recommendations, reduction of searching time, and reduction of delivery costs generates value. The second strategy aims to create 'stickiness' to simplify transaction recurrence, which is also congruent with the idea of lock-in as a source of value from Amit and Zott (2001). Similarly, Yen and Yao (2015) also note that one of the main strategies for e-commerce companies is their capacity to retain customers. They mention that 'stickiness' leads to value by retaining customers and by growing the volume of transactions. In doing so, they found e-commerce companies successfully creating 'stickiness' do the following: (1) Reward customers for their loyalty, (2) Allow them customise their products and services, (3) Form and develop virtual communities, and (4) Build a strong reputation of trust for their Internet transactions. These two generic strategies show a clear path to achieve profits, whereas transaction efficiency mainly looks at the supply side of the business, 'stickiness' mainly looks at the demand side.

Consider now the strategic framework from Shin (2001). It shows general guidelines about how innovative competitive strategies produce profits. He uses the Five Competitive Forces (i.e. threat of new entrants, threat of substitute products or services, bargaining power of customers, bargaining power of suppliers, and intensity of competitive rivalry) from Kotler (2008) and the

4Ps (i.e. promotion, place, price, and product) from McCarthy (1960) in the e-commerce context. Below an overview of the work of Shin (2001) combined with other related studies.

Promotion

Competitive strategies for e-commerce companies could emerge from user-centric promotion. Shin (2001) mentions one-to-one communication based on dialog allows e-businesses to collect data about specific customers to target them accurately. The author explains how creating experiences in tune with the brand makes them more competitive. He mentions these experiences should reflect authenticity and captivate customers through associations, emotions, and memories. Additionally, Shin (2001) proposes to capture profit from revenue-sharing (e.g. many-to-many marketing) in the form of affiliation programmes, which allows e-businesses to switch marketing and sales costs to perform-based rewards (e.g. commissions). These innovative user-centric promotion strategies block competitors and lock-in customers or create 'stickiness' as the sense of affiliation enhances customers' loyalty and the recurrence of transactions.

Place

Competitive strategies for e-commerce companies could also originate from new options to order and to receive products. Shin (2001) describes how subcontracting transport expert services and integrating online and offline presence are typical strategies to create new distribution options. He explains how a traditional book store in the United States integrated online ordering options and coffee shops within their stores to create value. The American book store known as Barnes and Noble is a story of success. The company's strategy delivers results in two ways. First, Barnes and Noble maintained their loyal customers and price levels despite increasing competition from giants, such as Amazon and Walmart. Second, the book store increased revenue through its coffee shops as customers gradually spend more time in the coffee shop section rather than in the bookshelves. The company remained competitive as it defended its customer base and attacked in the coffee shop business with its established offline presence. Ordering from home and picking up in-store (i.e. click and mortar) and ordering in-store and delivering at home are typical examples of innovative strategies in the distribution of goods (Chatterjee 2010). As traditional retailers add online presence and digital strategies, e-retailers which exclusively sell online should develop offline presence to remain competitive (Colla and Lapoule 2012; Enders and Jelassi 2000). Therefore, adding innovative options to order and to receive products could enhance the customer experience and may bring and maintain competitive advantages.

Price

The implicit negotiation between prices set by companies and purchasing decisions made by customers makes price a persistent ingredient in every competitive strategy. Typical pricing strategies come from price discrimination (Shin 2001). For example, 'price lining' involves delivering an offer at different quality levels at different prices. Sometimes these prices are radically low or even free (i.e. freemium) for new e-businesses aiming to take a big share of the market to later capitalise on network effects for example (Anderson 2009). Another price discrimination strategy comes from 'smart pricing' which uses customer's analytics to set the optimum price for a given customer. As Fortune companies struggle to take advantage of big data and customer's analytics with social media, this field has become a latent opportunity to develop competitive advantages for companies (Gartner Inc. 2013). Pricing is a field of major concern for retail companies selling through Internet as comparing prices of goods is readily available (Shin 2001). Innovative pricing models and algorithms become competitive strategies in the degree they serve to sale at optimum prices.

Product

E-businesses can build competitive strategies through their selection of products, customisation options, and convenience. In e-commerce, for example, one competitive strategy comes from 'product bundling' which promotes the benefits of a single point of sale (Shin 2001). The latter is in line with creating value from offering bundles of complementary products as proposed by Amit and Zott (2001). Another strategy is product innovation or the introduction of niche products aided by accessing directly to customers through the Internet as companies can collect and analyse their data according to Shin (2001). This helps companies to develop new products, to develop new services, to identify new markets, and to target new markets. Additionally, companies can also push their products to potential customers by allowing them to customise their product offerings online. Hence, the selection of products, customisation options, and product innovation offered by e-businesses are crucial in their competitive strategy.

Traditional business models adopting e-commerce

In today businesses, the growth of e-commerce has found a place within the multi-channel strategy as Fahey et al. (2014) explain. The authors draw on traditional consumer packaged goods companies as they struggle to successfully launch e-commerce options to their customers which pose different challenges for diverse business models. They explain how consumer packaged goods have been tackling e-commerce and digital expansion through a single business model based on business-to-consumer commerce. In doing so, they argue these companies must fully leverage multi-channel commerce to remain competitive. This requires integrating multiple channels with tailored operations to address new business models. These business models include business-to-business-to-customer coordination where maximising revenue and market share are the highest priorities. The authors conclude stating that the conceptual challenge is to keep the channel partners at the centre of each transaction. This implies to shift the 'catalogue mind-set' to an integrated perspective enabling easy-to-navigate sales and marketing channels to place orders and to restock inventories while maintaining a consistent customer experience. In addition, traditional companies must decide launching their own e-commerce platform or selling through established e-retailers (e.g. Amazon.com). They mention the best strategy for traditional companies may come from a combination of both options during the adoption process to later integrate e-commerce in their business models.

The role of e-commerce in the future of retail and logistics industries is outlined in four prospective scenarios developed by Ehrhart (2010). His four prospective scenarios show global trends and look forward to the year 2025 in order to consider possible implications for e-commerce. Below an overview of the work from Ehrhart (2010) combined with other related studies.

Scenario 1: Self-presentation in virtual communities

In this scenario the author shows that the global economy has grown quickly where this increase in prosperity is reflected in a robust and large consumption-oriented middle class. Individual lifestyles and self-realization are central for this class while social values have shifted away from work to leisure explains Ehrhart (2010). In doing so, he mentions life goes around feeling and being part of a community in which technology has gradually evolved. He describes how a plethora of wearable devices (e.g. smart glasses with video and photo capabilities) are very common and indispensable for the normal life of the middle class. The author mentions communities use these devices widely to share ideas and exchange experiences with other community members in real time. He also describes lifestyle products from golf clubs to skateboards with technological sensors transmitting data. This scenario concurs with recent developments surrounding the Internet of Things as explained by Yen and Yao (2015) in which connecting elements that were offline in the regular e-commerce model, lets retailers and manufacturers to analyse and to collect unprecedented quantities of information. The authors note this information about consumer requirements, experiences, and preferences will serve retailers and manufacturers to provide personalised products and services. Moreover, this information will serve companies to act in real time. In that line, the authors describe the Amazon Dash Button and their Dash Replenishment Service which were released in April of 2014. The Dash Button has a sensor connected to the Internet which helps to automate the ordering process of consumption goods, such as coffee grains or filters used by coffee machines or water pitches. Even Whirlpool partnered with Amazon to include the Dash Button for its new washer and dryer automating the ordering of laundry supplies. Ehrhart (2010) also mentions self-improvement is an integral part in this scenario where people will record their activities continually to share them with their communities.

In this scenario, the market share of online retail has significantly grown. The author explains the main e-commerce platforms benefit from a general increase in demand and their wide range of products serve the majority of the population. These e-commerce platforms also offer low-involvement products at good prices. However, the author highlights niche e-commerce platforms are taking the greatest profits as these are the central point of global and regional lifestyle communities. He explains this happens due to their dynamically changing and selective collections for individual lifestyles, which are the most important drivers of e-retail. Their physical presences such as local branches have become trendy and busy meeting places for diverse scenes. Dealers' selling arguments are based on uniqueness and quality as they are usually members of the community. The author explains departmental stores have picked up on the community notion and are structured according to diverse shopping experiences and theme worlds. Consumers can personalise their designs and create their own products in manufacturing stations equipped with 3D printers for example. The logistics sector has evolved dramatically because of the high economic development and prosperity, the ongoing transport volumes, and the growth of e-retail at international and national levels. Ehrhart (2010) describes how deliveries are regulated to evade traffic congestion and individual areas are served by only one integrated logistics company instead of several fragmented companies today. He mentions logistics companies have combined partnerships and many of them offer additional services, such as distribution consulting, while operating online platforms for start-ups. Product expertise is the only characteristic differentiating smaller logistics firms as these are members of a community and have in-depth product knowledge. Ehrhart (2010) concludes this lets them provide valuable insights about how to correctly use a purchased product when delivering it. The evolution of logistics as a result of the growth of e-commerce has been also noted by Yen and Yao (2015). For example, they explain that some observers have foreseen the Internet of Things would transform e-commerce by optimising inventory management.

Scenario 2: Hybrid consumer behaviour in convergent worlds of retailing

In another prospective scenario, Ehrhart (2010) depicts a moderate but steady growth in the global economy where the major driving forces come from Asian countries. The developed world (e.g. North America and Western Europe) has stable but low growth rates. The author describes a globally achievement-oriented society; weather in the United Kingdom, China, or Poland, personal achievement in the workplace defines and shapes people's daily lives. He mentions efficiency and convenience are the main premises of shopping. Additionally, the author highlights striking differences between regions regarding customers' shopping patterns. He also explains that convenience plays a fundamental role in developed countries (e.g. Germany or the United States), whereas price is crucial for the majority of the population in developing and emerging countries (e.g. Brazil and Indonesia).

Worldwide, e-commerce and stationary retailing have made advancements towards a merging as 'everywhere commerce' is widespread according to Ehrhart (2010). The author explains that retailing companies use a variety of channels to target customers. This is in line with how the Internet of Things will transform e-commerce business model through location-based or real time personalised recommendations and convenient shopping described by Yen and Yao (2015). Shopping is possible anywhere, anytime, and goods are delivered immediately continues Ehrhart (2010). He explains showrooms with several delivery options are common and using foldable and flexible displays of tablets and smartphones displace PCs and laptops when showing complex products to customers. Customers are accessible everywhere with the help of omnipresent interfaces in public places and the wide adoption of smartphones. The abundance of data helps manufacturing companies to predict customers' preferences and desires with considerable precision as a result of the evaluation of search patterns and purchasing behaviour. This is also in line with the development of big data analytics foreseen by studies and reports recently (e.g. Gartner Inc. 2013; Yen and Yao 2015). The raise of Internet connectivity of domestic appliances, development of advanced methods for big data analysis, and automated analytics technology provide a clearer insight into the behaviour of customers (Ehrhart 2010; Yen and Yao 2015). This leads to deliver precise and timely marketing messages and recommendations about products. Ehrhart (2010) explains how demand of logistics services is evident in all levels–from transnational to local traffic. He mentions few global companies control the e-retail sector, but small companies cover some regions with joint platforms specialised in additional services (e.g. goods assembly and installation). The author mentions convenience and speed are standard characteristics in urban centres where same-day delivery is possible when orders are placed early in the day. Finally, buildings equipped with pick-up stations and parcel boxes are common sight he concludes

Scenario 3: Collaborative consumption in a regionalised retailing landscape

In another prospective scenario, Ehrhart (2010) describes a difficult and decaying global economy. The second financial crisis has made severe damage. This is visible in all sectors of society whereas businesses are pushing high protectionist policies and regulatory frameworks. International retail growth is completely halted. The author explains how large increases in the cost of raw materials and energy with tight budgets in the private sector and a regionalisation of the economy drastically changed customers' patterns. He explains how developed countries (e.g. Germany, United Kingdom, and France) have increased their sense of community whereas the importance of private property and personal possessions has substantially diminished. According to the author, sharing and leasing models are very popular and available for most goods and services in this scenario. This is in line with the concept of 'sharing economy' involving the notion of sharing cars, bikes, or even your own house in new business models of companies such as, Uber, Zipcar, and Airbnb (Cohen and Kietzmann 2014; Matzler et al. 2015). It is because of exchange and lending models that many people in developing countries (e.g. India and Nigeria) access to durable goods mentions Ehrhart (2010).

The author also explains that energy efficiency and sustainability are the main factors in consumption and manufacturing. He explains environmental friendly production cycles with closed material cycles and high recycling rates as people have become socially engaged and aware of the ecological implications of retailers. Numerous tangible goods have a modular structure making them easier to repair. Domestic appliances and equipment are fitted with sensors in the leasing sector to indicate in advance repair and maintenance needs. The Amazon Dash Button described earlier is a good example of this scenario when referring to domestic appliances (see Yen and Yao 2015). Ehrhart (2010) explains how very diverse suppliers are establishing e-commerce capabilities whereas few regional companies specialise in leasing durable goods by swapping industrial equipment to a massive number of small companies. The author describes little convergence between stationary retail and e-retail but he notes how cooperative companies in maintenance and repair sectors converge between e-retail and stationary retail. In residential areas and shopping centres self-service stores for the production of daily use products are growing.

In this scenario, Ehrhart (2010) also depict a renewed specialist retailing offering products to borrow or buy. At the same time, he explains that most parcel deliveries and package companies operate within the same region since there is little growth in the demand of logistics and transportation services. Furthermore, the author describes that only very few major transportation and logistics companies are present in each region together with a great number of informal logistics services. He adds that cooperation between retailers and logistics companies grows whereas the vast majority of logistics companies include spare parts logistics, maintenance, and repair services. The author concludes explaining transportation and logistics companies do not deliver many tangible goods but replace many defective items of equipment in this scenario.

Scenario 4: Artificial intelligence in the digital retailing sphere

Although having a considerable volatility in recent years, a fresh and booming global economy is described by Ehrhart (2010) in this prospective scenario. He explains this happens due to the high-velocity of progress in the area of information technology innovation, particularly in automation. In general, technology has significantly advanced in many areas together with an advanced digital culture worldwide by the year 2025. The author describes smart contact lenses, smart glasses, and smartphones are all times in the lives of everyone. One example of these developments is the Google Glass project where a head-mounted display has a computer that works with Internet via voice commands as explained by Holey and Gaikwad (2014). The progress of technology therefore equips houses and streets with sensors while mobility and energy systems are surrounded by a data field according to Ehrhart (2010).

The author also explains how avatars are a strong concentration of the sales activity. These avatars are virtual consultants automatically assisting customers in buying decisions and activities. For example, an avatar places a purchase order, monitors the delivery of a good, and verifies its authenticity. Online shops adjust their offerings according to customer profiles in real time whereas avatars package and present products in 'shopping hubs' as noted by Ehrhart (2010). He describes how local showrooms and e-retailers use tailored simulations to customers' profiles making real time decorations and offerings' arrays in retail stores. Data analysis incorporate customers' interest and moods using advanced sensors leading to the development of new business models relying on predictive purchasing whereas customers receive goods they did not order says explains Ehrhart (2010). This also comes with enhanced after-sale relationships, going far beyond current e-commerce transactions over websites and mobile applications (Yen and Yao 2015). Is in this scenario where logistics companies benefit from reverse supply chain as products are returned. The author adds that the advantages of increased convenience and networked environments also come with new risks and privacy becomes a global problem. He also explains that there is an ongoing need for security due to cybercrime; hence, protecting private information in the digital space is a priority for most people. The author notes major logistics companies offer highly secured supply chains increasing transaction costs for those customers who want security. In the main cities, same-day delivery is very common as both logistics companies and retailers predict demand accurately ahead of time and deliver some products using drones. An example of this is the Prime Air from Amazon (2013). Finally, the author concludes mentioning customers can define the location of product delivery as needed in this scenario

These four prospective scenarios show how traditional retailers will pursue digital and multi-channel strategies building cross-channel and cross-functional capabilities has described by Noble et al. (2015). They explain how incorporating advanced analytics will help retailers to integrate inventory management systems and optimise the supply chain by allocating the right product in the right place at minimum time and cost. Looking into the future, traditional business models will embrace e-commerce and implement digital strategies in some way. Physical-digital innovations are changing almost every part of businesses today. For instance, think about reserving, ticketing, and paying airplane trips, the use of digital diagnostic equipment in healthcare, and 3D printing as Rigby and Tager (2014) explain. Their findings point in one clear direction where every industry will undergo to some extent a digital-physical transformation. Looking ahead, this transformation represents a both great threat and a great opportunity to discover new value sources for businesses (Fahey et al. 2014; Rigby and Tager 2014). Synergies between physical and digital channels are crucial to develop competitive advantages for traditional offline businesses and e-businesses as their business models evolve (Colla and Lapoule 2012; Enders and Jelassi 2000). One recent example of this are the openings of traditional physical stores by e-retailers, such as Amazon.com and Spartoo.com (M.E. 2015; Wakefield 2015). At the same time, these e-retailers reinvented their business models to take advantage of these synergies between physical and digital channels. Business models must include digital markets and an integral vision of the evolving value creation mechanisms surrounding customers' behaviour and technological innovations to remain competitive. This is particular relevant for e-retailers looking for new value sources in social media platforms today as the next section describes.

2.3 Overview of e-retailers' expansion to social media platforms

E-retailers have expanded widely to social media platforms. The consulting firm Burson-Marsteller (2012) reports that every month, companies in the Global Fortune Top 100s were mentioned in social media platforms 10.4M times on average and that they create multiple accounts to target different audiences. The Internet Retailer Magazine (2012) reports that more than 90% of the top 500 e-retailers in the United States use at least two social media platforms (e.g. Facebook, Twitter, or YouTube). Due to this wide adoption, consumers expect social links with brands and companies (Benkler 2006; Giamanco and Gregoire 2012). Gartner Inc. (2013) reports that more than 50% of the top organisations will have internal social media platforms and 30% of them will consider them critical for business communications by 2016, as firms leverage information from social media analytics. In addition, the consulting firm McKinsey (2013) explains that any inquiry on marketing influence and brand performance is unfinished without considering social media platforms. Therefore, expansion to social media platform affects the success of e-retailers.

E-retailers' expand to social media platforms due to their proximity —everything is just one click away— as social media platforms could drive traffic and sales. Several studies confirm the importance of this expansion to social media platform and their potential benefits for diverse industries although these benefits are hard to measure (e.g. Fisher 2009; Forrester Inc. 2010; Giamanco and Gregoire 2012; Hoffman and Fodor 2010; Kumar and Mirchandani 2012; Murdough 2009). Channel expansion in communications concurs with studies that see the Internet as a new market place (e.g. Frey et al. 2011; Hoffman and Novak 1997; Novak and Hoffman 1996; Wang et al. 2002). Therefore, e-retailers expand to social media platforms to gain and maintain market share through these communication channels: *"While it has been said for traditional media that the medium is the message with the Web it is also true that the medium is the market"* (Hoffman and Novak 1997 p. 12).

E-retailers' channel expansion

As explained earlier, channel expansion theory explains that information richness depends on the characteristics of the medium and on the users' skill with that medium (e.g. Carlson and Zmud 1999; D'Urso and Rains 2008; Dennis et al. 2008). As a consequence, inquiries about the effect of media on consumers are of subjective nature as the skill of each individual with a medium is different. E-retailers use social media platforms to promote their offers as more people use social media platforms and purchase online. Several authors have pointed out the advantage of channel expansion and its implications on the market success of e-businesses (e.g. Carlson and Zmud 1999; Friedman and Furey 1999; Hoffman and Novak 1997; Novak and Hoffman 1996). These studies suggest that new channels provide value as these channels emerge and potential consumers learn how to use them. For instance, how the Internet provides convenience for consumers and allows developing new services and points of sale. As the Internet provides new ways to shape industries, the literature in e-businesses notes the importance of channel expansion. It explores multi-channel management opportunities that come with adopting new channels and integrating cross-channel strategies (e.g. Choudhury and Karahanna 2008; Enders and Jelassi 2000; Geyskens et al. 2002; Keller 2010; Patel 2013). Therefore, it is common to identify e-business strategies that combine offline and online channels such as 'click and mortar' or 'click and drive' (e.g. Chatterjee 2010; Colla and Lapoule 2012; Naik and Peters 2009; Steinfield 2002) that show how e-retailers create value and reinvent their strategy while expanding their channels (e.g. Porter 2001; Shin 2001; Zott et al. 2000).

Channel expansion can drive incremental revenue for e-retailers in three ways (1) By reaching new markets, (2) Capturing customers from competitors, and (3) Selling more to existing customers as Geyskens et al. (2002) explain. Several studies explain that social presence and information richness in social media platform influence potential consumers (e.g. Gao and Bai 2014; Kaplan and Haenlein 2010; Mennecke et al. 2011; Rikakis et al. 2013; Sashi 2012; Weisberg et al. 2011).

Social media platforms arise from users' social involvement as social media platforms aim to reflect the social identity and presence of Internet users (Kaplan and Haenlein 2010). This inclusion of Internet users makes the social influence of social media platforms different from other media (e.g. radio, TV). Social influence positively affects information richness according to some authors (e.g. Carlson and Zmud 1999; D'Urso and Rains 2008). Many studies also note the effects of electronic word-of-mouth about companies is largely positive in social media platforms (e.g. Archak et al. 2011; Berger et al. 2010; Hu et al. 2009; Taylor et al. 2011; Vazquez-Casielles et al. 2013). A shared identity between members drives positive conversations and a sense of social belonging towards firms' offers and their virtual community as several studies explain (e.g. Gangadharbatla, 2008; Kietzmann, Hermkens, McCarthy, & Silvestre, 2011; Muniz Jr & O'Guinn, 2001; Schau, Muñiz, & Arnould, 2009). This positive trend in the socialisation process within virtual communities makes electronic word-of-mouth in social media platforms a natural marketing and advertising tool in business-to-consumer markets. For instance, studies have documented successful marketing and advertising campaigns in social media platforms for diverse companies such as Starbucks, Victoria Secret, or Hokey Pokey (see Hoffman and Fodor 2010; Kumar and Mirchandani 2012; Lipsman et al. 2012).

Customer service and market intelligence benefits of expansion to social media

Some companies have taken advantage of social media platforms to improve their customer service. For example, Zappos.com—an apparel e-retailer—use social media platforms to improve their customer service by encouraging employees to exhibit a genuine disclosure of their company culture (e.g. Hsieh 2010a; b).

Disclosure of information helps companies to build social capital, improve market intelligence, and social influence as some studies suggest (e.g. Ellison et al. 2007; Johnston et al. 2011; Nichols 2013; Rozwell and Sallam 2013).

Risks of expansion to social media

On the other hand, the inherent transparency within social media platforms has some risks. First, as transparency in social media platforms involves self-presentation and self-disclosure (Kaplan and Haenlein 2010), the misuse of social media platforms for identity theft or stalking behaviour raises serious privacy concerns (e.g. Bernstein 2012; Boyd and Ellison 2007; Dwyer et al. 2007; Farquhar 2009; Mitchell 2013; Patterson 2012; Reay et al. 2009). One study from Kachhi and

Link (2009) notes the privacy threats perceived by people using communication technologies. People are afraid of sharing personal and private information as it can expose them to security risks. This perception is also common among social media users as people are aware of these risks such as identity theft where criminals rely on triangulating information sources. Second, Aula (2010) argues that social media platforms could represent a risk because users typically post unverified information (true or false, and conflicting opinions). He explains how word-of-mouth changes beliefs about organisations and their product offerings (including ethical business practices and transparency of operations). He also reveals that companies who try to manipulate word-of-mouth to recommend their products might face a greater reputation risk because it is ethically questionable. *"Firms will find it increasingly hard to hide poor service, high pricing or unpopular practices, as technology makes them more visible to end-consumer"* (The Economic Intelligence Unit, 2012 p. 5). Transparency is a double-edged sword as privacy concerns are controversial and are at the core of sharing content and connections (Giles 2010). It can expose poor service of companies that serve end-consumers. For example, when United Airlines refused to compensate a passenger, Dave Carroll, for breaking his guitar; Dave complained publicly by recording a music video in YouTube (Aula 2010; Kietzmann et al. 2011; Noble et al. 2012). This video from Carroll (2009) received widespread coverage with more than 12M views and turned into a reputation disaster for United Airlines (Aula 2010; Kietzmann et al. 2011; Noble et al. 2012). As word-of-mouth changes understanding of companies' offers, companies cannot just look good but they have to be good to avoid reputation risks (Aula 2010).

Risk mitigation

Reputation is frail. Another stream of literature therefore looks to advise companies about how to mitigate negative effects of word-of-mouth (e.g. Bambauer-Sachse and Mangold 2011; Champoux et al. 2012). For example, Champoux et al. (2012) explains that since it is nearly impossible to predict users' interactions in social media platforms, companies must elaborate crisis plans. In the same line, Steiman and Hawkings (2010) suggest companies to watch word-of-mouth in social media platforms to avoid trademark and copyright misdeeds that could damage their reputation. Hence, corporate and individual users are required to be more transparent and responsible for their actions in social media platforms (Jones et al. 2009).

2.4 Marketing and advertising objectives of e-retailers' expansion

E-retailers expand their communication channels with social media platforms to promote their product offerings. Their objectives are to increase awareness and influence consumers' behaviour while switching marketing costs through these platforms. *"When a communication channel is established, each succeeding message after the first message yields a larger return"* (Wind & Mahajan 2002 p.

36). Social media platforms serve as promotion tools for firms as the literature explains (e.g. Constantinides et al. 2008; Edwards 2011; Felix 2012; Kaplan and Haenlein 2011; Kumar and Mirchandani 2012; Laroche et al. 2012, 2013; Lipsman et al. 2012). Indeed, consumers are active participants in the promotion process when they use social media platforms (Taylor et al. 2011). This allows firms to switch marketing costs to their consumers by addressing communications in social media platforms such as electronic word-of-mouth (e.g. Chintagunta et al. 2010; Sonnier et al. 2011). Potts et al. (2008) and Zailskaite-Jakste and Kuvykaite (2012) explain how social media platforms affect firms' market position with awareness while influencing on their members (e.g. fixing preferences). One of the reasons is that electronic word-of-mouth has a higher degree of credibility when it comes from someone familiar to the consumer (Steiman and Hawkings 2010). In addition, it references companies' product offerings and travel in a social network where co-produced stories create continuous feedback (Christodoulides et al. 2012; Lipsman et al. 2012). Therefore, social media platforms affect e-retailers' immediate promotional outcomes, from a consumer perspective: product awareness and perceived product quality. The following sections explain these outcomes as marketing objectives of e-retailers' expansion to social media platforms.

Product awareness

Marketing scholarship uses the concept of awareness defined in cognitive psychology as attention (e.g. Berger et al. 2010; Berger and Milkman 2011; Jansen et al. 2009; Trusov, Bucklin, et al. 2009). However, defining product awareness is a difficult task and involves defining each term separately.

On one hand, the literature refers to awareness as a threshold in the mind that allows people to recall, associate and recognise external stimulus or cues (e.g. Anderson 2004; Farris et al. 2010; Keller 2013; Merikle et al. 2001). According to some authors, awareness is the first response towards firms' offers (e.g. Funk 2012; Jansen et al. 2009; Rose 2008) and is a cognitive process of attention to external stimulus (e.g. Sylvester et al. 2007; Wijaya 2012). Firms provide external stimulus (e.g. products, brands) for people to be aware of and to buy them. On the other hand, firms' products are bundles of attributes capable of being exchanged or used to satisfy wants and needs in the market while providing value to individuals (American Marketing Association 2014; Kotler and Keller 2012; Kotler et al. 2006). Product is one of the core elements of the marketing mix (see McCarthy 1960; Yudelson 1999) and often refers to tangible goods (e.g. physical objects) but also refers to intangible goods (e.g. services).

Although defining with precision product awareness overlaps with other terms as brand consciousness or perception of objects, and other fields (e.g. neuroscience), this study considers a basic definition. Product awareness reflects a cognitive process of attention on tangible product categories (e.g. shoes, books). Product awareness is very important for e-retailers' promotion objectives in social media platforms. When consumers are not aware of products, it is unthinkable that they purchase them, so, awareness is the first step of market success. In fact, product awareness increases the likelihood of consumers to buy in the future even when there was initially a negative perception (Berger et al. 2010). The reason is that product awareness is the first step in getting into the mind of e-retailers' customers. There are several ways to cause product awareness (e.g. paid advertising, physical presence, word-of-mouth). Social media platforms contribute with product awareness through their user-generated content that serves as electronic word-of-mouth, this is how social media platforms influence promotion effectiveness (Wen et al. 2009; Zailskaite-Jakste and Kuvykaite 2012). Anderson (2009) explains that in the Internet, information is so abundant that consumers' attention (i.e. awareness) is so scarce. As a result, awareness of products has an intrinsic value because it captures people's attention.

Expansion to social media platforms leads to product awareness because these platforms capture attention. Social media platforms could be important in the attention economy as noted by Jansen et al. (2009) because electronic word-of-mouth increases awareness (Steyn et al. 2010; Trusov, Bucklin, et al. 2009). In addition, 'mere virtual presence' increases the attractiveness of offers as explained by Naylor et al. (2012) where awareness spreads and feeds word-of-mouth. As a result, it drives purchases (Vázquez-Casielles et al. 2013). In fact, Jansen et al. (2009) demonstrate how word-of-mouth influences the relationship between buyers and sellers through awareness that arises from social media platforms. In their research model, the authors posit awareness through electronic word-of-mouth from a social media platform as the first step to making a purchase.

Different studies assert that electronic word-of-mouth in social media platforms leads to an increase in product awareness (e.g. Berger et al. 2010; De Maeyer 2012). This relationship arises from two fronts: users of social media platforms may become aware of e-retailers offers from other users, or users of social media platforms may reflect their awareness through electronic word-of-mouth. In other words, electronic word-of-mouth is both the cause and the result of buying behaviour and preferences. Many studies recognise this cycle and show the importance of product awareness in social media platforms for marketing effectiveness (e.g. Christodoulides et al. 2012; Duan, Gu, and Whinston 2008; Duan, Gu, Whinston, et al. 2008; Litvin et al. 2008; Qin 2011; Xiang and Gretzel 2010; Ye et al. 2011). Although these studies concentrate on leisure and entertainment, the literature also relates social media platforms with diverse experience goods (e.g. Brown et al. 2007; Hung and Li 2007), search goods (e.g. Oestreicher-Singer and

Sundararajan 2012; Park and Lee 2008; Sung et al. 2010), and credence goods (e.g. Lee and Youn 2009; Steyn et al. 2010; Sung et al. 2010).

Consumers use social media platforms to manage their social and working lives and they also use them to get information about products and services as explained by Obal et al. (2011). Several studies conceptualise information seeking behaviour of Internet users and how they share user-generated content (e.g. Bera and Das 2011; Berinato et al. 2010; Jansen and Rieh 2010; Rose et al. 2011, 2012; Yao and Mela 2011). Therefore, expansion to social media platforms captures attention through user-generated content that serves as electronic word-of-mouth for e-retailers.

Perceived product quality

Expansion to social media platforms not only drives product awareness but it also influences consumers' evaluation about products such as perceived product quality. The reason is that information influences on the evaluation of products. Theories from information and cognitive psychology admit the convergence between external stimulus or information cues and an individual's understanding or mind cues (e.g. Carlson and Zmud 1999; Daft and Lengel 1986; Shannon and Weaver 1971; Vessey and Galletta 1991). Evaluating products is a cognitive task that involves comparisons of multiple product information cues (attributes) with their expected performance and against other products (Bredahl 2004; Steenkamp 1990; Szybillo and Jacoby 1974). Therefore, this thesis focuses on perceived product quality and how this changes with exposure to social media platforms as suggested by related studies (e.g. Ansari et al. 2000; Dellarocas 2003; Dellarocas et al. 2007; Hu et al. 2007; De Maeyer 2012).

Perceived product quality is a multidimensional construct that has several interpretations from the consumer and producer perspective as explained by Garvin (1984) and Stone-Romero et al. (1997). Studies explain that product quality involves judgements about subjective and objective attributes that closely mediate product value. (e.g. Garvin 1984; Ophuis and Trijp 1995; Steenkamp 1990; Szybillo and Jacoby 1974). These studies also conceptualise product attributes as information cues that serve to assess product quality. Particularly, the research of Steenkamp (1990) and Ophuis and Trijp (1995) describe models of the quality perception process and its subjectivity. In these models, consumers gather information cues and interpret them through an iterative mental process. This cognitive process resolves consumers' beliefs, expectations, and previous experience to form a single judgement about product quality. Perceived product quality summarises the evaluation of a product, it depends on several external cues. The price and the brand of the product have been closely related with perceived product quality (e.g. Erdem et al. 1999; Jacoby et al. 1971; Szybillo and Jacoby 1974). In addition, individual's characteristics cannot be disassociated from this subjective construct. In the words of Steenkamp (1990 p. 317),

"Perceived product quality is an idiosyncratic value judgment with respect to the fitness for consumption which is based upon the conscious and/or unconscious processing of quality cues in relation to relevant quality attributes within the context of significant personal and situational variables." This definition encompasses the subjective nature of measuring perceived product quality and factors affecting it—both internally and externally—to the individual who perceives product quality.

E-retailers' expansion to social media platforms affects consumers' perception of product quality

Expansion to social media platforms leads to changes in perceived product quality because these platforms produce external cues about product quality for potential consumers. The quality perception process that Steenkamp (1990) proposed, by adapting the lens model from Dudycha and Naylor (1966), explains how multiple external cues affect perceived product quality. Several other studies explain how environmental and atmospheric cues (e.g. sounds, smells, colours) in retail shops affect marketing objectives such as perceived product quality and communication performance (e.g. Babin and Attaway 2000; Bäckström and Johansson 2006; Baker et al. 1994, 2002; Daft and Lengel 1986; Daft and Macintosh 1981; Gardner 1985; Kotler 1973; Lengel and Daft 1988; Rayburn and Voss 2013). More recently, studies related with e-retailing reiterate the importance of such cues on consumer behaviour, attitudes, and consumer perceptions (e.g. Chang and Chen 2008; Gao and Bai 2014; Kim and Shim 2002; Mazaheri et al. 2014; Richard 2005). Consumers' perceptions and value judgements about products are formed through products' available information (Chang and Wildt 1994; Zeithaml 1988). As cues that come from social media platforms (including electronic word-of-mouth) can be sources of information about product quality, social media platforms affect perceived product quality.

Purchase intent

Purchase intent is important for market success because firms' sales largely depend on it (Morwitz et al. 2007; Mullet and Karson 1985; Sun and Morwitz 2010). Purchase intent is a popular indicator of media influence on consumers as it precedes buying behaviour (actual sales). It captures information on the willingness to buy. It does neither capture the buying act nor how much a consumer is willing to pay which involves resource availability and price sensitivity. However, purchase intent is probable the most important resolution just before the purchasing act as it results on firms' sales. It results from a cognitive process of awareness and evaluation about products as explained in the literature (e.g. Hosein 2012; Laroche et al. 1996; MacKenzie et al. 1986). It drives the purchasing act or purchasing behaviour as studies suggest (e.g. Ajzen and Fishbein 1980; Al-Ekam et al. 2012; Irshad 2012; Morwitz et al. 2007). The literature also relates purchase intent with consumers' satisfaction and loyalty (e.g. Bai et al. 2008; Parasuraman and

Grewal 2000; Singh and Sirdeshmukh 2000). In these studies, previous purchase experiences and affective attachments seem to impact purchase intent as Kwek et al. (2010) explain. Therefore, similar to perceived quality, purchase intent is of a subjective nature.

Perceived product quality affects online purchase intent

Expansion to social media platforms affects purchase intent because these platforms lead to product awareness and change perceived product quality. Purchase intent is possibly the most direct and important consequence of perceived product quality and awareness. Studies have found that perceived quality is closely related with purchase intent of retail products like furniture and clothes (e.g. Knight and Kim 2007; Wang et al. 2011). Several studies establish the relationship between consumers' perceptions and purchase intentions (e.g. Aghekyan-Simonian et al. 2012; Chang and Chen 2008; Kim and Shim 2002; Lafferty et al. 2002; Wood and Scheer 1996). This often helps to explain brand and product choice. In doing so, results from empirical studies appear to be consistent with the fact that perceived product quality and value are highly correlated and precede purchase intent (e.g. Bello Acebrón and Calvo Dopico 2000; Bredahl 2004; Knight and Kim 2007; Ophuis and Trijp 1995; Roest and Rindfleisch 2010). These studies also highlight the importance of risk and benefits embedded in consumers' perceived quality and confirm the explanations from Zeithaml (1988) and Chang and Wildt (1994) about how consumers' perceptions serve as primary drivers of purchase intentions. Therefore, it is plausible to argue that perceived quality and awareness drive purchase intent.

In the context of e-businesses, many studies concentrate on how website design affects purchase intentions (e.g. Chen et al. 2010; Hausman and Siekpe 2009; Hernández et al. 2009; Kim and Stoel 2004; Lee and Kozar 2006; Poddar et al. 2009; Rosen and Purinton 2004; Sam and Tahir 2009; Tan and Wei 2006). Their contributions serve to establish the relationship between consumer perceptions and purchase intention. In doing so, these studies remark the importance of website design (e.g. atmospherics) on behaviour of Internet users. This includes the moderating role of product awareness and perceived product quality that affects purchase intent. However, opposed to the majority of studies that explore web shops, this study focuses on social media platforms and their impact on perceived quality and purchase intention about e-retailers products. In this sense, the website atmospherics also seem to differentiate electronic word-of-mouth in social media platforms as recent studies suggest (e.g. Christodoulides et al. 2012; Lee and Youn 2009; Smith et al. 2012). These differences affect e-retailers' market success through product awareness and perceived product quality resulting in purchase intent.

Perceived product quality affects intention to recommend online

Consumers' perceptions about electronic services affect the intention to recommend them via electronic word-of-mouth (Finn et al. 2009) such as e-retail websites. As people manage their reputation in social media platforms, they would recommend only services or products of good quality (Kietzmann et al. 2011). They would do so due to their sense of social belonging to recommend or protect others by expressing their true perceptions about products (e.g. Hennig-Thurau and Walsh 2003; Hennig-Thurau et al. 2004, 2006). Therefore, perceived quality drives purchase intent affecting short-run sales and positive electronic word-of-mouth affecting long-run brand equity.

E-retailers aim to switch their marketing costs through expansion to social media platforms

E-retailers' market success seems to be a mix of awareness and influence. This literature review also showed that e-retailers aim to switch marketing costs as their third objective in their strategy of channel expansion to social media platforms (e.g. Shin 2001; Taylor et al. 2011). As surveyed in the literature, the concepts of awareness, perceived product quality, purchase intent, and intention to recommend seem to be consistent with e-retailers marketing objectives and can be empirically tested from the consumers' perspective. These concepts contribute to understand consumer's response to social media platforms and help to explain market success heterogeneity in e-retailers' expansion to social media platforms.

Summary of the literature review

Sections 2.1 and 2.2 provide a theoretical overview underpinning the conceptual framework of this thesis. These sections also provide and outlook of the competitive environment of e-businesses, their business models, and their strategies. From communication theory and the underlying theories of business model, each theoretical perspective described above gives insights on the value creation processes of e-commerce and social media. It draws attention to diverse generic strategies used in e-commerce and social media platforms pertaining to this research. In doing so, it reinforces the relevance of the many perspectives analysed above to improve the understanding of e-business and its future trends. Additionally, sections 2.3 and 2.4 concentrate on the objectives of e-retailers' expansion to social media platforms. These objectives describe the expected main effects social media platforms exert on e-retailers' performance from a consumer perspective in terms of awareness, perceived quality, purchase intent, and intention to recommend. Thus, Chapter 2 contributes to build the conceptual framework of this research presented in Chapter 3.

Chapter 3 Conceptual framework

3.1 Definitions

3.1.1 E-retailer and typology

E-retailers are entities that sell to end-consumers through the Internet. These sales involve transactions of goods and services in small quantities (Dennis et al. 2005; Shaw et al. 2011). According to Korgaonkar et al. (2006), e-retailers provide an ordering service for Internet users. Amazon, Sears.com, and Walmart.com are typical examples of e-retailers and there are at least four main typologies of e-retailers in the literature, most of them based on their product categories.

The first criterion to classify e-retailers depends on their commercial strategy. For example, Korgaonkar et al. (2006) categorise e-retailers in three types according to their competitive strategy. First, prestigious e-retailers leverage their offline reputation to attract customers. Second, discount e-retailers rely on low prices as the main way to sell. Third, prestigious and discount e-retailers have offline presence. In contrast, pure play e-retailers do not have offline presence and concentrate on developing specialised Internet services to attract customers.

The second criterion to classify e-retailers depends on their goods and services. Nelson (1970) and Obal et al. (2011) explain that goods and services differ according to how easy it is to evaluate their quality before consumption. First, search goods are the easiest to evaluate. Second, experience goods are harder to evaluate because an individual needs to experience them to assess their quality accurately. Third, credence goods are the hardest to evaluate even after consumption (Obal et al. 2011) *"Evaluating quality of credence goods accurately is beyond consumers' capabilities" (Olshavsky and Kumar 2001 p. 61).* Similarly, De Figueiredo (2000) proposes to distinguish goods according to how difficult it is to judge their quality. The author proposed another classification by listing commodity products, quasi-commodity products, look and feel goods, and look and feel goods with variable quality.

The third typology classifies goods and services according to consumers' motivations. Hedonic that provide pleasure and utilitarian that are functional (Childers et al. 2001; Dhar and Wertenbroch 2000).

The fourth typology classifies e-retailers' offers in four according to tangibility as offline goods, offline services, electronic goods and electronic services (Francis 2007, 2009).

Table 1 shows examples of types of e-retailers and their goods and services based on studies from Obal et al. (2011), De Figueiredo (2000), Francis (2007, 2009), Dhar and Wertenbroch (2000) and Korgaonkar et al. (2006).

E-retailers' strategy	Goods and services	
− Prestigious: Sears, Dillard's, Nordstrom, and Saks Fifth Avenue − Discount: Walmart, Aldi, and Tesco − Pure Play: Amazon, Zappos, and Overstock	− Search: books, printers, computers, and toasters − Experience: clothes, air flights, perfumes, and hotels − Credence: vitamins, consulting services, diet pills, and water purifiers − Commodity products: paper and oil − Quasi-commodity products: books, videos, and CDs − Look and feel goods: homes, suites − Look and feel goods with variable quality: art	− Hedonic goods: luxury watches and designer clothes − Utilitarian goods: computer desktops, and microwaves − Offline goods: groceries, flowers, clothing, and computer hardware − Electronic goods: digital books, software downloads, and video files − Offline services: tickets to travel, hotel accommodation, and car rental − Electronic services: subscriptions and investment services

Table 1 Examples of e-retailers and typologies

Content about physical product categories is the key to understand diverse types of e-retailer. Therefore, classifying product categories by their ease to evaluate quality before consumption serves to explore diverse types of e-retailer.

3.1.2 Social media platform and typology

Social media platforms are Internet companies that simplify content production and exchange. Several definitions in the literature coincide that social media platforms are Internet communication systems (Culnan et al. 2010; Hanna et al. 2011) that allow to create and to exchange user-generated content (Kaplan and Haenlein 2010). These platforms let users perform social functions such as managing conversations, sharing, reputation, relationships, groups, identity, and presence (Kietzmann et al. 2011). Table 2 shows selected definitions of social media platforms.

References	Definitions
Murthy (2013 p. 7)	"The many relatively inexpensive and widely accessible electronic tools that enable anyone to publish and access information, collaborate on a common effort, or build relationships"
Andzulis et al. (2012 p. 308)	"The technological component of the communication, transaction and relationship building functions of a business which leverages the network of customers and prospects to promote value co-creation"
Berthon et al. (2012 p. 263)	"Social media is the product of internet-based applications that build on the technological foundations of Web 2.0"
Tiryakioglu & Erzurum (2011 p. 138)	"Platforms such as social networks, blogs, micro-blogs, and forums where self-generated contents of users are shared by the user like a publisher"
Kaplan & Haenlein (2010 p. 61)	"A group of internet-based applications that build on the ideological and technological foundations of Web 2.0, and allow the creation and exchange of User-Generated Content"
Culnan et al. (2010 p. 246)	"Social media are essentially communication systems"

Table 2 Definitions of social media

Most of the definitions above concur on that social media platforms are networked systems of communication; the key to differentiate social media platforms from other forms of communication is their focus on user-generated content. User-generated content is in the form of words, text, images, and videos created and shared by millions of people (Berthon et al. 2012). According to Stoeckl et al. (2007), user-generated content must be mass-media oriented and consumers of this content become producers without immediate profit motivation. User-generated content could be seen as all forms people use of social media platforms (Kaplan and Haenlein 2010). It can be present everywhere on Internet like in Amazon.com reviews, videos in YouTube, or Facebook profiles (Akar and Topçu 2011).

There are at least eight categories of social media platforms identified by Hoffman and Fodor (2010), Kaplan and Haenlein (2010), and Thomas Aichner and Jacob (2015) according to their objectives. Table 3 summarises their classifications of social media platform.

Type	Description
1. Social networking sites	Also known as online social networks where individuals can generate personal profiles, communicate with other users that share a connection and navigate others profiles (Boyd and Ellison 2007). They allow people to preserve social relationships, find users and locate content shared by other users (Mislove and Marcon 2007)
2. Collaborative projects or co-creation sites	Enable creation and consolidation of content under the supposition that a project gets better results through a collective effort (Kaplan and Haenlein 2010). This collective effort is also known as 'crowdsourcing' which comes from two words 'crowd' and 'outsourcing' (Schenk and Guittard 2009)
3. Blogs	Traditional websites, usually, created and managed by sole users. These websites display updates with time stamps (OECD 2007). Users can read blogs, comment on them and create their own (Kilian et al. 2012)
4. Micro blogs	Restricted to small number of characters for each communication and with social networking capabilities (McFedries 2007). Micro-blogs are considered a broadcast medium that allows to share small elements of content (Kaplan and Haenlein 2011). Still, is a debate how to categorise Twitter and some consider it a news media because its information is of general interest, synthesised and fast (Kwak et al. 2010). While others consider it a social network due to its capability to generate follow and followed connections (Huberman et al. 2008). Micro-blogging is also known as micro-sharing and micro-updating that imply short comments delivered to a network of associates (Jansen et al. 2009)
5. Content communities	Form networks by letting individuals to upload and share media content. Profiles only contain basic information about users' identities (Kaplan and Haenlein 2010). This includes photo sharing and video sharing sites as acknowledged by Thomas Aichner and Jacob (2015).
6. Online forums and discussion boards	Manage and concentrate user-generated content forming virtual communities where visitors may read and write about topics of common interest
7. Review sites	Similar to an online forums but the major topic is about reviewing people, businesses, products, and services. They serve as a reference
8. Virtual worlds	Reproduce three-dimensional environments where users appear represented by avatars and interact as they would in real-life. These platforms offer the highest degree of information richness and encompass virtual social world and virtual game worlds (Kaplan and Haenlein 2010). This includes social gaming as identified by Thomas Aichner and Jacob (2015)

Table 3 Types of social media platforms

The objective of the first category is to connect people (e.g. social networking sites). The second category aims to build collective knowledge (e.g. collaborative projects). The third category empowers individuals to create websites and share about topics of interest (e.g. blogs). The goal of the fourth category is to develop a continual news feed of real time information (e.g. microblogs). The fifth category looks to concentrate content in rich file formats about interest topics (e.g. content communities). The sixth category looks to encourage debates about topics of common interest (e.g. online forums and discussion boards). The seventh concentrates electronic word-of-mouth about products and services (e.g. review sites). The eight category aims to entertain people, for example, in a video game (e.g. virtual worlds).

Scholars and practitioners commonly study social media platforms as virtual communities. According to Burnett (2000), a virtual community is both: a social network and a network of information. There are two types of virtual communities according to their network. Frey et al. (2011) labels the first type as explicit network where its members are aware others' identities. The authors refer to the second type as implicit networks in which its members are less aware of others' identities. The members of implicit networks connect with others based on current interests as opposed to the members of explicit networks that connect with real-world friends. In this line, van Dijck (2013) offers a concurring view based on actor-network theory with a political economy perspective where social media platforms are a set of relations that constantly need to be performed. This relations form virtual communities or microsystems that together build the ecosystem of connective media, a system that *"nourishes and, in turn, is nourished by social and cultural norms that simultaneously evolve in our everyday world" (van Dijck 2013 p. 21)*. Therefore, it is important to understand virtual communities as a bundle of interpersonal virtual ties building the network structure of these communities.

Interpersonal ties differ in their strength. *"The strength of a tie is (probably linear) combination of the amount of time, the emotional intensity, the intimacy (mutual confiding), and the reciprocal services which characterise a tie" (Granovetter 1973 p. 1361)*. For example, weak ties exist between acquaintances while strong ties exist between relatives (Granovetter 1973). This separation can be used to distinguish ties within members of virtual communities in social media platforms. Inferring from Frey et al. (2011), explicit networks will have more strong ties than weak ties as opposed to implicit networks. Therefore, social media platforms with weak ties have less dense networks than platforms with strong ties if the definition of network density is *"the mean strength of connections among units in a network, or (for dichotomous measurements) the proportion of links present relative to those possible" (Marsden 1990 p. 453-454)*.

Finally, two additional classifications for social media platforms arise from the work of Kaplan and Haenlein (2010). The first comes from social presence theory where social influence and self-disclosure are higher, both critical to develop close relationships. The second comes from information richness theory where the amount of information transmitted in a given time interval differs between social media platforms. Table 4 shows examples of social media platforms based on the studies from Kaplan and Haenlein (2010), Hoffman and Fodor (2010), and Frey et al. (2011).

Objectives of social media platforms	Social presence / Information richness	Social ties of virtual communities
– Social networking sites: Facebook, LinkedIn – Collaborative projects or Co-creation sites: Wikipedia – Blogs: Diverse providers for example WordPress and Blogger – Micro blogs: Twitter, Pinterest. – Content communities: YouTube, SlideShare, and Flickr – Online forums and discussion boards: Google Groups – Customer or product review sites: Amazon, Yelp, TripAdvisor – Virtual worlds: Second life and World of Warcraft	– Low social presence/information richness: collaborative projects as Wikipedia and blogs – Medium social presence/information richness: social networking sites as Facebook and content communities as YouTube – High social presence/information richness: Virtual social worlds as Second Life and virtual game worlds as World of Warcraft	– Strong ties: Social networking sites as Facebook and virtual social worlds as Second Life – Weak ties: Blogs, Review sites, Content communities and collaborative projects as YouTube and Wikipedia

Table 4 Examples of social media platforms and typologies

Analysing the types of user-generated content is the key to understand diverse types of social media platform. Therefore, tie strength, social presence, and information richness serve to explore diverse types of social media platform.

3.1.3 Business model and transaction content

The objective of this section is to outline the importance of business models and provide relevant definitions for this research. According to Zott et al. (2011), the literature concerning business models started to become more common with the arrival of the Internet during mid-1990s and has been gathering momentum since then. The importance of using business models to understand firms is widely supported in the literature (e.g. Baden-Fuller and Morgan 2010; Wirtz et al. 2010; Zott and Amit 2010; Zott et al. 2000). Table 5 shows selected definitions of a business model.

References	Definitions
Amit and Zott (2001 p. 511)	*"A business model depicts the content, structure, and governance of transactions designed so as to create value through the exploitation of business opportunities"*
Shafer et al. (2005 p. 202)	*"It can also be defined as "a representation of a firm's underlying core logic and strategic choices for creating and capturing value"*
Lumpkin and Dess (2004 p. 167)	*"A business model is a method and a set of assumptions that explains how a business creates value and earns profits in a competitive environment"*
Zott and Amit (2007 p. 181)	*"A business model elucidates how an organization is linked to external stakeholders, and how it engages in economic exchanges with them to create value for all exchange partners"*
Teece (2010 p. 173)	*"A business model articulates the logic and provides data and other evidence that demonstrates how a business creates and delivers value to customer"*
Casadesus-Masanell and Ricart (2010)	Business models concern to the logic of the firm but rather than be a strategy, a business model is a reflection of the firm's realised strategy
Baden-Fuller and Mangematin (2013)	A business model should not be descriptive but a cognitive instrument that captures the essence of the cause–effect relationships between customers, organisation, and money

Table 5 Definitions of a business model

A business model is an abstract image of the value operations of a firm, it allows to describe differences about how a firm produces value (Casadesus-Masanell and Ricart 2010). A business model serves as a tool to understand and explore firms' logic through diverse parameters. For example, Baden-Fuller and Mangematin (2013) mention that the main business model parameters are customer sensing, customer engagement, monetisation, and value chain and linkages. Similarly, Amit and Zott (2001) propose novelty, efficiency, complementarities, and lock-in as the main sources of value. For e-businesses, a model involves systems with content, governance, and structure (Zott and Amit 2010). Indeed, networks and content are recurring ideas to explain how firms create and secure value (e.g. Baden-Fuller and Mangematin 2013; Lumpkin and Dess 2004; Wirtz et al. 2010; Zott and Amit 2007, 2010). Content is widely considered as a key parameter in studies about competitive strategies of e-businesses (e.g. Enders et al. 2008; Lumpkin and Dess 2004; Teece 2010; Weill and Woerner 2013; Wirtz et al. 2010; Zott et al. 2000). According to Amit (2014), the links between business models' parameters and competitive advantages have not been fully explored.

One of these business model parameters is transaction content. It refers to *"the goods or information that are being exchanged and to the resources and capabilities that are required to enable the exchange" (Amit & Zott, 2001 p. 511)*. According to Amit and Zott (2001), studying transaction content allows to improve transaction efficiency and network effects, which serve as complementarities among resources-capabilities applicable in digital markets. The authors also explain that transaction structure and governance refer to how parties exchange goods and how information flows among them. This study focuses on transaction content because it is clearly different between e-retailers and social media platforms from a consumer perspective. One can identify transaction content as exchangeable goods and understand the business model of e-retailers through their product categories (see section 3.1.1). Similarly, one can easily perceive differences among the social media platforms through their content (see section 3.1.2). In contrast, other business model parameters such as transaction structure and governance are not as easy to identify from the consumer perspective and require technical knowledge to understand their differences. Additionally, some business model taxonomies focus on the business model alignment of information systems within organisations (e.g. Al-Debei 2010; Osterwalder 2004). In contrast, this research looks to explore business model alignment between organisations (e.g. e-retail and social media platforms) and the idea of transaction content serves this purpose. This thesis refer only to one parameter of business model: transaction content as this study focuses on marketing and communications. Therefore, transaction content serves to explore business model alignment and to understand e-business model typologies and their differences from a consumer perspective as this thesis explains in the following sections.

Transaction content of e-retailers

This study defines e-retailers' transaction content as products offerings because they are the source of value for e-retailers.

E-retailers' deliver value from the efficiency they provide through Internet capabilities (e.g. 24-hour-shop, unlimited display space for products, vast selection of product offerings). This reduces transaction costs of consumers when compared to traditional retail. Choudhury and Karahanna (2008) explain that e-retailers, in their role of market intermediaries, should reduce the costs of transactions for their users. The authors argue that individuals choose to buy online because they can save time and effort while completing their transactions. In that line, Amit and Zott (2001) and Zott et al. (2000) mention efficiency in searching costs also produces value for e-businesses.

Search costs and search patterns are key because consumers need to get information before buying online (Choudhury and Karahanna 2008; Kim et al. 2011). For these reasons, behavioural assumptions from transaction cost economics (opportunism and bounded rationality) help to explain consumers' decisions online (Hu et al. 2008). Consumers gather rapid information from others' opinions to decide what to buy (Huang and Chen 2006) increasing their product awareness. They choose to buy online depending on their understandings about the costs of transactions (Choudhury and Karahanna 2008; Hu et al. 2008). These understandings include enjoyment and risk associated with online transactions (Huang et al. 2009) as perceived quality and purchase intent. However, retailing and e-retailing coincide on their objective to produce a large volume of transactions. In doing so, e-retailers attract web traffic and potential consumers by concentrating product offerings.

With more product offerings, e-retailers can increase their volume of transactions as explained in the 'long tail' idea from Anderson (2008). The author notes that the future of e-retail is selling less of more. That is, e-retailers will increasingly diminish the quantity they sell per product but the diversity of their products will grow. This growth in the diversity of products suggests that products offerings are the main transaction content of the business model of e-retailers because more products cause more transactions overall. Therefore, e-retailers' product typologies as transaction content depict e-retailers business models. In addition, consumers' information needs vary according to product categories. *"Consider Amazon's retail customer digital business model. Amazon's content — what is consumed — includes digital products like movies and software, as well as information about the physical products it sells or brokers"* (Weill and Woerner 2013 p. 73).

Transaction content of social media platform

This study defines transaction content of social media platforms as user-generated content because it is the source of value for social media platforms.

Social media platforms provide value through efficiency in communications as they simplify production and consumption of user-generated content. In addition, these platforms lock-in users through social networks. These characteristics give advantages over traditional media (e.g. content personalisation and co-creation) that eventually reduce costs of content. Consequently, social media platforms concentrate a large volume of content at no cost. This abundance of content motivates non-monetary exchanges (e.g. awareness-attention) in information economies that are typical of business models based on the Internet as Anderson (2009) explains. This is relevant for the business model of social media platforms as the literature highlights the importance of content for competitive strategies and e-business models (e.g. Enders et al. 2008; Lumpkin and Dess 2004; Teece 2010; Wirtz et al. 2010; Zott et al. 2000). Social media platforms are essentially media businesses. Their business model is primarily based on advertising, it relies on user-generated content to increase their growth and value as referred to in the literature (e.g. Dwyer 2007; Enders et al. 2008; Shriver et al. 2013; Teece 2010). Like in any other media business, the value of social media platforms varies according to the time people spend on user-generated content as explained in the attention economies from Anderson (2009).

Social media platforms aim to entertain by centralising and simplifying exchanges (including production and consumption) of user-generated content (Enders et al. 2008; Lumpkin and Dess 2004; Teece 2010). Similar to e-retailers' product offerings, diversity in user-generated content in social media platforms results in a 'long tail' that increases overall transactions of content (Enders et al. 2008). The reason is that the more diverse and great the user-generated content is, the more users and attention that a social media platform will attract. This suggests that user-generated content is the main transaction content of social media platforms. As more user-generated content could increase information transactions among their users, it also increases the value of the social media platform. Therefore, typologies of user-generated content from social media platforms as transaction content depict business models of social media platforms.

Characterising business models of e-business in terms of their transaction content has many advantages to do empirical research. Particularly, the main transaction content of e-retailers and social media platforms is readily available. Therefore, the next section describes the empirical paradigm used in this thesis.

3.2 The Stimulus-Organism-Response paradigm

The Stimulus-Organism-Response (S-O-R) paradigm provides a perspective to develop knowledge based on empirical research. First, this paradigm is convenient because several studies use it to support the influence of information cues in traditional retailing (e.g. Chang et al. 2011; Grewal et al. 1998; Lee et al. 2011; Michon et al. 2005; Turley and Milliman 2000; Wu et al. 2013). It is also used in e-retail contexts (e.g. Eroglu et al. 2001; Fang 2012; Kim and Lennon 2012; Rose et al. 2012; Wang et al. 2011) despite studies focus on services instead of products (e.g. Chang et al. 2014; Gao and Bai 2014; Kawaf and Tagg 2012). It is well established in the advertising literature underlying this study where information cues affect consumers' responses (e.g. Chang and Chen 2008; Jang and Namkung 2009). In addition, early literature has operationalised this paradigm to study media influence. For example, Baker and Churchill Jr. (1977) propose scales to empirically assess media influence compatible with this paradigm. Second, using this paradigm will provide a more complete explanation as it incorporates individual's characteristics (organism).

A closer survey of the literature shows that involvement of individuals also drives consumers' responses (e.g. Jacoby 2002; Sautter et al. 2004; Slama and Tashchian 1987). Third, the S-O-R paradigm allows this study to capture alignment of transaction content from a consumer perspective by comparing responses of treatment groups exposed to e-retailer and social media platform (stimulus). The influence of media channels influence on e-retailers' multi-channel strategies and objectives can be deduced from many related studies (e.g. Baron and Kenny 1986; Fang 2012; Hsieh et al. 2012; Li et al. 2012; Mousavi and Demirkan 2013; Qu et al. 2013; Richard 2005; Rose et al. 2011). Therefore, the S-O-R paradigm sets the basis to compare the influence of e-retailer and social media platform.

```
        ┌──────────┐
        │ Stimulus │
        └────┬─────┘
             │
             ▼
        ┌──────────┐
        │ Organism │
        └────┬─────┘
             │
             ▼
        ┌──────────┐
        │ Response │
        └──────────┘
```

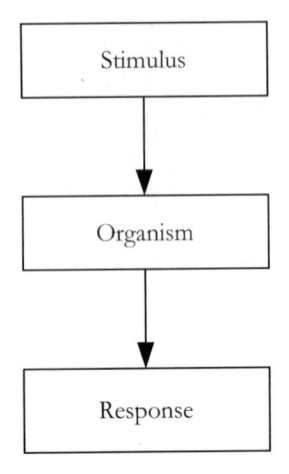

Figure 1 S-O-R paradigm

Figure 1 shows a basic representation of the S-O-R paradigm adapted from several studies (e.g. Li et al. 2012; Sautter et al. 2004; Slama and Tashchian 1987; Wang et al. 2011).

As explained in section 2.4, social media platforms influence the perception of e-retailers' potential consumers by producing external cues about the quality of products (e.g. Chang and Chen 2008; Gao and Bai 2014; Kim and Shim 2002; Mazaheri et al. 2014; Richard 2005). Perceived quality is highly correlated with value and precedes purchase intent of retail products as several studies suggest (e.g. Bello Acebrón and Calvo Dopico 2000; Bredahl 2004; Knight and Kim 2007; Oude Ophuis and Van Trijp 1995; Roest and Rindfleisch 2010; Wang et al. 2011). Furthermore, consumers' perceptions about electronic services affect the intention to recommend them via electronic word-of-mouth (Finn et al. 2009) such as in e-retail websites. As people manage their reputation in social media platforms, they would recommend only services or products of good quality (Kietzmann et al. 2011). As explained earlier, they would do so due to their sense of social belonging (Hennig-Thurau and Walsh 2003; Hennig-Thurau et al. 2004, 2006). Therefore, perceived quality drives purchase intent and positive electronic word-of-mouth affecting long-run brand equity and short-run sales.

Figure 2 serves to understand the influence of e-retailer and social media platform external cues (i.e. stimuli) on consumer (i.e. organism) and their perceived quality (i.e. response). A variety of studies support the proposed mediating path in this causal chain (e.g. Chang and Wildt 1994; Kim and Lennon 2012; De Maeyer 2012; Merikle et al. 2001). Note that individual's characteristics (i.e. organism) will be considered in the methodology section as controls.

```
          ┌─ ─ ─ ─ ─Treatment─ ─ ─ ─ ─┐
          │   ╱Type of e-retailer and type of╲   │
          │  (    social media platform    )  │
          │   ╲_____╱   │
          └─ ─ ─ ─ ─ ─│─ ─ ─ ─ ─ ─ ─ ─ ─ ─┘
                     ▼
               ╱Perceived quality╲
              (                  )
               ╲_____╱
                 ╱           ╲
                ▼             ▼
      ╱Online purchase intent╲  ╱Intention to recommend online╲
```

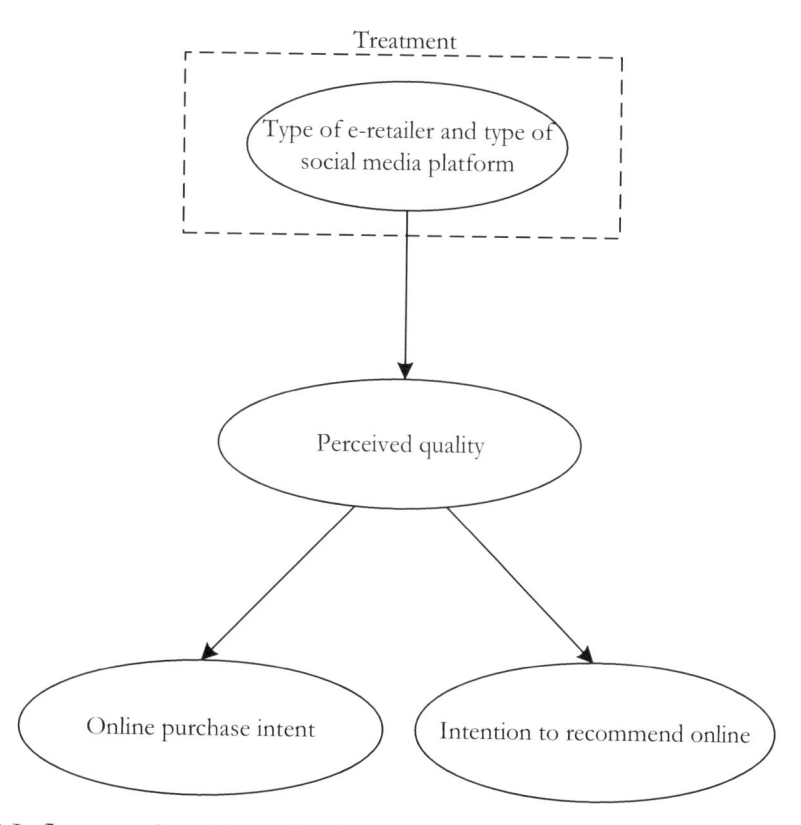

Figure 2 Influence of social media platforms on consumers of e-retailers' products

Stimulus: Virtual community of e-retailer in social media platform as an ongoing advertisement

The literature on virtual brand communities has established how these communities drive positive attitudes and perceptions about products in consumers. For example, Habibi et al. (2014) and Felix (2012) explain how virtual brand communities based on social media platforms for brands such as Harley Davidson, Yamaha, and Jeep are successful. User-generated content is equivalent to electronic word-of-mouth when is brand-related as Christodoulides et al. (2012) explain. In addition, a virtual brand community based on a social media platform serves as a unit of analysis for individuals whose information task is to evaluate firms' offers as used in related studies (e.g. Laroche et al. 2012, 2013). Therefore, virtual communities of e-retailers in social media platforms can be studied as ongoing advertisements.

Communication and information theories contribute to study virtual communities of e-retailers in social media platforms as ongoing advertisements. The strength of weak ties theory from (Granovetter 1973, 1983) helps to explain information diffusion in virtual communities. Social presence theory serves to understand the influence of social media platforms on e-retailers' customers. As social presence *"is the degree to which we as individuals perceive another as a real person and any interaction between the two of us as a relationship" (Wood and Smith 2001 p. 72)*, it can boost social influence. Individuals tend to imitate others in online environments where they do not know how to respond (Bonabeau 2004). Indeed, being mindful about others, a sense of community and interpersonal interactions are essential to understand the influence of social presence (e.g. Rice 1993; Short et al. 1976; Tu and McIsaac 2002; Wrench and Punyanunt-Carter 2007). According to Daft and Macintosh, (1981 p. 210), information is *"that which alters a mental representation"* and information richness is *"the ability of information to change understanding within a time interval"* (Daft and Lengel 1986 p. 560). This richness serves to resolve ambiguities in communication (Daft and Lengel 1986; Dennis et al. 2008) such as the ones present in the subjectivity of perceived product quality.

Organism (e.g. individual): Individuals' characteristics affecting their responses

People respond to media and change their initial perceptions in different ways. As explained earlier, information richness depends on the characteristics of the medium and on the users' skill with that medium (e.g. Carlson and Zmud 1999; D'Urso and Rains 2008; Dennis et al. 2008). In addition, cognitive fit theory from Vessey and Galletta (1991) explain variations on the effectiveness of cognitive processing when information fits users' favourite cognitive mode. Therefore, individuals' characteristics should be taken into account to better understand the subjectivity of their behavioural responses to external stimuli (see section 4.1.2 page 80 about control items).

Response: Influence on individuals' behaviour towards e-retailer's products

Recent studies show the influence of social media platforms on perceptions about products. For instance, Obal et al. (2011) demonstrates how the effect of electronic word-of-mouth in social media platforms vary according to diverse products. Additionally, Laroche et al. (2013) found that virtual brand communities in social media platforms have a positive effect on judgements about brands and products. This is in line with the literature reviewed in section 2.4 page 52 where the marketing and advertising objectives of e-retailers aim to influence potential customers in terms of perceived quality, purchase intent, and intention to recommend. Therefore, by comparing people's responses in diverse treatment groups it is possible to drive conclusions about the different influence of two or more social media platforms on products' perceptions.

3.3 Transactional content alignment of e-retailer and social media platform

Using the framework from Amit and Zott (2001), this thesis conceptualises transaction content of e-retailers' in terms of their product categories. The search-experience-credence classification has been found valid and relevant for e-retail as Girard and Dion (2010) and Nakayama et al. (2010) explain. It fits the context of e-retail and social media platforms because it is based on the information available about quality of product categories (Nelson 1970). As consumers categorise objects based on their similarity to the schema (Neisser 1976), product categories facilitate consumers' responses (Boush and Loken 1991). The study also defines transaction content of social media platforms in terms of user-generated content. Differences among user-generated content of social media platforms could affect positively channel richness expansion and advertising performance (e.g. Kaplan and Haenlein 2010; Timmerman and Madhavapeddi 2008). Typologies of social media platforms based on communication and information theories are the logical path to develop hypotheses regarding social media platforms as previous studies suggest (e.g. Frey et al. 2011; Kaplan and Haenlein 2010). Therefore, the role of transactional content alignment of e-retailer and social media platform may be explored by analysing responses to diverse e-retailer's product category and user-generated content of social media platform.

3.3.1 H1: Alignment of search goods and tie strength

Evaluation of search goods depends on weak ties because of their information immediacy. First, search goods are the easiest to evaluate before consumption and information about their quality is much more abundant than information from experience or credence goods (Ekelund et al. 1995; Nelson 1970; Obal et al. 2011). Finding information opportunely therefore is the key to promote search goods. As weak ties produce less dense networks than strong ties, information travels faster in weak ties rather than in strong ties (see Granovetter 1973, 1983). This produces higher information immediacy that helps to learn faster about search goods from weak ties than from strong ties. Second, weak ties validate information about search goods faster than strong ties due to the triangulation of information sources. As strong ties need more resources (e.g. time, intimacy, and emotional intensity), weak ties outnumber strong ties (Granovetter 1973, 1983). The average individual would have much more weak ties than strong ties. In addition, an individual would rely more on advice from experts than advice from peers for search goods (Obal et al. 2011). Experts of specific search goods would be typically weak ties rather than strong ties due to the scarcity of strong ties versus weak ties. Thus, information from weak ties has a greater positive influence on consumers of search goods than information from strong ties.

H1a: Social media platforms with weak ties will have a greater positive influence on consumers' perceived quality of e-retailer's search goods than social media platforms with strong ties.

H1b: Social media platforms with weak ties will have a greater positive influence on consumers' intention to purchase online search goods of e-retailer than social media platforms with strong ties.

H1c: Social media platforms with weak ties will have a greater positive influence on consumers' intention to recommend online e-retailer with search goods than social media platforms with strong ties.

3.3.2 H2: Alignment of experience goods and social presence

Evaluation of experience goods depends on social presence as it helps fitting information from other people about them. First, as the evaluation of experience goods is relatively easy immediately after consumption (Nakayama et al. 2010; Nelson 1970; Obal et al. 2011), electronic word-of-mouth from past consumers becomes crucial. The most reliable sources are the most personal (Obal et al. 2011) and this is more relevant for experience goods than credence or search goods: (1) As credence goods are impossible to evaluate even after consumption, word-of-mouth will have a lower impact, and (2) As search goods are the easiest to evaluate before consumption, personal sources are not necessary to assess them. In contrast, experience goods are easily evaluated but only after consumption. This makes electronic word-of-mouth more useful and credible in social media platforms where people disclose their identities as a basis for socialisation (e.g. Kaplan and Haenlein 2010; Kietzmann et al. 2011). Second, identity disclosure serves to triangulate and validate information among sources (see Chakravarty et al. 2010; Cheung et al. 2009; Obal et al. 2011). It serves to evaluate similarity with sources of information as demonstrated in studies that distinguish between word-of-mouth of peers and experts (e.g. Brown et al. 2007; Obal and Kunz 2013; Paek et al. 2011; Yang et al. 2012). This similarity serves to establish a better cognitive fit between information-source-meaning for someone evaluating experience goods (see Vessey and Galletta 1991). Third, herding behaviour is present in social contexts where people follow others' opinions and attitudes (Bonabeau 2004; Huang and Chen 2006) that is the case of social media platforms with higher social presence which tend to have higher social influence. Thus, information with high social presence has a greater positive influence on consumers of experience goods than information with low social presence.

H2a: Social media platforms with high social presence will have a greater positive influence on consumers' perceived quality of e-retailer's experience goods than social media platforms with low social presence.

H2b: Social media platforms with high social presence will have a greater positive influence on consumers' intention to purchase online experience goods of e-retailer than social media platforms with low social presence.

H2c: Social media platforms with high social presence will have a greater positive influence on consumers' intention to recommend online e-retailer with experience goods than social media platforms with low social presence.

3.3.3 H3: Alignment of credence goods and information richness

Evaluation of credence goods depends on information richness as indirect cues form beliefs in consumers' minds about them. As the evaluation of credence goods is beyond consumers' capabilities (Obal et al. 2011; Olshavsky and Kumar 2001), cues about the benefits of the these goods play a key role. The reason is that these cues persuade and form beliefs about quality in consumers' minds. Triangulating diverse information cues provides a more persuasive, realistic, and validated message (Todd 1979), therefore, social media platforms with videos will be more effective to promote credence goods. For instance, Phillips (1998) concludes that video communications are more persuasive than written communications. As information richness resolves ambiguities (Kaplan and Haenlein 2010) and credence goods are the most ambiguous goods (Obal et al. 2011), information richness change beliefs faster (Daft and Lengel 1986; Dennis et al. 2008). Thus, information with high information richness has a greater positive influence on consumers of credence goods than information with low information richness.

H3a: Social media platforms with high information richness will have a greater positive influence on consumers' perceived quality of e-retailer's credence goods than social media platforms with low information richness.

H3b: Social media platforms with high information richness will have a greater positive influence on consumers' intention to purchase online credence goods of e-retailer than social media platforms with low information richness.

H3c: Social media platforms with high information richness will have a greater positive influence on consumers' intention to recommend online e-retailer with credence goods than social media platforms with low information richness.

These hypotheses assume that the effect of social media platforms is largely positive as several studies suggest (e.g. Archak et al. 2011; Berger et al. 2010; Gangadharbatla 2008; Kietzmann et al. 2011; Muniz Jr and O'Guinn 2001; Schau et al. 2009; Taylor et al. 2011; Vázquez-Casielles et al. 2013). Although the mediating effect of perceived quality on purchase intent and intention to recommend is acknowledged in section 3.2, the research hypotheses aim to evaluate main effects. It does so because the objective of this thesis is to explore the role of transactional content alignment by comparing the effect of diverse social media platforms on the performance of diverse e-retailers. Figure 3 summarises the research hypotheses operationalised with the methodology proposed in Chapter 4.

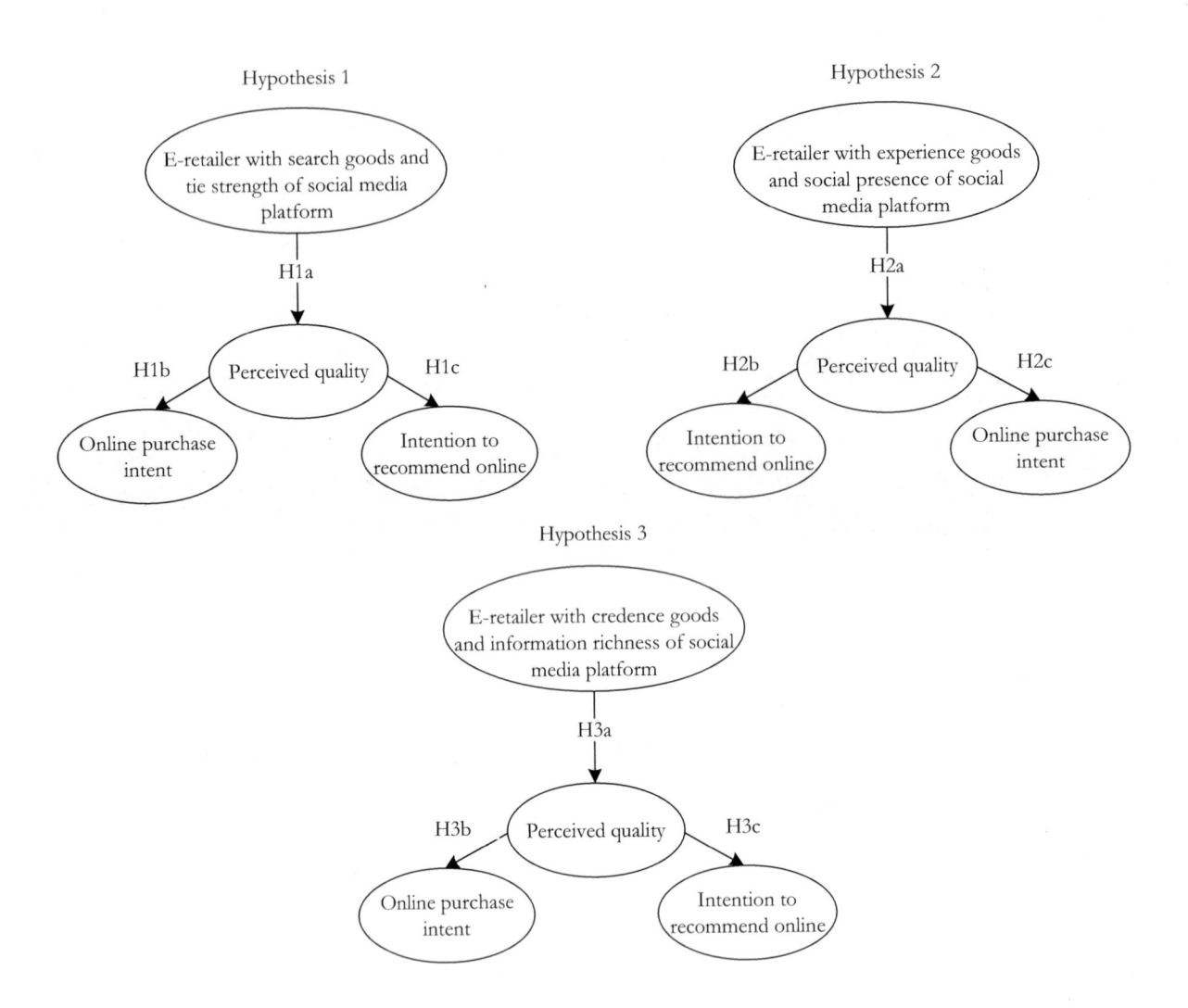

Figure 3 Research hypotheses

Chapter 4 Methodology

4.1 Research design

An experimental design for each e-retailer characterised by search, experience, and credence goods with one factor and different levels of tie strength, social presence, and information richness represented by social media platforms serves to test the hypotheses. This experimental design is mainly prepared for between subject comparisons for those individuals unfamiliar with selected e-retailers. Additionally, it selectively captures qualitative data from participants as a way to explore justifications of their responses in a complementary analysis.

An experiment using surveys matches the needs of this study. First, experiments are appropriate for testing the research hypotheses of this study, since they allow assessment of differences between two groups of respondents to be attributed to a treatment condition (Visser et al. 2000). Further, experiments with surveys allow *"to say how much direct causal impact a variable has" (De Vaus 2011 p. 70)* on consumers. Second, experiments with surveys serve to get qualitative and quantitative primary data from consumers for within-subject and between-subject analyses. This permits the use of mixed designs that combine the benefits and complexities of both analyses (Charness et al. 2012; Creswell and Clark 2007). Third, De Maeyer (2012) mentions that experiments with surveys are better to measure consumers' attitudes and behaviours than data from companies. Finally, experimenting with surveys adds originality to this study as most studies about electronic word-of-mouth and online reviews use data from companies instead of surveys.

The resulting instrument consists of 34 items. Additionally, the short length of the survey (around 6 minutes) and its presentation makes it friendly to participants as Deutskens et al. (2004) recommend. This design allows the study to gather data for its between-subject analysis to compare the effects of transactional content alignment between e-retailer and social media platform.

4.1.1 Selection of empirical context

To select e-retailers according to the research hypotheses (i.e. search, experience, and credence e-retailers), this study uses existing research on this topic. For e-retailers with search goods, this research considers an e-retailer of computers, electronics, and appliances such as PCs, MP3 players, CDs, microwaves, printers, and cartridges. This is in line with previous empirical studies that consider computers, electronics and appliances as search goods (e.g. Korgaonkar et al. 2006 p. 273; Nakayama et al. 2010 p. 256; Obal et al. 2011 p. 40). For e-retailers with experience goods, this study considers an e-retailer specialised in apparel and accessories such as clothes, shoes, accessories as experience goods (e.g. Ekelund et al. 1995 p. 36; Girard and Dion 2010 p. 1081; Korgaonkar et al. 2006 p. 273; Obal et al. 2011 p. 40). For e-retailers with credence goods, this thesis considers an e-retailer specialised in nutritional supplements such as vitamins, herbal supplements, and diet pills. This is in line with extant empirical research that considers nutritional supplements as credence goods (e.g. Girard and Dion 2010 p. 1081; Korgaonkar et al. 2006 p. 273; Nakayama et al. 2010 p. 256; Obal et al. 2011 p. 40). For details see link 1 and link 2.

Similarly, to select social media platforms pertaining to the research hypotheses, this research uses existing studies. For social media platforms with weak ties, this research considers a social media platform with less dense social networks as the basis of its user-generated content. The low density network of Twitter makes it a social media platform with weak ties as several studies indicate (e.g. Garg et al. 2011; Kivran-Swaine et al. 2011; Kwak et al. 2010; Kwon and Han 2013; Lin and Peña 2011; Myers et al. 2012; Qian and Ya 2012; Smith et al. 2012; Yagan et al. 2013). In contrast, dense networks such as the one of Facebook, represents a social media platform with strong ties. For social media platforms with high social presence, this thesis considers a social media platform where users build robust social profiles and updates as the basis of its user-generated content. Robust profiles and content are forms of identity and identification that make Facebook the most popular social media platform with high social presence as previous research suggests (e.g. Ellison et al. 2007; Farquhar 2009; Heidemann et al. 2010; Johnston et al. 2011; Kavada 2012; Lipsman et al. 2012; Reagans 2005). In contrast, this study considers social media platforms that have users with short social profiles and content updates such as Twitter to represent a social media platform with low social presence. For social media platforms with high information richness, this thesis considers a social media platform with videos as its main user-generated content. Videos from YouTube have the richest information available in popular social media platforms as several studies acknowledge (e.g. Biel and Gatica-Perez 2010; Hanson and Haridakis 2008; Pace 2008; Smith et al. 2012; Snelson 2011; Waters and Jones 2011). In contrast, this study considers social media platforms with text as its main user-generated content such as Twitter to represent a social media platform with low information richness.

For creating the empirical context of the experimental study, three existing e-retailer firms were selected through a Google search for each type of e-retailer. It was ensured that selected e-retailers used Facebook, Twitter, and YouTube as their social media platform. The e-retailers: Samsung, Currys, and Pixmania were selected for e-retailer with search goods. For e-retailer with experience goods: ASOS, Next, and boohoo.com were selected, while for e-retailer with credence goods: Healthspan, iHerb, and PROZIS were selected. To further narrow the e-retailers selected, brand familiarity was measured for the nine e-retailers. Brand familiarity accumulates consumer's experiences with the brand (Keller 1993), it is capable of influencing consumers' responses

(Laroche et al. 1996; Zhou et al. 2009), blurring the effect of the experimental design. Hence, e-retailers with low brand familiarity were selected to avoid the confounding effect of familiarity with the brand. To measure brand familiarity, a pilot study was conducted for each e-retailer. Participants were exposed to the logo and name of each selected e-retailer and answered survey questions about brand familiarity. Brand familiarity was measured by adapting a ten-point Likert scale comprising three items (see Table 6) developed by Bruner (2013 p. 98).

Items	Cronbach's α
1. Please evaluate how familiar you are with the brand above from 1 (this brand is very unfamiliar to me) to 10 (this brand is very familiar to me). 2. Please evaluate how much you know about the brand above from 1 (I'm not at all knowledgeable about this brand) to 10 (I'm very knowledgeable about this brand). 3. Please evaluate how much you have seen the brand above from 1 (I have never seen advertisements about this brand in the mass media) to 10 (I have seen many advertisements about this brand in the mass media).	.91 from the original scale developed by Bruner (2013 p. 98)
Note: All items capture responses from 'strongly disagree' to 'strongly agree'	

Table 6 Adapted scales to brand familiarity

For e-retailers with search goods, participants were less familiar with Currys (M = 1.4, SD = 1.3) than Samsung (M = 8.4, SD = 1.4). Similarly, they were less familiar with Currys than Pixmania (M = 1.5, SD = 1.4). Due to its low score, Currys was selected as the e-retailer with search goods, such as computer-electronics and appliances.

For e-retailers with experience goods, participants were less familiar with boohoo.com (M = 1.4, SD = 1.3) than ASOS (M = 2.1, SD = 2.3). Similarly, they were less familiar with boohoo.com than Next (M = 1.7, SD = 1.5). Due to its low score, boohoo.com was selected as the e-retailer with experience goods, such as apparel and accessories.

For e-retailers with credence goods, results show that participants were less familiar with PROZIS (M = 1.3, SD = 1.2) than Healthspan (M = 1.5, SD = 1.1). Similarly, they were less familiar with PROZIS than iHerb (M = 1.4, SD = 1.2). Due to its low score, PROZIS was selected as the e-retailer with credence goods, such as nutritional supplements.

4.1.2 Measures

The study adapts reliable measures for its dependent variables. Scale reliability is important because it allows the study to give similar results in repeated occasions (De Vaus 2011), which is a quality standard in research. To assess the reliability of the measures, this research uses the Alpha (α) coefficient from Cronbach (1951). The Cronbach's α coefficient assessment depends on heuristics. While a score higher than .70 is recommended for exploratory studies, a score higher than .80 is recommended for confirmatory studies (Nunally and Bernstein 1967; Peterson 1994).

The Likert measures in this study use nine-point scales to maximise the reliability of the measurements as Preston and Colman (2000 p. 6-7) suggest.

Dependent variables

Perceived quality of an e-retailer

This study measures perceived quality of an e-retailer by adapting a Likert scale. The effects of information cues on perceived product quality have been studied extensively (e.g. Bello Acebrón and Calvo Dopico 2000; Breivik and Thorbjørnsen 2008; Ekelund et al. 1995; Jo 2007; Stone-Romero et al. 1997). People make inferences based on external stimuli and memories (Dover 1982; Olson 1978), such inferences can be about product quality. Breivik and Thorbjørnsen (2008) and Jo (2007) present a Likert scale of absolute product quality consisting of five items. Absolute quality of the product is *"used to measure a person's assessment of a product's quality made without comparison to any referent product" (Bruner 2012 p. 519)*. Quality of product is a valid measure for this research because it is *"the consumer's judgment about a product overall excellence or superiority" (Zeithaml 1988 p. 3)*, which is compatible with perceived product quality as reviewed earlier (see section 2.4 page 55). In addition, inferences about product quality can be extended to make quality assessments about product categories (e.g. Hahn et al. 1994; Lim and Olshavsky 1988; Sujan 1985). Therefore, this study measures perceived product quality of an e-retailer by adapting a scale of absolute product quality. Table 7 shows adapted items to measure absolute quality for e-retailer with search goods as an example.

Items	Cronbach's α
1. [Computer-electronics and appliances like PCs, MP3 players, printers, printer cartridges, microwaves, and mixers from Currys] have excellent quality. 2. [Computer-electronics... from Currys] look to be reliable and imperishable (credence goods) / look to be reliable and resistant (experience goods) / look to be reliable and durable (search goods). 3. [Computer-electronics... from Currys] have fewer performance problems like unwanted side effects (credence goods) / have fewer defects like fabrication flaws (experience goods) / have fewer problems like malfunctioning (search goods). 4. [Computer-electronics... from Currys] have excellent quality properties (credence and experience goods) / have excellent quality features. 5. [Computer-electronics... from Currys] provide an excellent experience.	.81 - .90 from the original scale developed by Bruner (2012 p. 519)
Note: All items capture responses from 'strongly disagree' to 'strongly agree'	

Table 7 Adapted scales to measure perceived quality

Intention to purchase online from an e-retailer

This research measures intention to purchase products online from an e-retailer by adapting a Likert scale. There are strong empirical foundations showing ways to measure the effect of Internet marketing on purchase intent and sales in several studies (e.g. Brown et al. 2007; Jansen et al. 2009; Lee and Youn 2009; Obal et al. 2011; Oestreicher-Singer and Sundararajan 2012; Park and Lee 2008; Stephen and Galak 2012; Wang et al. 2011; Yang 2012). The work from Wang et al. (2011) provides measures of purchase intent at the website. *"The scale measures the probability that a customer will buy something at a particular website right after having looked at some of its pages" (Bruner 2013 p. 285)*. This is a valid measure for this study because it is compatible with purchase intent as reviewed earlier (see 2.4 page 56). Discriminant tests support the validity of these measures in the study of Wang et al. (2011). Additionally, intention to buy a product can also be extended to study buying products from an e-retailer (e.g. Liaw et al. 2005; Pan et al. 2013; Rahtz and Moore 1989). Table 8 shows adapted items to measure intent to purchase products online for an e-retailer with search goods.

Items	Cronbach's α
1. I intend to purchase online [Computer-electronics and appliances like PCs, MP3 players, printers, printer cartridges, microwaves, and mixers from Currys] immediately. 2. The likelihood of me purchasing online [Computer-electronics… from Currys] immediately is… 3. I rate my chances of purchasing online [Computer-electronics… from Currys] immediately as…	.91 from the original scale developed by Bruner (2013 p. 285)
Note: Item 1 capture responses from 'strongly disagree' to 'strongly agree', item 2 from 'very unlikely' to 'very likely'; and item 3 from 'very low' to 'very high'	

Table 8 Adapted scales to measure intent to purchase online

Intention to recommend online an e-retailer

This study measures intention to make an online recommendation of an e-retailer by adapting a Likert scale. There are many empirical studies about recommendation through word-of-mouth (e.g. Berger and Schwartz 2011; Gelbrich 2011; Kozinets et al. 2010; Oestreicher-Singer and Sundararajan 2012; Vázquez-Casielles et al. 2013). The work from Gelbrich (2011) shows a way to measure intention to recommend. This scale measures *"a person's willingness to recommend a particular merchant to friends if they are in the market for a certain product" (Bruner 2013 p. 420)*. Table 9 shows adapted items to measure intent to make an online recommendation for an e-retailer with search goods.

Items	Cronbach's α
1. I would recommend online [Computer-electronics and appliances like PCs, MP3 players, printers, printer cartridges, microwaves, and mixers from Currys] for [product category] to my online audience (friends, acquaintances, etc.). 2. If my online audience (friends, acquaintances, etc.) were looking for [product category] I would tell them online to try [Computer-electronics… from Currys]. 3. I would advise my online audience (friends, acquaintances, etc.) to buy [product category] from [Computer-electronics… from Currys].	.83 - .93 from the original scale developed by Bruner (2013 p. 420)
Note: All items capture responses from 'strongly disagree' to 'strongly agree'	

Table 9 Adapted scales to measure intent to recommend online

Control items

Demographics

Individual's characteristics may affect the evaluation and use of a particular online channel (Montoya-Weiss et al. 2003). Several studies acknowledge that (1) Age affects individual's behaviour (e.g. Kilian et al. 2012; Moore 2012; O'Reilly and Marx 2011). Age differences affect information processing in terms of ability to learn, susceptibility to social influence and receptivity (Phillips and Sternthal 1977; Taylor et al. 2011). Although Strutton et al. (2011) empirically show motivations and behaviours across age groups are similar, they also show differences in the media used across age groups. To exacerbate this point, Kilian et al. (2012) show that behaviour related with social media among 'millennials' is less homogeneous than literature suggests. Additionally, Chen and Green (2012) mentions that age of participants affects behaviour of retailer shoppers in terms of perceived quality and brand associations. Slama and Tashchian (1985) explain that purchasing behaviour depends on socioeconomic demographic characteristics. They mention that (2) Gender, (3) Income, and (4) Education are readily available and often used for segmenting. Due to this fact, controlling for these demographic variables is easy and would add more control to between subject comparisons in this study.

There is also literature supporting the influence of these demographic variables on consumer's behaviour. First, consumer's responses vary according to gender as several studies have shown. Consumers vary on how they perceive media (e.g. Baker and Churchill Jr. 1977; Clipson et al. 2012; Molyneaux et al. 2008; Taylor et al. 2011; Yang et al. 2010). Second, consumer responses may vary according to income group as it has been used in several marketing studies (e.g. Van den Bulte and Stremersch 2004; Childers et al. 2001; Hyllegard et al. 2005; Kim and Stoel 2004; Montoya-Weiss et al. 2003; Ramcharran 2013; Seiders et al. 2005). Third, education level affects purchasing behaviour as previous studies suggest (e.g. Montoya-Weiss et al. 2003; Slama and Tashchian 1985). For instance, security concerns about online transactions are lower for consumers with more education (Montoya-Weiss et al. 2003 p. 452).

Finally, this study also controls for (5) Racial-ethnicity, and (6) Geographic location (i.e. longitude and latitude). Several studies acknowledge consumer's response differences according to their culture and ethnicity (e.g. Amersdorffer et al. 2012; Burton et al. 2012; Maclaran et al. 2011; Matei and Ball-Rokeach 2001; Mazaheri et al. 2014; Obal and Kunz 2013; Park et al. 2012; Schultz 2010; Seraj 2012; Xiu-he et al. 2011). Park et al. (2012) show how consumers' trust towards e-retailers varies across western and eastern cultures for example. They explain consumers also differ on how they interact with e-retailers in terms of willingness to depend on e-retailers and perceived risk when dealing with them. Similarly, Mazaheri et al. (2014) explain that consumers' attitudes toward the website and service vary significantly across cultures. The following items aim to control for demographic differences between individuals:

1. My year of birth is...

    Note: This item captures a positive number with four digits.

2. Select your gender

    Note: This item offers types of responses from 'female' or 'male'

3. What was your annual family household income in 2013?

    Note: This item offers nine types of responses: (1) Less than $15,000 USDs, (2) $15,000 - $24,999 USDs, (3) $25,000 - $34,999 USDs, (4) $35,000 - $49,999 USDs, (5) $50,000 - $74,999 USDs, (6) $75,000 - $99,999 USDs, (7) $100,000 - $149,999 USDs, (8) $150,000 - $199,999 USDs, and (9) $200,000 USDs or more. Based on ranges used by the United States Census Bureau (2014 p. 23) and the United Kingdom Office for National Statistics (2013b p. 4)

4. My level of education is...

    Note: This item offers fifteen types of responses: (1) None, (2) 1st - 4th grade, (3) 5th - 6th grade, (4) 7th - 8th grade, (5) 9th grade, (6) 10th grade, (7) 11th grade, (8) High school graduate, (9) Some college, no degree, (10) Associate degree, occupational, (11) Associate degree, academic, (12) Bachelor's degree, (13) Master's degree, (14) Professional degree, and (15) Doctoral degree. Based on classifications used by United States Census Bureau (2013) and the United Kingdom National Archives (2012)

5. The ethnical / racial group that I belong is...

    Note: This item offers six types of responses: (1) African American / Black, (2) Asian American, (3) Caucasian / White, (4) Hispanic / Latino, (5) Native American, and (6) Other _____. Based on classifications used by United States Census Bureau (2014 p. 5) and the United Kingdom Office for National Statistics (2013a p. 5)

6. Two automated controls for geographic location estimate longitude and latitude according to the IP address of each participant.

Time of exposure

Time affects consumer's responses (see Deutskens et al. 2004; Hu et al. 2008; Malhotra 2008). This research controls for response time with automated time controls that track the first click, the last click, and page submit click in the survey screen dedicated to the treatment. This allows controlling for time participants spent in the treatment.

4.1.3 Pilot study

The pilot study serves to ensure the surveys use common language and avoid leading respondents in one direction as recommended by Évrard (1993), Zikmund et al. (2012), and Malhotra and Birks (2007). First, three graduate students reviewed a paper version of the questionnaire and responded to a semi-structured interview about the experiment. This helps to review that each item is easy to understand and the suitability of their sequence. Second, a pilot online survey provided feedback from a convenience sample. Lexical and validation improvements served to build final versions of the six questionnaires. Improvements in wording of six items were included. The pilot showed that the survey looks well in different computer devices (e.g. PC, Smartphones, Tablets, and Laptops). Third, the data from the pilot study was used to check the appropriateness of selected e-retailers in terms of the search-experience-credence classification. Fourth, the data was also used to check the suitability of selected social media platforms in terms of tie strength, social presence, and information richness. Finally, a time analysis serves to verify that participants spent similar times on different social media platforms.

Checking classification of e-retailers

Participants compared the three e-retailers' product categories to check the search-experience-credence classification. Three items, one per product category, serve to survey participants about the ease to evaluate each product category.

Results show the search-experience-credence classification, indicating successful manipulation. All participants responded to the first items of the questionnaire about the search-experience-credence classification (n = 90). Based on the items' scores, the results are conclusive. These results empirically validate three levels of goods according to the ease to evaluate their quality before consumption. Computer-electronics and appliances (i.e. search goods) are easier to evaluate than apparel and accessories (i.e. experience goods), $t(89) = 2.5$, $p = .02$ ($M_S = 4.2$, $SD_S = 2.0$ and $M_E = 4.8$, $SD_E = 2.2$ respectively). At the same time, apparel and accessories are easier to evaluate than nutritional supplements (i.e. credence goods), $t(89) = 3.6$, $p < .01$ ($M_E = 4.8$, $SD_E = 2.2$ and $M_C = 5.9$, $SD_C = 2.3$ respectively). Figure 4 displays estimated means for the three product categories.

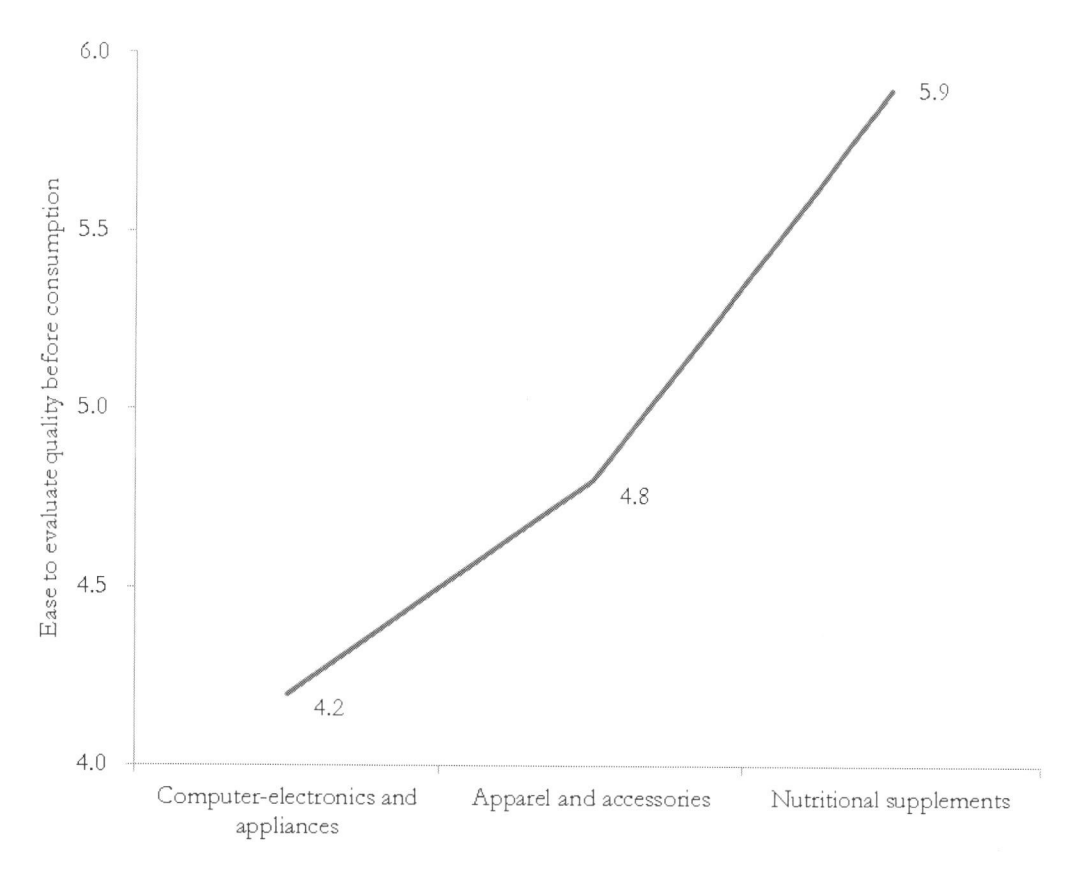

Figure 4 Three product categories represent the search-experience-credence classification

Checking classifications of social media platforms

Participants compared two social media platforms to check the classification according to tie strength of social media platform. A ten-point Likert scale comprising three adapted items serve to survey participants about tie strength of social media platform. Two items come from two scales of Bruner (2012 p. 681-682) which measure tie strength and one item is deduced from Granovetter (1983) and Krackhardt (1992). These three items form a reliable scale for comparisons between Twitter (Cronbach's α = .86) and Facebook (Cronbach's α = .86). Results show that participants considered virtual ties of Twitter as weaker (M = 2.8, SD = 2.0) than the ones of Facebook (M = 6.4, SD = 2.3), this difference was significant, t (54) = -8.6, p < .01. Therefore, these social media platforms will serve to test the first set of research hypotheses (i.e. search goods and tie strength).

Participants compared two social media platforms to check the classification according to social presence of social media platform. A ten-point Likert scale comprising three adapted items serve to survey participants about social presence of social media platform. Two items come from a scale of Bruner (2012 p. 639) which measures similarity and one item comes from another scale of Bruner (2012 p. 465) which measures community social value. These three items form a reliable scale for comparisons between Facebook (Cronbach's α = .87) and Twitter (Cronbach's α

= .88). Results show that participants considered Facebook has higher social presence (M = 4.9, SD = 2.5) than Twitter (M = 3.7, SD = 2.5), this difference was significant, t (45) = 3.2, p < .01. Therefore, these social media platforms will serve to test the second set of research hypotheses (i.e. experience goods and social presence).

Participants compared two social media platforms to check the classification according to information richness of social media platform. A ten-point Likert scale comprising two adapted items serve to survey participants about social presence of social media platform. One item comes from a scale of Bruner (2013 p. 265) which measures Persuasiveness of the Ad and one item is deduced from (Daft and Lengel 1986 p. 560). These two items form a reliable scale for comparisons between YouTube (Cronbach's α = .87) and Twitter (Cronbach's α = .84). Results show that participants considered YouTube has higher information richness (M = 6.1, SD = 2.5) than Twitter (M = 3.5, SD = 2.3), this difference was significant, t (50) = 5.9, p < .01. Therefore, these social media platforms will serve to test the third set of research hypotheses (i.e. credence goods and information richness).

Validity of scales used for checking classification of social media platforms

The proposed scales have acceptable convergent and discriminant validity to measure tie strength, social presence, and information richness of social media platform. First, items one, two, and three are highly correlated (see Table 10 for correlations) indicating convergent validity for tie strength of social media platform. Second, items 4 to 6 are highly correlated indicating convergent validity for social presence of social media platform. Third, items 7 to 8 are also highly correlated indicating convergent validity for information richness of social media platform. On the other hand, items 1 to 3 are not highly correlated with any other item. Similarly items 4 to 6 are not highly correlated with any other item. Finally, items 7 to 8 are not highly correlated with any other item indicating discriminant validity (see for Table 11 descriptions of items).

Table 10 shows the correlation matrix between items measuring these constructs for Twitter because it is the only social media platform measured in the three dimensions. An exploratory factor analysis with varimax rotation shows three factors are sufficient to represent the eight items, χ^2 (7) = 5.7, p = .57. Factor loadings indicate that the group of items used for each manipulation check support the theory. In fact, the factor loadings concentrate on each of the three latent constructs: tie strength, social presence, and information richness. Table 11 shows these results.

n = 46		Tie strength			Social presence			Information richness	
		Item1	Item2	Item3	Item4	Item5	Item6	Item7	Item8
Tie strength	Item 1								
	Item 2	**.68**							
	Item 3	**.60**	**.83**						
Social Presence	Item 4	-.05	.10	.09					
	Item 5	-.08	.06	.03	**.75**				
	Item 6	-.15	-.13	-.12	**.61**	**.77**			
Information richness	Item 7	.19	.04	.09	.09	.18	.12		
	Item 8	.18	-.08	-.08	.08	-.01	.08	**.71**	

Note: Highly significant correlations above .50 with p < .01 are bold.

Table 10 Item-correlation matrix

	Factor loadings		
Item	Tie strength	Social presence	Information richness
1. Please evaluate connections in Twitter from 1 (weak) to 10 (strong)	.72		.2
2. Please rate your relationships with people in Twitter from 1 (not close) to 10 (close)	.97		
3. What is the likelihood of you spending a free afternoon with someone from you are connected in Twitter? Please evaluate from 1 (not likely) to 10 (very likely)	.86		
4. Please evaluate from 1 (No) to 10 (Yes) People in Twitter make me feel they are similar to me...		.76	
5. Please evaluate from 1 (No) to 10 (Yes) People in Twitter make me feel we have a lot in common...		.99	
6. Please evaluate from 1 (No) to 10 (Yes) I rely on the personal support I get from others in Twitter...	-.16	.78	
7. Please evaluate Twitter content from 1 (not useful to learn about products) to 10 (very useful to learn about products)		.16	.72
8. Please evaluate Twitter from 1 (does not influences my opinion about products) to 10 (influences my opinion about products)			.99
Eigenvalue	2.3	2.2	1.6
Variance explained	27.8%	27.6%	19.6%
Cumulative variance explained	**75.0%**		

Table 11 Exploratory factor analysis

Time analysis

Statistical analyses were performed with data from the pilot study. Using non-parametric tests from Gao et al. (2008), no significant differences (p > .1) were found between time participants spent visiting diverse social media platforms. However, these analyses unveiled a left-skewed distribution (i.e. less total time of survey) and a considerable difference between the 10% fastest respondents and the typical ones (i.e. 158 versus 263 seconds) as Figure 5 shows.

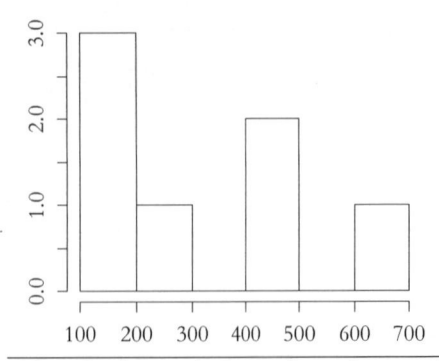

Accumulated percentage (%)	Total time (seconds)
10	158
15	175
20	179
50 (median)	263
80	446
85	480
90	660

Note: In the graph the y axis are frequencies and the x axis are seconds.

Figure 5 Histogram – Total time of pilot study

This study uses Amazon Mechanical Turk to recruit participants and pays them per completed survey. This payment is depends on the average time they spend answering the survey; but because they respond at different times, a time threshold was established to trigger 'why' questions to normalise their response times. The minimum length required in each question is based on Karat et al. (1999 p. 571), Arif and Stuerzlinger (2009 p. 101) and Wolfram Alpha (2014). The authors explain written composition takes 19 words per minute and each word is around 5 characters. Considering the latter, 1.58 characters per second (i.e. 19÷60×5) determine the length of written composition to compensate the time of 105 seconds (i.e. 263−158) between typical and fast respondents. The fast participants hence require answering 'why' questions with a minimum text length of 66 characters (i.e. 105÷1.58) also providing qualitative insights for the complementary analysis explained below (see page 91). Table 12 serves to evaluate costs of using Amazon Mechanical Turk.

References	Time per survey (minutes)	Cost per survey in study (USDs)	Cost per minute in study (USDs)
Jacquet (2011 p. 2)	60	1.4	.0233
Paolacci et al. (2010 p. 412-415)	3	.1	.0333
	5	.1	.0200
Casler et al. (2013 p. 2157)	10	.5	.0500
	12	.5	.0417
Buhrmester et al. (2011 p. 2)	10	.1	.0100
	5	.1	.0200
	30	.1	.0033
Ipeirotis (2010 p. 2)	3	.1	.0333
Ross et al. (2010 p. 10)	60	1.67	.0278
Berinsky et al. (2012 p. 353)	7	.15	.0214
	6	.75	.1250
Crump et al. (2013 p. 3)	5	.1	.0200
		Mean	**.0330**
		Median	**.0233**

Table 12 Estimation of monetary awards of participants

As Buhrmester et al. (2011) and Berinsky et al. (2012) mention, paying above 2 cents per minute just affects the time required to collect data but not its quality. Based on the pilot study, the estimated time for the final survey is around 6 minutes. Therefore, this study pays participants between 12 and 24 cents per survey (i.e. 2 and 4 cents per minute).

4.2 Research procedure

The research procedure is simple. Participants are randomly assigned to a treatment group and answer items. Each treatment group drives participants to the official website of selected e-retailer within the selected social media platform. For the main study, participants respond to items about dependent variables after treatment.

4.2.1 Data collection

The study collects data through Internet exclusively. First, online quantitative surveys have lower costs and faster responses (Deutskens et al. 2004). Second, this procedure helps participants to recall. As previous experience with e-retail or social media platforms comes from online environments, online surveys help participants to recall. The reason is that retrieval context increases participants' recalling skills when it matches their encoding context (e.g. Godden and Baddeley 1975, 1980; Tulving and Thomson 1973). As most control questions at the beginning of the survey require participants to recall, surveying online is important. Third, an online survey is an easy way to expose participants to stimuli from e-retailers in social media platforms. Participants can easily access a link that exposes them to e-retailer and social media platform as confirmed in the pilot study. In fact, other studies have applied similar procedures (e.g. Hamouda and Tabbane 2013; Lee and Youn 2009). Furthermore, it is easier to administer online surveys than offline surveys and randomise treatment groups, survey blocks, items and response options (Evans and Mathur 2005). This is important to avoid primacy effects that produce biased responses (Holbrook et al. 2007; Krosnick and Alwin 1987; Malhotra 2008; Schwarz et al. 1992). Therefore, using online questionnaires is widely accepted in related empirical studies (e.g. Chen, Hsu, & Lin, 2010; Cheng et al., 2012; Gruen et al., 2006; Lin & Lu, 2011; Teltzrow et al., 2007; Xiu-he et al., 2011).

The study uses Qualtrics to setup the online survey and uses Amazon Mechanical Turk to distribute and to pay participants. On one hand, Qualtrics is a tool widely used by empirical researchers (e.g. Gillin 2008; Hart and Dale 2014; Limbu et al. 2012; Liu et al. 2013; Peer and Paolacci 2012). It has the features needed for this study such as randomisation, validation, conditional displaying of items, and collection of time data. For instance, this online survey randomises treatment groups to avoid non-equivalent groups and randomises control items to avoid carry over effects.

This research also uses Amazon Mechanical Turk because it has many advantages as a distribution mechanism and as a platform for payments. First, it has been validated by empirical researchers related with the topic of this study (e.g. Archak et al. 2011; Biel et al. 2011; Crump et al. 2013; Hart and Dale 2014; Holden et al. 2013; Montgomery and Cutler 2013; Paolacci and Chandler 2014). Second, it allows to assign random treatments and target online populations (e.g. Berinsky et al. 2012; Wright 2005). Third, even though Amazon Mechanical Turk has been questioned in linguistics research and has been labelled as an unregulated labour market (e.g. Fort et al. 2011; Pavlick et al. 2014), it delivers results of good quality within hours and at low cost (e.g. Archak et al. 2011; Christensen and Glick 2013). Therefore, using these online tools for data collection can be valid and even superior than in-person data collection in some cases (Casler et al. 2013).

By using Qualtrics and Amazon Mechanical Turk, this research is able to collect quantitative and qualitative data. After the completion of each survey, participants can claim their monetary award in Amazon Mechanical Turk. Qualtrics blocks participant's IP address to avoid multiple responses from the same participant. It also allows collecting additional data such as web browser and approximate location of the participants, which can serve as additional controls. All this contributes to conduct a transparent and rigorous procedure. The research therefore exposes participants of the web survey to one of the selected empirical contexts. Figure 6 and Figure 7 show screenshots as examples of the experimental treatment in the next page, to see the complete web survey visit the following link:

https://co1.qualtrics.com/SE/?SID=SV_a9Ipbj2CMiLEyIT&Preview=Su...

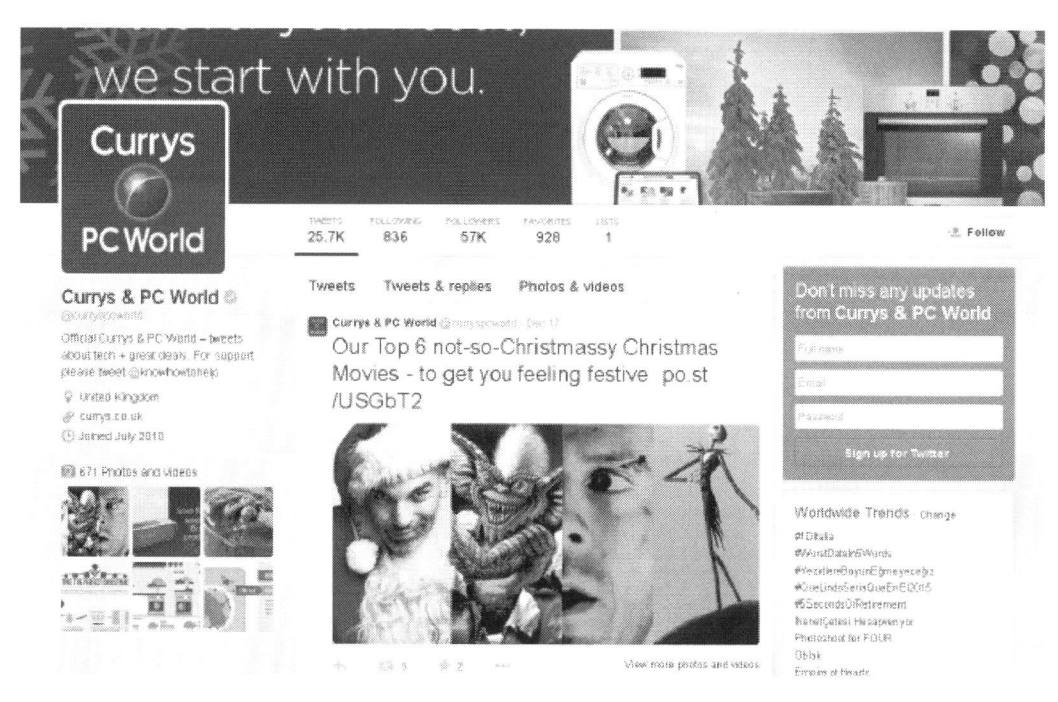

Figure 6 Screenshot of Experimental Treatment for Group 1

E-retailer with computer-electronics and appliances (i.e. search goods) and Twitter (i.e. social media with weak ties)

Figure 7 Screenshot of Experimental Treatment for Group 2

E-retailer with computer-electronics and appliances (i.e. search goods) and Facebook (i.e. social media with strong ties)

4.2.2 Sample

This research gathers a convenience sample of online shoppers in the United States. It surveys residents of the United States because it is the largest e-retail market in the world as A.T. Kearney Korea LLC. (2013) reported. It contributed with sales of $268 billion in 2013 according to Centre for Retail Research (2014). The United States has the second largest population of Internet users in the world. Internet World Stats (2012) and Internet Live Stats (2014) report that 87% of the population in the United States use Internet (est. 280 million active users) from which 64% (est. 204 million) use at least one social media platform. In addition, the use of Facebook, Twitter, and YouTube is more typical in the United States than in other countries. Furthermore, during 2005 and 2013 sales in e-retail as a proportion of total retail sales steadily grew from 2.4% to 6% (United States Census Bureau News 2014). Finally, it is possible to get a representative sample of the online population in the United States with Amazon Mechanical Turk (Berinsky et al. 2012). Thus, surveying residents of the United States is relevant and provides enough data for this research.

Consumers' responses in each treatment group may vary following a normal distribution as explained by the central limit theorem (see Cramer 1946; McClave et al. 2008). Although surveying more than 30 individuals randomly is enough to make inferences about a population, a larger sample size produces more significance (McClave et al. 2008). Therefore, this study aims to survey more individuals per treatment group.

Treatment groups

The main study contemplates six treatment groups for participants unfamiliar with the e-retailer. Table 13 shows treatment groups of the experimental research design.

Treatment Group 1 Search goods (computer-electronics and appliances) and Weak ties (Twitter)	Treatment Group 3 Experience goods (apparel and accessories) and High social presence (Facebook)	Treatment Group 5 Credence goods (nutritional supplements) and High information richness (YouTube)
Treatment Group 2 Search goods (computer-electronics and appliances) and Strong ties (Facebook)	Treatment Group 4 Experience goods (apparel and accessories) and Low social presence (Twitter)	Treatment Group 6 Credence goods (nutritional supplements) and Low information richness (Twitter)

Table 13 Treatment groups of the experiment

4.2.3 Data analysis

All statistical analyses are carried out using the open source R-Cran because it provides all statistical analyses required for this study at no cost. It also allows documenting step by step the data analysis, one element that is neither easily detailed nor publicly available in many research papers. See http://rpubs.com/erikernestov/source-code...

The effect of exposure to e-retailer and social media platform in the main experimental design is captured by comparing the means of dependent variables between groups. This is done directly with t-tests. To avoid misleading the analyses of means between groups, the analysis first cleans the data by looking for extreme values exceeding the upper or lower quartile by three times the interquartile range. Meyers et al. (2013) suggest considering the removal of extreme values if they represent more than 5% of the sample. Additionally, as a robustness check, Wilcoxon rank sum tests serves to test if one group ranks higher than the other does, thus double-checking the conclusions of the t-tests. Finally, the main dataset is available online to be scrutinised. See https://docs.google.com/spreadsheets/d/11HW...

Complementary qualitative and exploratory analysis

The interpretation of responses to open-ended questions follows the context of the research framework and hypotheses. There are 'why' questions conditionally triggered to the fastest participants after items measuring dependent variables. To study the responses of participants, the research follows basics of interpretative studies; such as the principle of suspicion that looks for possible biases in the narratives of the participants (Klein and Myers 1999). Instead of using inter-coder reliability to verify the quality of the interpretations (Cho 2008; Freelon 2010), this study looks to interpret the justifications in the context of the results obtained in the experiment and classifies selected responses according to elements related to the research framework and hypotheses. These responses therefore serve only as a complementary analysis for the results of hypothesis tests in this research.

Chapter 5 Results

5.1 Hypothesis testing

Sample description

The sample fairly represents the geographic distribution of the Internet population as described by United States Census Bureau (2012). It contains responses of 559 participants from 45 states and 356 cities in the main regions of the country. Figure 8 shows the geographic location of participants and Table 14 shows a comparison of the sample and the United States Census Bureau (2012) by State. See https://www.google.com/fusiontab...

Figure 8 Geographic distribution of the sample[1]

---

[1] Geopolitical boundaries and coordinates of cities (latitude and longitude) come from the United States Census Bureau, data from the MAF/TIGER database, and Global Communications. Geolocation coordinates of participants come from Qualtrics that approximates them based on their Internet Service Provider (ISP). The equation to estimate distances between the central coordinates of the cities and the location of participants in a curved surface was validated through United States 2010 Census Bureau, Hedges Experiments, and bluemm blog. This equation works for locations around 39° from the equator (e.g. approximately the latitude of Washington, DC in United States). It considers 6,671 kilometres as the radius of the earth. This served to compute distances between participants and the centre of cities in order to assign participants to the closest city and obtain the list of cities involved in the study. The code to display the map chart is based on code from the molecular ecologist for the open source R-Cran; participants from Hawaii and Alaska are not displayed in the map to simplify its presentation.

State	Sample *Online shoppers n	Sample *Online shoppers %	Census *Internet population %
Alaska	1	.2	.2
Alabama	10	1.8	1.5
Arizona	17	3.0	2.1
Arkansas	3	.5	.9
California	58	10.4	12.1
Colorado	7	1.2	1.6
Connecticut	6	1.1	1.2
Florida	30	5.4	6.2
Georgia	21	3.8	3.1
Idaho	2	.4	.5
Illinois	32	5.7	4.1
Indiana	9	1.6	2.1
Iowa	5	.9	1.0
Kansas	9	1.6	.9
Kentucky	11	2.0	1.4
Louisiana	12	2.1	1.5
Maine	2	.4	.4
Maryland	10	1.8	1.9
Massachusetts	16	2.9	2.1
Michigan	22	3.9	3.2
Minnesota	10	1.8	1.7
Mississippi	3	.5	.9
Missouri	9	1.6	1.9
Nebraska	4	.7	.6
Nevada	2	.4	.9
New Hampshire	4	.7	.4
New Jersey	23	4.1	2.8
New Mexico	3	.5	.7
New York	33	5.9	6.3
North Carolina	15	2.7	3.1
Ohio	24	4.3	3.7
Oregon	6	1.1	1.3
Pennsylvania	18	3.2	4.1
Rhode Island	3	.5	.3
South Carolina	4	.7	1.5
Tennessee	16	2.9	2.1
Texas	44	7.9	8.2
Utah	4	.7	.9
Virginia	17	3.0	2.6
Washington	14	2.5	2.2
West Virginia	3	.5	.6
Wisconsin	7	1.3	1.9
Hawaii, Oklahoma, Vermont, and Unspecified	10	1.8	3.3
Total	559	100	100

Table 14 Estimated geographic location of participants

The sample has participants with ages between 18 and 67 years (M = 31.8, SD = 9.8) where 284 are females and 275 males. Participants also come from all income levels proposed in the questionnaire. The largest bracket earns between $35K and $50K (19.1%) and the smallest earns above $200K (1.4%). The majority of participants have bachelor's degrees (31.3%) or some college (31.1%), participants with an educational level below high school are the minority (1.1%). The sample represents all ethnical racial groups proposed in the questionnaire. The large majority (71.8%) are White / Caucasian followed by African American / Black (11.6%). Table 15 compares the demographic distributions of the sample (online shoppers) with Nielsen (2014) and the United States Census Bureau (2014b).

		Sample *Online shoppers n	Sample *Online shoppers %	Nielsen *Online shoppers %	Census *Internet population %
Age	< 20	41	7.3	5-9	
	21-28	219	39.2	52-63	
	29-34	111	19.9		
	35-49	160	28.6	25-30	
	> 50	28	5	6-13	
Gender	Female	284	50.8		48.9
	Male	275	49.2		51.1
Income	< $25K	124	22.2		23.7
	$25-$50K	171	30.6		23.9
	$50K-$100K	170	30.4		29.8
	$100K-$150K	68	12.2		12.7
	> $150K	26	4.6		9.9
Education	< High School	6	1.1		11.5
	High school	62	11.1		25.3
	Some college / associate deg.	240	42.9		30.6
	Bachelor's and graduate's degree	251	44.9		32.5
Racial ethnicity	African American / Black	64	11.5		12.2
	Asian American	39	7		4.3
	Caucasian / White	402	71.9		71.0
	Hispanic / Latino	41	7.3		12.5
	Native American	3	.5		-
	Other	10	1.8		-
	Total	**559**	**100**	**100**	**100**

Table 15 Sample description

The age distribution of the sample is similar to the online shopping population reported by Nielsen (2014). Due to the data collection procedure, females are overrepresented in the sample (Berinsky et al. 2012), however, these results are very close to the ones reported by the United States Census Bureau (2014b). The income distribution of the sample is similar to the one reported by the United States Census Bureau (2014b). The same report shows that the sample underrepresents lower educated segments of the Internet population (below high school level 11.5% versus 1.1%). The reason is that the data collection procedure targets online shoppers who are usually from higher educated segments (Perea y Monsuwé et al. 2004). In conclusion, the sample fairly represents the Internet population of online shoppers in the United States.

Verifying equivalency of groups

One must compare equivalent groups to conduct a valid experimental analysis (Hernández Sampieri et al. 2014). Table 16 shows the treatment groups.

Treatment Group 1 Search goods (computer-electronics and appliances) and Weak ties (Twitter) n = 103	Treatment Group 3 Experience goods (apparel and accessories) and High social presence (Facebook) n = 79	Treatment Group 5 Credence goods (nutritional supplements) and High information richness (YouTube) n = 93
Treatment Group 2 Search goods (computer-electronics and appliances) and Strong ties (Facebook) n = 110	Treatment Group 4 Experience goods (apparel and accessories) and Low social presence (Twitter) n = 80	Treatment Group 6 Credence goods (nutritional supplements) and Low information richness (Twitter) n = 94

Table 16 Treatment groups

	Treatment Group	1	2	3	4	5	6
Age	< 20	12	8	6	6	4	5
	21-28	39	38	24	35	40	43
	29-34	14	23	23	14	22	15
	35-49	30	35	21	22	25	27
	> 50	8	6	5	3	2	4
Gender	Female	51	62	36	38	44	53
	Male	52	48	43	42	49	41
Income	< $25K	25	23	17	15	22	22
	$25-$50K	29	36	22	23	31	30
	$50K-$100K	23	36	27	28	27	29
	$100K-$150K	18	11	12	9	10	8
	> $150K	8	4	1	5	3	5
Education	< High School	1	1	0	1	3	0
	High school	8	16	9	6	13	10
	Some college / associate deg.	52	45	34	31	31	47
	Bachelor's and graduate's degree	42	48	36	42	46	37
Racial-ethnicity	African American / Black	10	9	9	13	14	9
	Asian American	6	8	6	9	2	8
	Caucasian / White	79	81	59	50	65	68
	Hispanic / Latino	7	10	4	4	8	8
	Native American	0	0	0	1	2	0
	Other	1	2	1	3	2	1
Geographic location (means in coordinates)	Latitude	38.1	37.4	37.1	36.4	38.3	37.6
	Longitude	-90.1	-89.2	-88.5	-86.7	-87.9	-91.0
Time of exposure (means in seconds)	First click	9.2	9.7	10.6	11.1	9.1	9.5
	Page submit click	63.7	61.5	63.0	62.0	60.2	63.5
Familiarity with e-retailer (means in 9-point Likert item)		1.5	1.5	1.4	1.5	1.4	1.3
	Total	103	110	79	80	93	94

Table 17 Equivalency of treatment groups

Table 17 describes the treatment groups. To verify that groups are equivalent; age, income, education, location coordinates, and time of exposure of participants are evaluated comparing group means with t-tests while gender and racial-ethnicity are evaluated with chi-square tests as suggested by De Winter (2013) and Campbell and Swinscow (2011) respectively. In addition, by adapting an item of brand familiarity from Bruner (2013 p. 98) and surveying participants before treatment, this research double checks low familiarity with e-retailer and equivalency of groups. Results show that each pair of groups to be compared are probabilistically equivalent (p > .1) in all these variables.

Reliability of dependent variables

The reliability of items that measure each dependent variable meets the standards for confirmatory analysis for the three product categories. Therefore, by combining their scores, these items form three scales to measure dependent variables. Table 18 shows the Cronbach's α for dependent variables in each product category.

Scale	Cronbach's α		
	Search goods	Experience goods	Credence goods
Quality of products from e-retailer (absolute)	.93	.89	.92
Online purchase intention of products from e-retailer at the social media platform	.93	.95	.96
Intention to recommend online products from e-retailer	.96	.94	.94

Table 18 Reliability of scales measuring dependent variables

5.1.1 H1: Alignment of search goods and tie strength

First, estimated means show greater perceived quality for search goods of e-retailer and social media platform with weak ties (M = 6.2, SD = 1.2) than social media platform with strong ties (M = 5.5, SD = 1.6). This effect is significant, t (211) = 3.6, p < .01, thus supporting H1a: Social media platforms with weak ties will have a greater positive influence on consumers' perceived quality of e-retailer's search goods than social media platforms with strong ties. Second, estimated means show greater purchase intent for search goods of e-retailer and social media platform with weak ties (M = 3.5, SD = 2.1) than social media platform with strong ties (M = 3.1, SD = 1.8). This effect is significant, t (211) = 1.6, p = .10, thus supporting H1b: Social media platforms with weak ties will have a greater positive influence on consumers' intention to purchase online search goods of e-retailer than social media platforms with strong ties. Third, estimated means show greater hypothetical positive word-of-mouth for search goods of e-retailer and social media platform with weak ties (M = 4.8, SD = 2.2) than social media platform with strong ties (M = 3.8, SD = 2.1). This effect is significant, t (211) = 3.6, p < .01, thus supporting H1c: Social media platforms with weak ties will have a greater positive influence on consumers' intention to recommend online e-retailer with search goods than social media platforms with strong ties. Figure 9 shows a graphic comparison of the estimated means.

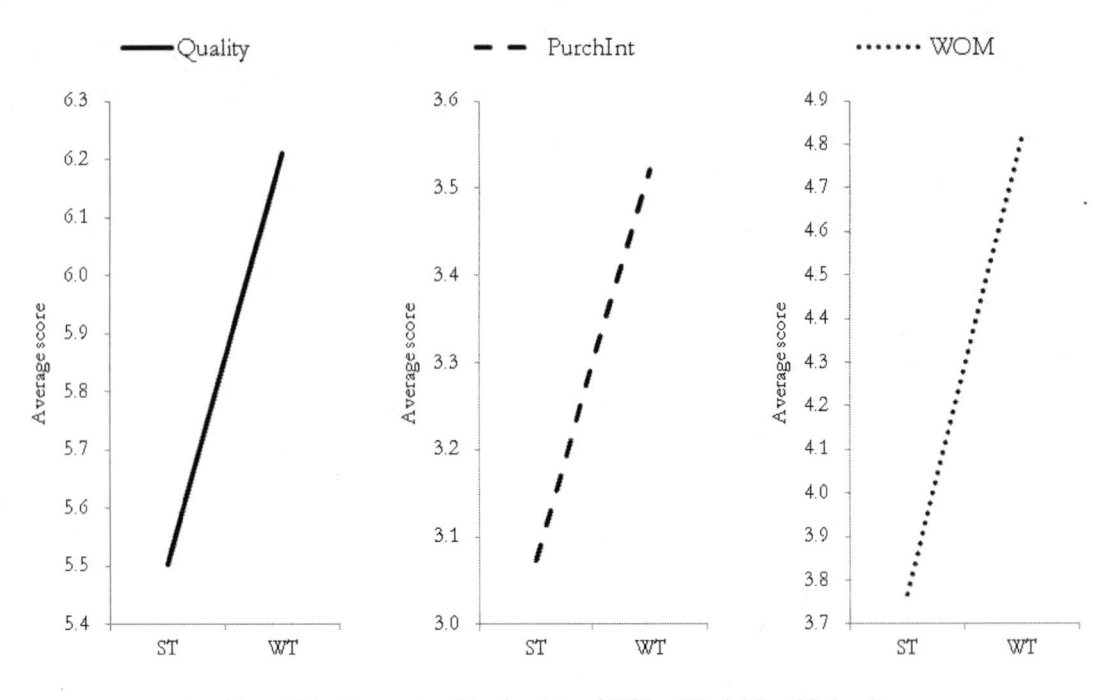

Note: ST= Strong ties (Facebook) and WT = Weak Ties (Twitter)

Figure 9 Tie strength affects e-retailer with search goods

5.1.2 H2: Alignment of experience goods and social presence

First, estimated means show similar perceived quality for experience goods of e-retailer and social media platform with high social presence (M = 5.8, SD = 1.1) than social media platform with low social presence (M = 5.8, SD = 1.2). This effect is not significant, t (157) = .3, p = .79, thus not supporting H2a: Social media platforms with high social presence will have a greater positive influence on consumers' perceived quality of e-retailer's experience goods than social media platforms with low social presence. Second, estimated means show similar purchase intent for experience goods of e-retailer and social media platform with high social presence (M = 3.0, SD = 1.8) than social media platform with low social presence (M =3.0, SD = 2.0). This effect is not significant, t (157) = -.1, p = .95, thus not supporting H2b: Social media platforms with high social presence will have a greater positive influence on consumers' intention to purchase online experience goods of e-retailer than social media platforms with low social presence. Third, estimated means show similar hypothetical positive word-of-mouth for experience goods of e-retailer and social media platform with high social presence (M = 4.4, SD = 1.9) than social media platform with low social presence (M = 4.2, SD = 2.1). This effect is not significant, t (157) = .5, p = .58, thus not supporting H2c: Social media platforms with high social presence will have a greater positive influence on consumers' intention to recommend online e-retailer with experience goods than social media platforms with low social presence. Figure 10 shows a graphic comparison of the estimated means.

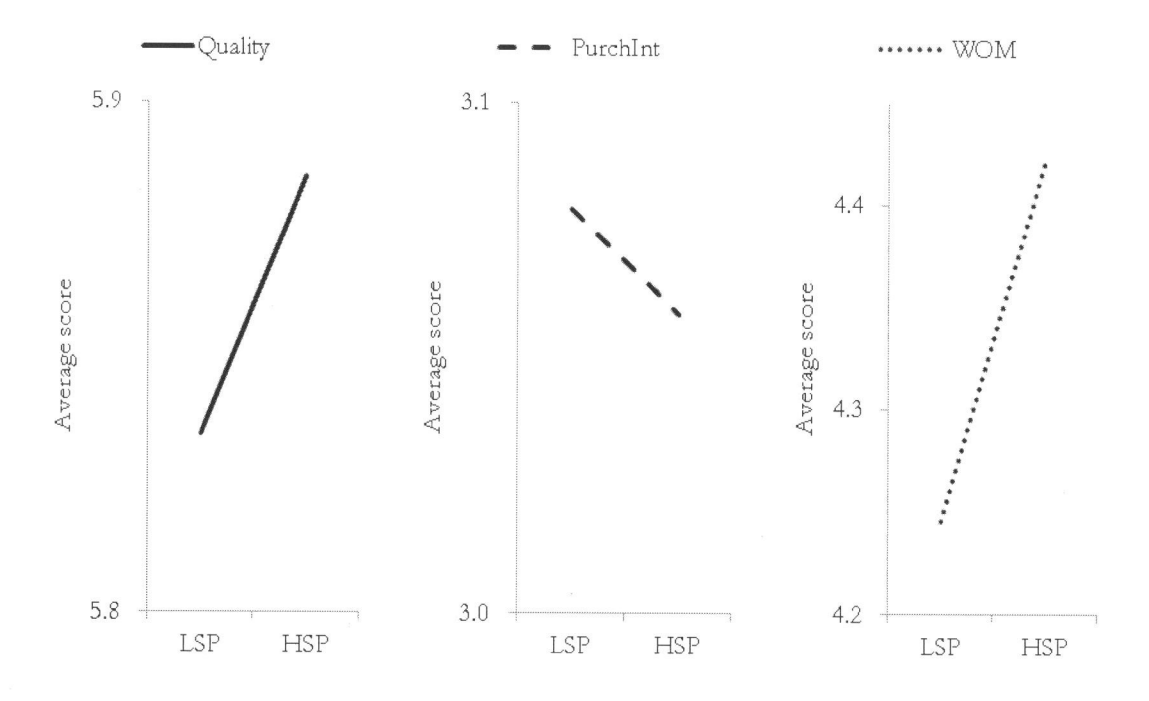

Note: LSP = Low Social Presence (Twitter) and HSP = High Social Presence (Facebook)

Figure 10 Social presence not affects e-retailer with experience goods

5.1.3 H3: Alignment of credence goods and information richness

First, estimated means show greater perceived quality for credence goods of e-retailer and social media platform with high information richness (M = 5.5, SD = 1.2) than social media platform with low information richness (M = 5.1, SD = 1.5). This effect is significant, t (185) = 2.3, p = .02, thus supporting H3a: Social media platforms with high information richness will have a greater positive influence on consumers' perceived quality of e-retailer's credence goods than social media platforms with low information richness. Second, estimated means show greater purchase intent for credence goods of e-retailer and social media platform with high information richness (M = 3.3, SD = 1.9) than social media platform with low information richness (M = 2.4, SD = 1.7). This effect is significant, t (185) = 3.2, p < .01, thus supporting H3b: Social media platforms with high information richness will have a greater positive influence on consumers' intention to purchase online credence goods of e-retailer than social media platforms with low information richness. Third, estimated means show greater hypothetical positive word-of-mouth for credence goods of e-retailer and social media platform with high information richness (M = 4.1, SD = 2.0) than social media platform with low information richness (M = 3.6, SD = 2.1). This effect is significant, t (185) = 1.9, p = .06, thus supporting H3c: Social media platforms with high information richness will have a greater positive influence on consumers' intention to recommend online e-retailer with credence goods than social media platforms with low information richness. Figure 11 shows a graphic comparison of the estimated means.

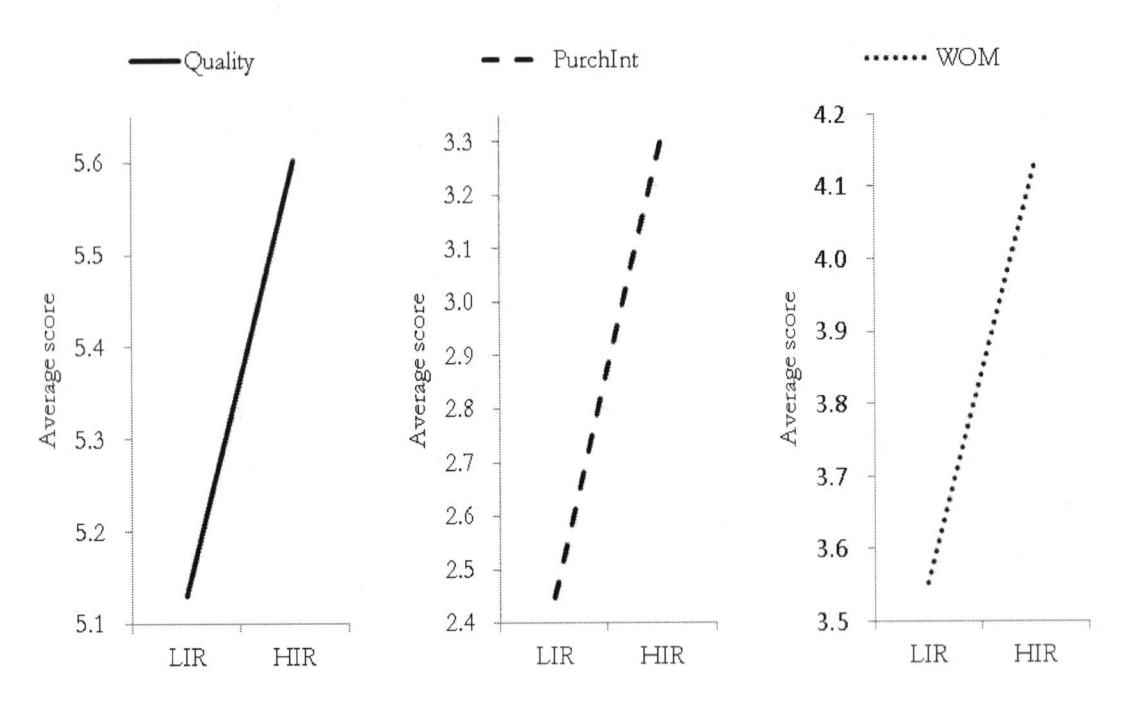

―― Quality　　　― ― PurchInt　　　······ WOM

Note: LIR = Low Information Richness (Twitter) and HIR = High Information Richness (YouTube)

Figure 11 Information richness affects e-retailer with credence goods

5.2 Complementary qualitative and explorative analysis

All complementary analyses aim to enrich the research by exploring the phenomena further. These analyses help to overcome the narrowness of experimental designs and aim to complement this thesis by portraying a more real picture of the topic under study.

Search goods and tie strength

Open-ended questions captured justifications of participants. Participants expressed the ease to evaluate computer-electronics and appliances (i.e. search goods) from Currys by relying on their brands and assessing directly specific offers:

They are a reseller of a lot of name brands [9]
I read a tweet about a self cleaning oven they offer [19]

Participants also justify their responses of perceived quality based on comments from customers and the popularity of the e-retailer:

No customer service and the social media for this company is a disaster [11]
It looks like a good put together page and it has over 400k likes [16]
it seems they care for their clients [17]

There seem to be a decent amount of comments blasting the company. But most customers who have a good experience don't comment [18]

They seem to have active online engagement with a community of people who support their products [21]

I can not tell much from the twitter page, but they do respond to their fans [26]

There were some complaints on the Facebook page [35]

It looks like this company has bad customer service, especially when merchandise breaks [36]

A lot of people had tweeted about how amazing the company was [40]

As the quality of search goods is easy to evaluate before consumption, some participants focus on cost when determining their purchase intent:

It would depend on shipping costs [14]

It's in the United Kingdom and doesn't seem to have deals any better than those I can get at home [18]

Participants will prefer familiar e-retailers rather than Currys.

I typically only buy from Amazon, I may look for their product there [19]

Doesn't seem as good as Amazon [28]

I don't know them. I'd use Amazon or NewEgg instead [32]

Finally, participants also justified why they would use a particular social media platform if they were to recommend online Currys, showing their knowledge of social media platforms:

Facebook is the easiest social media to get the word out [5]

Many of my contacts would want to visit the site [7]

Yelp is the best venue for this [8]

Facebook is where I talk to people about products if I do [12]

I don't know real world people on twitter whereas i do on facebook [20]

I would chose to use Facebook considering I am more connected to family and friends in that aspect and would ask for opinions about the site itself [23]

I don't use social networking sites to offer recommendations, unless it's the same as a word of mouth one to a close friend via private message on one of these networks [33]

I share most of my favorite brands, stores, music, etc through pinterest rather than other social networking sites which I use primarily for socializing with friends [38]

I don't really have a lot of \"followers\" anywhere else [39]

I've used Yelp before and find the reviews reliable [40]

Experience goods and social presence

Participants expressed the difficulties to evaluate apparel and accessories (i.e. experience goods) from boohoo.com:

> *Hard to evaluate clothing and accessories without trying in person [17]*
>
> *They looked nice but there's no way of knowing until trying the products [37]*
>
> *I like to touch clothing before I buy [43]*
>
> *I can't really tell what the quality is like just by watching the video [56]*
>
> *I cannot thoroughly rate clothing just by looking at it [59]*
>
> *Clothing is difficult to determine unless you touch it or test it out in person [96]*

They also expressed that they would rely on reviews and that fit is very subjective, this suggests that a higher level of social presence would be more convincing for this type of goods:

> *Purely from pictures it is hard to gauge quality, personal reviews would provide more of an insight [14]*
>
> *I will make a purchase if the clothes have the possibility of fitting [47]*
>
> *Clothing and apparel quality and fit is very subjective [61]*
>
> *Everyone in the ad is skinny, so I am guessing they don't sell items for larger people like myself [59]*
>
> *I think I'm older than their target market; I don't wear clothes like the ones they sell very often anymore [82]*
>
> *They are not my style of clothing. I am a male and it looks like a female clothing store [87]*
>
> *I dont need clothes, need to lose weight [88]*
>
> *Just seems like more of a woman site [83]*
>
> *The style seemed to be more fitting for females rather than males and thus it doesn't correlate to my taste [96]*
>
> *I also don't usually buy clothing from places online that I haven't before, because I have no idea how things will fit [97]*
>
> *The clothing is not my style [105]*

They also brought insights that come from triangulating with other people and assessing their fit with apparel and accessories from boohoo.com (e.g. style), this suggests that a higher level of social presence would be more convincing for this type of goods:

> *They seem nice for younger women [19]*
>
> *They look like clothes my daughter would like [29]*
>
> *There are alot of different styles, and there always seems to be a sale going on [38]*
>
> *I don't think they are for me a middle aged fat woman [70]*

Participants also inferred the quality of experience goods from boohoo.com based on social presence (people):

> *The e-saler seems to have a good grasp on what they sell and are enthusiastic about thier products [12]*
>
> *they seem to be designed by people who care about them [21]*
>
> *It was a very popular Facebook page with over two million likes so it would seem as though it was quite reputable [24]*
>
> *BooHoo is active with sales, retweeting pictures of people wearing product, and connecting with customers [48]*
>
> *the site looked fun and trendy [63]*

In as much as any clothes provide an experience, I think this high-class brand does so [64]

It looks like I could wear these clothes out for a good time [69]

because good looking people wear them [73]

They do participate in community events, \"Save the Children\ [81]

It is hard to make decisions about clothes and quality from looking at pictures... Also the site is in french which I can not read [85]

Products provide a stylish appearance [89]

you have to have the best to look the best [90]

They look fun and as if they would make they wearer feel happy [92]

The people wearing their products were hot. I was thinking that I would like to go to the store and meet some customers [95]

They are foreign and interesting. It would make me feel unique while wearing whatever I bought from there [100]

There are some likes of different items, but I don't see any comments on the items [105]

This also influenced participants on their intention to buy online from boohoo.com:

The style is a little too young for my taste [1]

NOT MY TYPE OF CLOTHING OR ACCESSORIES [4]

I am a man. They appear to cater towards women's clothes [6]

Their fashion style does not match mine very well [8]

However, participants were reluctant to buy as they already have purchased from other e-retailers for apparel and accessories:

I don't have enough information, and i already have other sites i trust [5]

I'm not familiar enough with the company to make a purchase from them"[24]

I like to buy my clothes from discount online stores [25]

I have other stores that I frequent [28]

I would be more likely to choose a shopping site more familiar and trusted to me [30]

I've never heard of this company. So I can't say that I am actually going to go out and buy something from them [56]

I am not familiar with the store. [59]

I am very used to the brands I currently use and prefer them [60]

I also don't usually buy clothing from places online that I haven't before, because I have no idea how things will fit [97]

Some participants were reluctant to recommend, as their friends are loyal to other stores or due to their fit with the products:

Because I know alot of my friends are store loyal and rarely stray from their stores [38]

> *Most people I know prefer to purchase their clothing, accessories, etc. through more well-known retailers rather than Boohoo [41]*
>
> *I am a fat and unfashionable person, nobody would listen to me and I wouldn't try to advise [70]*

Other participants justified their intention to recommend online boohoo.com with perceived quality and knowledge of their social circle:

> *I would want others to see the good choices offered [2]*
>
> *Casual mention to close friends [3]*
>
> *I think a lot of my family and friends with enjoy boohoo.com [35]*
>
> *Boohoo appears to sell trendy clothing that would appeal to my audience. I would suggest them as another e-shopping option [47]*
>
> *My friends would enjoy the trendy clothing and free shipping. I would share my experiences on Facebook and Twitter once I received my order [48]*
>
> *If a friend said they were looking for xmas themed clothing, I would forward them this youtube link on facebook [53]*
>
> *I will buy those apparel and will suggest to my friends as well [68]*
>
> *My guy friends will love the models [95]*

Credence goods and information richness

Participants expressed the difficulties to evaluate nutritional supplements (i.e. credence goods) from PROZIS:

> *You can never be sure if anything will work for sure, everyone's body is different [2]*
>
> *I have a hard time judging the quality of a product by pictures… Whether or not it actually works is usually very hard to tell without breaking down ingredients, researching, or seeing a pattern of long use by people [5]*

Participants also inferred the quality of credence goods from PROZIS based on information richness:

> *All of the individuals that have used PROZIS looked to be happy with the results they have achieved! [4]*
>
> *From what was seen on the Youtube page, Prozis provides practical information and tips on how to maximize use of their products [10]*
>
> *Everyone in the video seems very healthy and like what they have accomplished [13]*
>
> *The commercial looked well produced, made me feel confident in product [18]*
>
> *They seem to have a good fan base and reviews. Good informative videos [24]*
>
> *They crossfit athletes who are using their products [27]*
>
> *They make you look really good because they improve muscle tone [30]*
>
> *Based on the video reviews and information I watched on YouTube it appears that the quality and performance of the product is great [37]*

> *The customer pictures and testimonials appear to speak to the good quality of the product [38]*
> *The video seemed very educational on all matters [40]*
> *The pictures on the twitter account looked nice and professional [44]*
> *It looked like a very legitimate and respectable brand [49]*
> *The videos are high quality and there are a lot of interviews, so I'd assume the product is quality [51]*
> *They provide pictures of athletes at their prime, exhibiting that the product results great benefits [53]*
> *Everyone looked very happy in all of the posts, which leads me to believe that they are all satisfied with their products. Also, it seems that they are all in really good shape, which makes me think that the products actually work [55]*
> *From the photos it looks like Prozis' products help people get in great shape [73]*

This also influenced participants on their intention to buy online from PROZIS where perceived quality precedes this effect:

> *because they show me how it works [23]*
> *They appear reliable and effective [41]*
> *They seem like a legitimate business [55]*

Additionally, the convenience of the channel affected purchase intent:

> *i would order online as its more convient for me [21]*

Perceived quality also precedes intention to recommend online PROZIS:

> *They seem like a good brand worth recommending [19]*
> *Advertisements matters for good supplements and natures herbal products [20]*
> *I find videos more helpful than that of pictures and words [38]*
> *It seems like a product that I would love to show to new people [49]*
> *People are trusted on youtube because they are verbalizing their experience with the product [54]*
> *It is a good source of nutritional supplements [63]*
> *I would recommend PROZIS because they seem like a good company [68]*

Finally, participants also justified why they would use a particular social media platform if they were to recommend online PROZIS, showing their knowledge of social media platforms:

> *YouTube, and Facebook can give you much needed info on the product [2]*
> *Referring a friend the correct supplements would be easiest through facebook. For those who I don't know youtube, because it's easier for me to sell the product by telling the benefits [9]*
> *I would probably just leave a comment under one of the videos or something like that [60]*
> *I would get people to know the name on Twitter but get people to learn more about the product and love it from YouTube [74]*

Summary of the complementary qualitative and exploratory analysis

The complementary analysis above serves to improve the understanding of the context in which the research hypotheses were tested. As explained earlier, participants' responses, therefore, help to complement the results obtained from the hypothesis tests. This complementary analysis provides an outlook of the limitations of this research and the many possibilities for further studies as Chapter 6 describes.

Chapter 6 Conclusions

6.1 Concluding remarks

The role of transactional content alignment in e-retailers' expansion to social media platforms can provide a competitive advantage for e-businesses in business-to-consumer markets. Consider, for example, the use of online experiments to explore the perception of e-retail consumers towards a communication channel, which exemplify the far-reaching ramifications of aligning transactional content. One of them shows how cognitive categorisations related with social media platforms and goods are relevant to how managers conceive their channel strategies. In doing so, firms in e-retail must grapple with fundamental marketing and advertising communications decisions. The most competitive channels to communicate with consumers provide e-retailers with an advantage that leads them to achieve greater market success than those e-retailers unaware of the role of transactional content alignment.

Theorists and practitioners benefit from this research. It complements previous studies by bringing new insight to bear on an important decision that managers face when assigning resources across communication channels. This study does so by examining e-retailers with diverse categories of consumption products and multiple social media platforms widely adopted. It helps to solve the traditional problem in marketing and advertising communications by optimising resources: *"Half the money I spend on advertising is wasted; the trouble is I don't know which half" John Wanamaker 19th Century*. This research conceptually argues and empirically shows the role of transactional content alignment between e-retailer and social media platform bringing valuable insights to theorists and practitioners.

6.2 Research implications

6.2.1 Theoretical and methodological implications

By answering the research questions, this thesis contributes to extend the literature about e-businesses, multi-channel marketing and communication strategy. For business-to-consumer e-commerce and new media the implications are straightforward. On one hand, it supports the search-experience-credence classification for e-retailers' goods, which represents their main transaction content as it was validated prior to testing hypotheses. Following channel expansion and cognitive fit theories, it explores how to measure the perception of information richness, social presence, and tie strength of social media platforms as dimensions that represent their main transaction content. This is particularly relevant as it helps to translate the subjectivity involved in media perceptions outlined in the channel expansion and cognitive fit theories into a low information richness of social media platform. On the other hand, it supports the application of the strength of weak ties theory (H1) and information richness theory (H3) in a new context. In doing so, the most substantial theoretical implication is connecting the strength of weak ties, social presence, and information richness theories with the search-experience-credence classification of goods. This connects transaction content about e-businesses of retail and media. Thus, this thesis builds a bridge between theories of marketing communications, transaction content of e-business model, and strategy behind these two types of e-businesses.

This study extends the research of Habibi et al. (2014), Laroche et al. (2013), and Smith et al. (2012) by combining channel expansion and quality perspectives to analyse the impact of social media platforms on diverse product categories and types of e-retailers. The thesis also links this line of research with the literature about multi-channel strategy and transaction content from e-business model (e.g. Amit and Zott 2001; Keller 2010; Zott et al. 2000). This research is congruent with the work from Obal et al. (2011) which demonstrates people use more advice from weak ties than from strong ties when evaluating search products (e.g. MP3 player, books, toaster oven). Additionally, this study extends the work from Obal et al. (2011) by adding dimensions of social media platforms (information richness and social presence) to explain their effect on search, experience, and credence goods. By adding the information richness dimension, for example, this research suggests to consider it when testing advice-related hypotheses for credence goods as in the work of Obal et al. (2011). Additionally, this research proposes to represent experience goods with tangible retail products rather than to represent them with services, which is usually present in the literature. For instance, to represent experience goods this study uses apparel and accessories whereas previous studies have used hair salons, hotels, fitness studios, welding services, or carpet cleaning (e.g. Ekelund et al. 1995; Obal et al. 2011). This specification also helps the present study to contribute not only in the theory but in the practice. The reason is that the paper can also be relevant to the practice as it is directly linked to the retail sector often concentrated in tangible consumption products.

This paper also answers calls from Christodoulides (2012), Lee and Youn (2009), and Smith et al. (2012) who encourage the study about how diverse virtual communities affect consumer behaviour. It does so by assessing the competitiveness of diverse social media according to the effect they produce on diverse types of e-retailers' product categories. It joins to the literature that links content from social media platforms with business competitiveness (e.g. Asur and Huberman 2010; Bollen et al. 2011; Kumar and Mirchandani 2012). In line with Teece (2010) and Weill and Woerner (2013), this research provides an illustrative example of how content, customer experience, and platforms provide competitive advantages while optimising two types e-businesses. Consequently, the complementarities of e-retailers and social media platforms also depict an image of how cognitive configurations such as customer sensing and customer engagement within social media platforms lead to user-added value (Baden-Fuller and Mangematin 2013; Wirtz et al. 2010). The cognitive approach in this study also extends the research in transaction content as it is useful to unlock innovation through data from consumers (see Martins et al. 2015; Mikusz et al. 2015; Wirtz et al. 2010). For example, applying the quality perspective to classify e-retailers in the environment of social media platforms shows the potential to innovate the conceptualization of their transaction content. Similarly, classifying social media platforms by their dimensions of tie strength, social presence, and information richness shows the potential to innovate taxonomies used to describe social media platforms. Therefore, this study extends research by combining its unique perspectives to classify e-retailers and social media platforms.

The study provides a guideline to explore and analyse online shopping behaviour, by showing the different effects of social media platforms on e-retailers' customers by product category. Its major methodological implication arises from showing another way of studying e-retail products by using broad categories of products rather than narrow specific products (e.g. Obal et al. 2011; Oestreicher-Singer and Sundararajan 2012). This is faster and can deliver results in cases where data from companies is limited and when product categories are sufficient to drive conclusions. This methodological implication is essential to design and replicate online experiments and produce knowledge with less resource than studying specific products for organisations researching product categories. Some advantages of the methodology include the following: (1) less time for data analysis, (2) fewer treatment groups, (3) less time for data collection, and (4) less computer processing power. Additionally, exploring measures to classify social media platforms and e-retailers provides a starting point to build cognitive instruments for other business model parameters as proposed by Baden-Fuller and Mangematin (2013). This is particularly important for e-businesses where primary data is readily available for empirical researchers. Although classifications are merely theoretical, exploring and analysing how consumers sense them provide a glimpse into how classifications shape knowledge about online shopping behaviour as this methodology shows.

The methodology also shows the reliability and flexibility of low cost and open source tools to get and analyse data. For instance, it gets representative samples of online shoppers using Amazon Mechanical Turk and it gets results from advanced statistical analyses and maps using R-Cran. Although statistical analysis served to test effects of diverse social media platform and research hypotheses, this thesis also explores the following. First, narratives of participants justifying their responses are important for understanding in depth the phenomena and generalisation of the results. Therefore, the methodology also shows an original way of mixing qualitative and quantitative methods while taking confirmatory and exploratory perspectives simultaneously.

6.2.2 Managerial implications

For those managers of e-retailers using simultaneously multiple social media platforms, the study provides a road map that helps them to select and focus on social media platforms according to their main product category. This improves the practice of category management often used in retail. First, it is possible to make better predictions about product choice in buying decisions by analysing the network of consumers in diverse social media platforms (Bowler et al. 2011). This study swiftly shows so by analysing consumers' relationships with diverse e-retailers and social media platforms. In fact, the implications of these analyses can be integrated into predictive models concerning supply and demand of e-retail products and content in social media platforms. Second, it is possible to segment markets in new ways by understanding the variability of social media platforms. This could be useful when traditional segmentation fails and the market is compounded by very heterogeneous groups (Brandt et al. 2011). This research shows a way to segment consumers relying on their perceptions about product categories and social media platforms; therefore, it serves to segment e-retail consumers and consumers of content in social media platforms. It also provides guidelines to order e-retail content within social media platforms and to avoid promotion and information overload to their consumers. Consequently, this study provides advantages to managers of e-retailers targeting many diverse customers with diverse product categories simultaneously. Third, it is possible to allocate resources better among social media platforms by understanding their differences (Smith et al. 2012). The most substantial managerial implication of this study suggests, all other things remaining equal and relative to competitors, to allocate more resources on:

- Twitter instead of Facebook for e-retailers that sell computer-electronics and appliances.
- YouTube instead of Twitter for e-retailers that sell nutritional supplements.

These recommendations bring a starting point for companies to begin prioritising their resources between diverse social media platforms according to their product offerings. Additionally, this can turn into a competitive advantage for those business-to-consumer e-commerce companies that incorporate them into their current budgeting procedures for marketing and advertising expenses in social media platforms. For those companies without sophisticated budgeting procedures for their marketing and advertising expenses in social media platforms, this study provides them with actionable insights. It does so by showing how to prioritise advertising and marketing expenses between Facebook, Twitter, and YouTube.

Prioritising advertising and marketing investments properly between social media platforms according to product offerings improves the profitability of companies. On one hand, it can increase demand generation due to the higher effect exemplified in this study for some combinations of e-retailers and social media platforms. This provides firms with a potential source of additional revenue relative to those firms that do not prioritise their investments between social media platforms. On the other hand, it can decrease marketing and advertising expenses as firms can switch more of these expenses to engaged users of social media platforms. Consider, for example, the added value provided by advocates and users of social media platforms that spread positive electronic word-of-mouth about companies and their products. This can produce a snowball effect decreasing marketing and advertising expenses between social media platforms in the long-run. As a result, two outcomes are possible from prioritising properly advertising and marketing investments. First, direct effects from marketing and adverting lead to demand generation and additional revenue from sales in the short-run. Second, indirect effects from electronic word-of-mouth serve as a mechanism of companies to switch some of their marketing and advertising expenses to users of social media platforms in the long-run. This is a consequence of increasing brand equity. Therefore, prioritising advertising and marketing investments between social media platforms can increase revenue while decreasing operating expenses leading e-retailers to achieve higher levels of profitability.

This research provides practitioners with a better understanding of how e-retail product categories and social media platforms interact and affect the effectiveness of marketing and advertising efforts. At the same time, it offers a better comprehension of how relevant social media platforms such as Facebook, Twitter, and YouTube are perceived by e-retail's customers. This serves as a guideline to design experiments that will help companies to evaluate their allocation of resources across multiple channels and improve their resource management. For instance, practitioners may test their own classifications of goods and their own classifications of social media platforms by following the steps provided in this research. The methodology presented in this thesis provides managers with a guide to implement open source and low-cost tools to investigate which communication channel is more competitive for their products categories. Furthermore, the methodology can be extended to test others types of media. This can add value to the traditional approach that just counts the number of impacts between channels rather than evaluating the effect of media and offers on consumers. Therefore, this study provides practitioners with a road map to apply and produce knowledge in their unique

6.3 Limitations and further research

This research has several limitations. This paper implies e-retailers' marketing messages are positive and consistent through social media as it concentrates on the effect produced by different channels on e-retailer's performance. A larger sample of e-retailers would provide a more precise evaluation of the effect of social media platform on e-retailer's performance to validate the findings of this research. As the effect size is small and the hypothesis testing procedure accepts only 66% of the research hypotheses, repeating this experiment is necessary to improve the validity of the conclusions. Although there is a noticeable difference between the effects produced by two distinct social media platforms, the small effect size could undermine the importance of this study. So, rather than running field experiments, one could gauge the effect size in a more controlled setting such as in a laboratory experiment. Additionally, reducing the complexities involved in e-business models of retail and media to their transaction content and typologies limits the exploration of other characteristics of e-business models. For instance, there are several classifications of social media platforms and goods that were neither fully explored nor tested. On one hand, all products possess attributes from the search-experience-credence classification. This produces ambiguity and subjectivity in the participant, which were not fully dissected in this study, leaving behind the multiple dimensions embedded in the products. Increasing the sample size of e-retailers would improve the external validity to generalise the conclusions regarding each product category. This study can only validate conclusions about the three e-retailers involved in the experiment. On the other hand, dichotomies used to classify social media platforms based on tie strength, social presence, and information richness show a broad view of social media platforms. This makes the study to lack of an exploration of other specific design and usability elements embedded in each social media platform, which could also be important. Colour and shape of the platform's interface or its reachability and loading time are some examples. Another limitation from this research comes from the measures used to evaluate the proposed dimensions of social media platforms. These measures require further exploration and development. For instance, this study only confirms convergent and discriminant validity of these dimensions for Twitter (see page 85). It does not test the three dimensions in other social media platforms (e.g. Facebook or YouTube).

Additional limitations of this research arise from the exploratory and qualitative analysis of participants' justifications. First, as the sentiment and polarity of comments within the social media platforms were not controlled, large differences may have affected results of the online experiment. Second, the study did not control e-retailers use the same language across social media platforms nor the target market of e-retailer was a niche. These two factors may have obscured results of hypothesis 2 in the main experiment (i.e. experience goods and social presence). Qualitative analyses of participants' responses suggest they were upset because the Facebook page of boohoo.com was in French and not in English. In contrast, the Twitter page of boohoo.com was in English. The same exploratory analyses suggest this e-retailer has a clear focus on females for example. Therefore, further research should aim to test again the hypothesis 2 of this study with another e-retailer of apparel and accessories.

Countless possibilities arise for further research from the cognitive configuration view of business models from Baden-Fuller and Mangematin (2013). For instance, the study of how transactional content alignment affects the monetisation of goods and services, customer engagement, or customer sensing. One way to empirically explore this line of research may looks at effects on pricing. Does transactional content alignment of e-retailer and social media platform affect pricing of hedonic and utilitarian goods? If so, is this effect general to all goods or exclusive to some of them? For example, what would be the difference between luxury versus non-luxury goods? Finally, other business model parameters may guide further research such as positive network externalities, efficiency of search costs, or selection range of products and even services as described by Amit and Zott (2001).

Further research of transaction content could lead to develop tools in order to better measure the sentiment and the polarity of comments. For instance, associating positive and negative words with a numerical score (e.g. Stieglitz and Dang-Xuan 2013). The use of computer tools for content analysis (e.g. NVivo and QDA Miner) as proposed by Silver (2014) and Leech and Onwuegbuzie (2011) may guide new research to expand the theoretical and methodological boundaries of this study. Diverse methods to control and to measure the attention span of online shoppers could optimise online experiments. This can produce more insight for content design in multiple Internet channels. For example, instead of using an average reading speed per minute (e.g. Bell 2001; Noyes and Garland 2008; Ziefle 1998), a new study may test reading speed individually before the experiment to generate a baseline. The date and time of comments in social media platforms may also serve to develop strict controls about text and content consumption. Measuring and controlling the speed of content consumption for video and images are broad and interesting paths for further research. These would help to optimise experiments and to produce better insights for content design across channels, thus, improving the allocation of resources in multiple channel strategies. The research models in this thesis account for direct main effects only; further research may explore and add relevant mediating variables to clarify more the mechanism within the independent and dependent variables in this study. Finally, further research may also consider exploring questions such as: How does social media channels are related with their messages? What is the effect of social media channels compared to other

References

A.T. Kearney Korea LLC. (2013), "The 2013 Global Retail E-Commerce Index: Online retail is front and center in the quest for growth."

Aaker, David A. (1995), *Building Strong Brands*, Free Press.

——— (1996), "Measuring brand equity across products and markets," *California Management Review*, 38(3).

Aaker, David A., James M. Carman, and Robert Jacobson (1982), "Modeling advertising-sales relationships involving feedback: A time series analysis of six cereal brands," *Journal of Marketing Research*, 19(1), 116–25.

Acedo, Francisco Josê, Carmen Barroso, and José Luis Galan (2006), "The resource based theory: dissemination and main trends," *Strategic Management Journal*, 27(7), 621–36.

Adams, Frederick (2003), "The Informational Turn in Philosophy," *Minds and Machines*, 13(4), 471–501.

Aghekyan-Simonian, Mariné, Sandra Forsythe, Wi Suk Kwon, and Veena Chattaraman (2012), "The role of product brand image and online store image on perceived risks and online purchase intentions for apparel," *Journal of Retailing and Consumer Services*, 19(3), 325–31.

Ahmad, Muhammad A., and Ankur Teredesai (2006), "Modeling Spread of Ideas in Online Social Networks," *Reproduction*, 61, 185–90.

Ahn, June (2012), "Teenagers' Experiences With Social Network Sites: Relationships to Bridging and Bonding Social Capital," *The Information Society*, 28(2), 99–109.

Ajzen, Icek, and Martin Fishbein (1980), *Understanding attitudes and predicting social behavior*, Englewood Cliffs, NJ: Prentice Hall.

Akar, Erkan, and Birol Topçu (2011), "An Examination of the Factors Influencing Consumers' Attitudes Toward Social Media Marketing," *Journal of Internet Commerce*, 10(1), 35–67.

Al-Debei, Mutaz M. (2010), "The Design and Engineering of Innovative Mobile Data Services: An Ontological Framework Founded on Business Model Thinking," Brunel University West London.

Al-Ekam, Jamal Mohammed Esmail, Nik Kamariah Nik Mat, Salniza Md. Salleh, Norashikin Binti Baharom, Tuan Rohasnida Binti Tuan Teh, Noor Aida Binti Noh, and Nor Ermawati Binti Hussain (2012), "The influence of trust, advertising, family on intention and actual purchase of local brand in Yemen," *American Journal of Economics*, June(Special), 64–68.

Aljukhadar, Muhammad, Sylvain Senecal, and Denis Ouellette (2010), "Can the Media Richness of a Privacy Disclosure Enhance Outcome? A Multifaceted View of Trust in Rich Media Environments," *International Journal of Electronic Commerce*.

Amazon (2013), "Prime Air Video," <http://youtu.be/98BIu9dpwHU>.

American Marketing Association (2014), "American Marketing Association Dictionary," <https://www.ama.org/resources/Pages/Dictionary.aspx?dLetter=P>.

——— (2015), "American Marketing Association Dictionary," <http://www.marketingpower.com/_layouts/Dictionary.aspx?dLetter=W>.

Amersdorffer, D., F. Bauhuber, and J. Oellrich (2012), "The economic and cultural aspects of the social web: Implications for the tourism industry," *Journal of Vacation Marketing*, 18(3), 175–84.

Amit, Raphael (2014), "Business Models in a World of Networks: Theory and Practice," *Strategic Management Society*, <http://madrid.strategicmanagement.net/call_for_proposals.php>.

Amit, Raphael, and Paul J. H. Schoemaker (1993), "Strategic assets and organizational rent," *Strategic management journal*, 14(August 1992), 33–46.

Amit, Raphael, and Christoph Zott (2001), "Value creation in E-business," *Strategic Management Journal*, 22(6-7), 493–520.

——— (2002), "Value drivers of e-commerce business models," in *Creating value: Winners in the new business environment*, A. Hitt, R. Amit, C. Lucier, and R. D. Nixon, eds., Blackwell, 15–47.

Anderson, Chris (2008), *The Long Tail: Why the Future of Business is Selling Less of More*, New York, New York, USA: Hyperion.

——— (2009), *Free: The future of radical price*, New York, New York, USA: Hyperion.

Anderson, John R. (2004), *Cognitive psychology and its implications*, Worth Publishers.

Andrews, Kenneth R. (1987), "The concept of corporate strategy," in *The concept of corporate strategy*, Dow Jones-Irwin, 13–34.

Andzulis, James Mick "Mick," Nikolaos G. Panagopoulos, and Adam Rapp (2012), "A Review of Social Media and Implications for the Sales Process," *Journal of Personal Selling & Sales Management*, 32(3), 305–16.

Ansari, Asim, Skander Essegaier, and Rajeev Kohli (2000), "Internet Recommendation Systems," *Journal of Marketing Research*, 37(3), 363–75.

Ansoff, H. Igor (1965), *Corporate Strategy, Management*, McGraw-Hill.

Archak, Nikolay, Anindya Ghose, and Panagiotis G. Ipeirotis (2011), "Deriving the Pricing Power of Product Features by Mining Consumer Reviews," *Management Science*, 57(8), 1485–1509.

Archer-Brown, Chris, Niall Piercy, and Adam Joinson (2013), "Examining the information value of virtual communities: Factual versus opinion-based message content," *Journal of Marketing Management*, 29(3-4), 421–38.

Argyle, Michael, and Janet Dean (1965), "Eye-contact, distance and affiliation," *Sociometry*, 28, 289–304.

Arif, Ahmed Sabbir, and Wolfgang Stuerzlinger (2009), "Analysis of text entry performance metrics," in *Science and Technology for Humanity (TIC-STH), Toronto International Conference*, Institute of Electrical and Electronics Engineers, 100–105.

Asur, Sitaram, and Bernardo A. Huberman (2010), "Predicting the future with social media," in *Proceedings of the International Conference on Web Intelligence and Intelligent Agent Technology*, 492–99.

Aula, Pekka (2010), "Social media, reputation risk and ambient publicity management," *Strategy & Leadership*, 38(6), 43–49.

Babin, Barry J., and Jill S. Attaway (2000), "Atmospheric affect as a tool for creating value and gaining share of customer," *Journal of Business Research*, 2963(99).

Bäckström, Kristina, and Ulf Johansson (2006), "Creating and consuming experiences in retail store environments: Comparing retailer and consumer perspectives," *Journal of Retailing and Consumer Services*, 13(6), 417–30.

Baden-Fuller, Charles, and Vincent Mangematin (2013), "Business models: A challenging agenda," *Strategic Organization*, 11(4), 418–27.

Baden-Fuller, Charles, and Mary S. Morgan (2010), "Business Models as Models," *Long Range Planning*, 43(2-3), 156–71.

Bai, Billy, Rob Law, and Ivan Wen (2008), "The impact of website quality on customer satisfaction and purchase intentions: Evidence from Chinese online visitors," *International Journal of Hospitality Management*, 27(3), 391–402.

Baker, Julie, Dhruv Grewal, and A. Parasuraman (1994), "The influence of store environment on quality inferences and store image," *Journal of the Academy of Marketing Science*, 22(4), 328–39.

Baker, Julie, A Parasuraman, Dhruv Grewal, and Glenn B. Voss (2002), "The influence of multiple store environment cues on perceived merchandise value and patronage intentions," *Journal of Marketing*, 66(2), 120–41.

Baker, Michael J., and Gilbert A. Churchill Jr. (1977), "The impact of physically attractive models on advertising evaluations," *Journal of Marketing Research*, 14(4), 538–55.

Bambauer-Sachse, Silke, and Sabrina Mangold (2011), "Brand equity dilution through negative online word-of-mouth communication," *Journal of Retailing and Consumer Services*, 18(1), 38–45.

Barney, Jay B. (1991), "Firm Resources and Competitive Advantage," *Journal of Management*, 17(1), 99–120.

——— (1997), *Gaining and Sustaining Competitive Advantage*, Boston, Massachusetts, United States: Addison-Wesley Publishing Company.

——— (2001), "Resource-based theories of competitive advantage: A ten-year retrospective on the resource-based view," *Journal of Management*, 27(6), 643–50.

Barnlund, Dean C. (1970), "A transactional model of communication," in *Language behavior: A book of readings*, 43–61.

Baron, Reuben M., and David A. Kenny (1986), "The moderator-mediator variable distinction in social psychological research: conceptual, strategic, and statistical considerations.," *Journal of Personality and Social Psychology*, WISICT '04, (E. Inc, ed.), 51(6), 1173–82.

Barry, TE (1987), "The development of the hierarchy of effects: An historical perspective," *Current issues and Research in Advertising*.

Bell, Timothy (2001), "Extensive reading: speed and comprehension," *The Reading Matrix*, 1(1).

Bellman, R., C. E. Clark, D. G. Malcolm, Clifford J. Craft, and F. M. Ricciardi (1957), "On the Construction of a Multi-Stage, Multi- Person Business Game," *Operations Research*, 5(4), 469–503.

Bello Acebrón, Laurentino, and Domingo Calvo Dopico (2000), "The importance of intrinsic and extrinsic cues to expected and experienced quality: an empirical application for beef," *Food Quality and Preference*, 11(3), 229–38.

Benkler, Yochai (2006), *The Wealth of Networks: How Social Production Transforms Markets and Freedom*, *Social Science Computer Review*, Yale University Press.

Bera, Sasadhar, and Prasun Das (2011), "An attempt to modeling rule base real time web funnel structure," *Journal of Business and Retail Management Research*, 5(2), 31–43.

Berger, Charles R., and Richard J. Calabrese (1975), "Some Explorations In Initial Interaction And Beyond: Toward A Developmental Theory Of Interpersonal Communication," *Human Communication Research*, 1(2), 99–112.

Berger, Jonah, and Katherine L. Milkman (2012), "What Makes online Content Viral?," *Journal of Marketing Research*, 49(2), 192–205.

Berger, Jonah, and Eric M. Schwartz (2011), "What drives immediate and ongoing Word of Mouth?," *Journal of Marketing Research*, 48(5), 869–80.

Berger, Jonah, Alan T. Sorensen, and Scott J. Rasmussen (2010), "Positive Effects of Negative Publicity: When Negative Reviews Increase Sales," *Marketing Science*, 29(5), 815–27.

Berinato, Scott, and Jeff Clark (2010), "Six ways to find value in Twitter's noise," *Harvard Business Review*, 88(June), 34–36.

Berinsky, Adam J., Gregory A. Huber, and Gabriel S. Lenz (2012), "Evaluating Online Labor Markets for Experimental Research: Amazon.com's Mechanical Turk," *Political Analysis*, 20(3), 351–68.

Berlo, David Kenneth (1960), *The process of communication: An introduction to theory and practice*, New York, New York: Holt, Rinehart, & Winston.

Bernstein, Ethan S. (2012), "The Transparency Paradox: A Role for Privacy in Organizational

Berthon, Pierre R., Leyland F. Pitt, Kirk Plangger, and Daniel Shapiro (2012), "Marketing meets Web 2.0, social media, and creative consumers: Implications for international marketing strategy," *Business Horizons*, 55(3), 261–71.

Biel, Joan-Isaac, Oya Aran, and Daniel Gatica-Perez (2011), "You Are Known by How You Vlog: Personality Impressions and Nonverbal Behavior in YouTube," in *Artificial Intelligence*, AAAI, 446–49.

Biel, Joan-Isaac, and Daniel Gatica-Perez (2010), "Vlogcast yourself: Nonverbal behavior and attention in social media," in *International Conference on Multimodal Interfaces and the Workshop on Machine Learning for Multimodal Interaction*, ICMI-MLMI '10, ACM, 50.

Björkdahl, Joakim (2009), "Technology cross-fertilization and the business model: The case of integrating ICTs in mechanical engineering products," *Research Policy*, 38(9), 1468–77.

Blumer, Herbert (1980), "Mead and Blumer: The Convergent Methodological Perspectives of Social Behaviorism and Symbolic Interactionism," *American Sociological Review*, 45(3), 409.

——— (1994), "Society as symbolic interaction," in *Human behavior and social processes*, A. M. Rose, ed., Houghton Mifflin, 179–92.

Blyler, Maureen, and Russell W Coff (2003), "Dynamic capabilities, social capital, and rent appropriation: ties that split pies," *Strategic Management Journal*, 24(7), 677–86.

Bollen, Johan, Huina Mao, and Xiao-Jun Zeng (2011), "Twitter mood predicts the stock market," *Journal of Computational Science*, 1–8.

Bonabeau, Eric (2004), "The perils of the imitation age," *Harvard Business Review*, (June), 1–8.

Borgatti, Stephen P., and Pacey C. Foster (2003), "The Network Paradigm in Organizational Research: A Review and Typology," *Journal of Management*, 29(6), 991–1013.

Borgatti, Stephen P., and Daniel S. Halgin (2011), "On Network Theory," *Organization Science*, 22(5), 1168–81.

Borgatti, Stephen P., Ajay Mehra, Daniel J. Brass, and Giuseppe Labianca (2009), "Network analysis in the social sciences.," *Science*, 323(5916), 892–95.

Borgmann, Albert (1999), *Holding on to Reality: The Nature of Information at the Turn of the Millennium*, Chicago, Illinois, USA: University of Chicago Press.

Boulton, Barry D., and Steve M. Samek Libert (2000), "A business model for the new economy," *Journal of Business Strategy*, 21(4), 29–35.

Boush, David M., and Barbara Loken (1991), "A process tracing study of brand extension evaluations," *Journal of Marketing Research*, 28, 16–28.

Bowler, Wm. Matthew, Robert Dahlstrom, Matthew T. Seevers, and Steven J. Skinner (2011), "The Ties That Buy: The Role of Interfirm Social Contagion Across Customer Accounts," *Journal of Personal Selling and Sales Management*, 31(1), 7–20.

Boyd, Danah M., and Nicole B. Ellison (2007), "Social Network Sites: Definition, History, and Scholarship," *Journal of Computer-Mediated Communication*, 13(1), 210–30.

Brandt, Celine, Charles Pahud de Mortanges, Christian Bluemelhuber, and Allard C.R. van Riel (2011), "Associative networks: A new approach to market segmentation," *International Journal of Market Research*, 53(2), 189.

Bredahl, Lone (2004), "Cue utilisation and quality perception with regard to branded beef," *Food Quality and Preference*, 15(1), 65–75.

Breivik, Einar, and Helge Thorbjørnsen (2008), "Consumer brand relationships: an investigation of two alternative models," *Journal of the Academy of Marketing Science*, 36(4), 443–72.

Brodie, Roderick J., Ana Ilic, Biljana Juric, and Linda Hollebeek (2013), "Consumer engagement in a virtual brand community: An exploratory analysis," *Journal of Business Research*, 66(1), 105–14.

Brown, Jo, Amanda J. Broderick, and Nick Lee (2007), "Word of mouth communication within online communities: Conceptualizing the online social network," *Journal of Interactive Marketing*, 21(3), 2–20.

Bruner, Gordon C. (2012), *Marketing Scales Handbook Multi-Item Measures for Consumer Behavior and Advertising Research*.

——— (2013), *Marketing Scales Handbook Multi-Item Measures for Consumer Insight Research*.

Buhrmester, M., T. Kwang, and S. D. Gosling (2011), "Amazon's Mechanical Turk: A New Source of Inexpensive, Yet High-Quality, Data?," *Perspectives on Psychological Science*, 6(1), 3–5.

Van den Bulte, Christophe, and Stefan Stremersch (2004), "Social Contagion and Income Heterogeneity in New Product Diffusion: A Meta-Analytic Test," *Marketing Science*, 23(4), 530–44.

Burnett, Gary (2000), "Information exchange in virtual communities: a typology," *Information Research*, 5(4), 1–25.

Burson-Marsteller (2012), "Global social media check-up," New York, New York, USA.

Burt, Ronald S. (1987), "Social Contagion and Innovation: Cohesion versus Structural Equivalence," *American Journal of Sociology*, 92(6), 1287.

——— (2001), "Structural holes versus network closure as social capital," in *Social capital: Theory and research*, Transaction Publishers.

——— (2004), "Structural Holes and Good Ideas," *American Journal of Sociology*, 110(2), 349–99.

Burton, Paul, Yu Wu, Victor R Prybutok, and Gina Harden (2012), "Differential Effects of the Volume and Diversity of Communication Network Ties on Knowledge Workers' Performance.," *IEEE Transactions on Professional Communication*, 55(3), 239–53.

Büyüközkan, Gülçin, Orhan Feyzioğlu, and Erdal Nebol (2008), "Selection of the strategic alliance partner in logistics value chain," *International Journal of Production Economics*, 113(1), 148–58.

Camarero-Izquierdo, Carmen, and Rebeca San José-Cabezudo (2011), "Social and attitudinal determinants of viral marketing dynamics," *Computers in Human Behavior*, 27(6), 2292–2300.

Campbell, Michael J., and Thomas Douglas Victor Swinscow (2011), *Statistics at square one*, West Sussex, UK: John Wiley & Sons, Inc.

Carlson, John R., and Robert W. Zmud (1999), "Channel expansion theory and the experiential nature of media richness perceptions," *Academy of Management Journal*, 42(2), 153–70.

Carroll, Dave (2009), "United Breaks Guitars Video," <http://youtu.be/5YGc4zOqozo>.

Casadesus-Masanell, Ramon, and Joan Enric Ricart (2010), "From Strategy to Business Models and onto Tactics," *Long Range Planning*, 43(2-3), 195–215.

Casler, Krista, Lydia Bickel, and Elizabeth Hackett (2013), "Separate but equal? A comparison of participants and data gathered via Amazon's MTurk, social media, and face-to-face behavioral testing," *Computers in Human Behavior*, 29(6), 2156–60.

Centre for Retail Research (2014), "Online Retailing: Britain, Europe and the US 2014," Newark, United Kingdom.

Chakravarty, Anindita, Yong Liu, and Tridib Mazumdar (2010), "The Differential Effects of Online Word-of-Mouth and Critics' Reviews on Pre-release Movie Evaluation," *Journal of Interactive Marketing*, 24(3), 185–97.

Champoux, Valerie, Julia Durgee, and Lauren McGlynn (2012), "Corporate Facebook pages: when 'fans' attack," *Journal of Business Strategy*, 33(2), 22–30.

Chandler, Alfred Dupont (1962), *Strategy and Structure: Chapters in the History of the American Industrial Enterprise, Business History Review*, Cambridge, Massachusetts, USA: Massachusetts Institute of Technology Cambridge.

Chandy, Rajesh K., and Jaideep C. Prabhu (2011), "Innovation typologies," in *Wiley International Encyclopedia of Marketing*, 1–9.

Chandy, Rajesh K., Jaideep C. Prabhu, and Kersi D. Antia (2003), "What will the future bring? Dominance, technology expectations, and radical innovation," *Journal of Marketing*, 67(3), 1–18.

Chandy, Rajesh K., and Gerard J. Tellis (1998), "Organizing for radical product innovation: the overlooked role of willingness to cannibalize," *Journal of Marketing Research*, 35(4), 474–87.

Chang, Ching-Hung, Shihtung Shu, and Brian King (2014), "Novelty in Theme Park Physical Surroundings: An Application of the Stimulus–Organism–Response Paradigm," *Asia Pacific Journal of Tourism Research*, 19(6), 680–99.

Chang, Hsin Hsin, and Su Wen Chen (2008), "The impact of online store environment cues on purchase intention: Trust and perceived risk as a mediator," *Online Information Review*, 32(6), 818–41.

Chang, Hyo-Jung, Molly Eckman, and Ruoh-Nan Yan (2011), "Application of the Stimulus-Organism-Response model to the retail environment: the role of hedonic motivation in impulse buying behavior," *The International Review of Retail, Distribution and Consumer Research*, 21(3), 233–49.

Chang, Tung-Zong, and Albert R. Wildt (1994), "Price, Product Information, and Purchase Intention: An Empirical Study," *Journal of the Academy of Marketing Science*, 22(1), 16–27.

Charness, Gary, Uri Gneezy, and Michael A. Kuhn (2012), "Experimental methods: Between-subject and within-subject design," *Journal of Economic Behavior & Organization*, 81(1), 1–8.

Chatterjee, Patrali (2010), "Multiple-channel and cross-channel shopping behavior: role of consumer shopping orientations," *Marketing Intelligence & Planning*, 28(1), 9–24.

Chen, Hui-chu, and Robert D. Green (2012), "To Increase Brand Equity: The differences between age groups," *International Business Economics Research*, 11(2), 241–54.

Chen, Ying-Hueih, I-Chieh Hsu, and Chia-Chen Lin (2010), "Website attributes that increase consumer purchase intention: A conjoint analysis," *Journal of Business Research*, 63(9-10), 1007–14.

Cheng, Xu, Jiangchuan Liu, Haiyang Wang, and Chonggang Wang (2012), "Coordinate Live Streaming and Storage Sharing for Social Media Content Distribution," *IEEE Transactions on Multimedia*, 14(6), 1558–65.

Chesbrough, Henry (2007), "Business model innovation: it's not just about technology anymore," *Strategy & Leadership*, 35(6), 12–17.

Chesbrough, Henry, and Richard S. Rosenbloom (2002), "The role of the business model in capturing value from innovation: evidence from Xerox Corporation's technology spin-off companies," *Industrial and Corporate Change*, 11(3), 529–55.

Cheung, Man Yee, Chuan Luo, Choon Ling Sia, and Huaping Chen (2009), "Credibility of Electronic Word-of-Mouth: Informational and Normative Determinants of On-line Consumer Recommendations," *International Journal of Electronic Commerce*, 13(4), 9–38.

Childers, Terry L., Christopher L. Carr, Joann Peck, and Stephen Carson (2001), "Hedonic and utilitarian motivations for online retail shopping behavior," *Journal of Retailing*, 77(4), 511–35.

Chintagunta, Pradeep K., Shyam Gopinath, and Sriram Venkataraman (2010), "The Effects of Online User Reviews on Movie Box Office Performance: Accounting for Sequential Rollout and Aggregation Across Local Markets," *Marketing Science*, 29(5), 944–57.

Cho, Young Ik (2008), "Intercoder Reliability," in *Encyclopedia of Survey Research Methods*, P. J.

Choudhury, Vivek, and Elena Karahanna (2008), "The relative advantage of electronic channels: A multidimensional view," *MIS Quarterly*, 32(1), 179–200.

Christensen, Dino P., and David M. Glick (2013), "Crowdsourcing panel studies and real-time experiments in MTurk," *The Political Methodologist*, 20(2), 27–32.

Christodoulides, George (2012), "Brand equity," *Brand*, 5(1), 1–14.

Christodoulides, George, Colin Jevons, and Jennifer Bonhomme (2012), "Memo to Marketers: Quantitative Evidence for Change -- How User-Generated Content Really Affects Brands," *Journal of Advertising Research*, 52(1), 53.

Christopher, Martin (2011), *Logistics & Supply Chain Management*, Harlow, United Kingdom: Pearson Education Limited.

Chung, Walter W. C., Anthony Y. K. Yam, and Michael F. S. Chan (2004), "Networked enterprise: A new business model for global sourcing," *International Journal of Production Economics*, 87(3), 267–80.

Clipson, Timothy W., S. Ann Wilson, and Debbie D. DuFrene (2012), "The Social Networking Arena: Battle of the Sexes," *Business Communication Quarterly*, 75(1), 64–67.

Cohen, Boyd, and Jan Kietzmann (2014), "Ride On! Mobility Business Models for the Sharing Economy," *Organization & Environment*, Vol. 27(3), 279–96.

Colla, Enrico, and Paul Lapoule (2012), "E-commerce: exploring the critical success factors," *International Journal of Retail & Distribution Management*.

Colliander, Jonas, and Micael Dahlen (2011), "Following the Fashionable Friend: The Power of Social Media - Weighing the Publicity Effectiveness Of Blogs versus Online Magazines," *Journal of Advertising Research*, 51(1), 313.

Combs, Kathryn L. (2000), "Information Rules: A Strategic Guide to the Network Economy by Carl Shapiro and Hal R. Varian. Review," *The Journal of Technology Transfer*, 25(2), 250–52.

Constantinides, Efthymios, Carlota Lorenzo Romero, and Miguel A. Gómez Boria (2008), "Social Media: A New Frontier for Retailers?," *European Retail Research*, 22, 1–28.

Cook, Karen S., Coye Cheshire, Eric R. W. Rice, and Sandra Nakagawa (2013), "Social Exchange Theory," in *Handbook of Social Psychology*, Amsterdam, Netherlands: Springer Netherlands, 61–88.

Craig, Robert T. (1999), "Communication Theory as a Field," *Communicaction Theory*, 9, 119–61.

Cramer, Harald (1946), *Mathematical Methods of Statistics*, New Jersey, United States: Princeton University Press.

Creswell, John W., and Vicki L. Plano Clark (2007), *Designing and conducting mixed methods research*, Thousand Oaks, CA. United States: SAGE Publications.

Cronbach, Lee J. (1951), "Coefficient alpha and the internal structure of tests," *Psychometrika*, 16(3), 297–334.

Cropanzano, R. (2005), "Social Exchange Theory: An Interdisciplinary Review," *Journal of Management*, 31(6), 874–900.

Crump, Matthew J. C., John V. McDonnell, and Todd M. Gureckis (2013), "Evaluating Amazon's Mechanical Turk as a tool for experimental behavioral research.," *PLOS ONE*, 8(3), e57410.

Cui, Guoqiang, Barbara Lockee, and Cuiqing Meng (2012), "Building modern online social presence: A review of social presence theory and its instructional design implications for future trends," *Education and Information Technologies*, 18(4), 661–85.

Culnan, Mary J., Patrick J. Mchugh, and Jesus I. Zubillaga (2010), "How Large US Companies Can Use Twitter and Other Social Media to Gain Business Value," *MIS Quarterly Executive*, 9(4), 243–60.

D'Urso, Scott C., and Stephen A. Rains (2008), "Examining the Scope of Channel Expansion: A Test of Channel Expansion Theory With New and Traditional Communication Media," *Management Communication Quarterly*, 21(4), 486–507.

Daft, Richard L., and Robert H. Lengel (1986), "Organizational Information Requirements, Media Richness and Structural Design," *Management Science*, 32(5), 554–71.

Daft, Richard L., and Norman B. Macintosh (1981), "A tentative exploration into the amount and equivocality of information processing in organizational work units," *Administrative Science Quarterly*, 26(2), 207–24.

Deetz, Stanley (1996), "Crossroads--Describing Differences in Approaches to Organization Science: Rethinking Burrell and Morgan and Their Legacy," *Organization Science*, 7(2), 191–207.

Dellarocas, Chrysanthos (2003), "The Digitization of Word of Mouth: Promise and Challenges of Online Feedback Mechanisms," *Management Science*, 49(10), 1407–24.

Dellarocas, Chrysanthos, Xiaoquan (Michael) Zhang, and Neveen F. Awad (2007), "Exploring the value of online product reviews in forecasting sales: The case of motion pictures," *Journal of Interactive Marketing*, 21(4), 23–45.

Dennis, Alan R., Robert M. Fuller, and Joseph S. Valacich (2008), "Media, tasks, and communication processes: A theory of media synchronicity," *MIS Quarterly*, 32(3), 575–600.

Dennis, Alan R., and Susan T. Kinney (1998), "Testing media richness theory in the new media: The effects of cues, feedback, and task equivocality," *Information Systems Research*, 9(3), 256–74.

Dennis, Alan R., and Joseph S. Valacich (1999), "Rethinking media richness: Towards a theory of media synchronicity," in *Hawaii International Conference on System Sciences*, 1–10.

Dennis, Charles, Tino Fenech, and Bill Merrilees (2005), "Sale the 7 Cs: teaching/training aid for

Deutskens, Elisabeth, Ko De Ruyter, Martin Wetzels, and Paul Oosterveld (2004), "Response Rate and Response Quality of Internet-Based Surveys: An Experimental Study," *Marketing Letters*, 15(1), 21–36.

Dhar, R, and K Wertenbroch (2000), "Consumer choice between hedonic and utilitarian goods," *Journal of Marketing Research*, 37(1), 60–71.

Dholakia, Utpal M., Richard P. Bagozzi, and Lisa K. Pearo (2004), "A social influence model of consumer participation in network- and small-group-based virtual communities," *International Journal of Research in Marketing*, 21(3), 241–63.

van Dijck, José (2013), *The culture of connectivity: a critical history of social media*, New York, NY: Oxford University Press.

Dover, Philip A. (1982), "Inferential Belief Formation: an Overlooked Concept in Information Processing Research," *Advances in Consumer Research*, (A. Mitchell, ed.), 9(1), 187–89.

Duan, Wenjing, Bin Gu, and Andrew B. Whinston (2008a), "Do online reviews matter? — An empirical investigation of panel data," *Decision Support Systems*, 45(4), 1007–16.

——— (2008b), "The dynamics of online word-of-mouth and product sales—An empirical investigation of the movie industry," *Journal of Retailing*, 84(2), 233–42.

Dudycha, Linda Weathers, and James C. Naylor (1966), "Characteristics of the human inference process in complex choice behavior situations," *Organizational Behavior and Human Performance*, 1(1), 110–28.

Dwyer, Catherine, Starr Hiltz, and Katia Passerini (2007), "Trust and privacy concern within social networking sites: A comparison of Facebook and MySpace," in *Proceedings of the Thirteenth Americas Conference on Information Systems*.

Dwyer, Paul (2007), "Measuring the value of electronic word of mouth and its impact in consumer communities," *Journal of Interactive Marketing*, 21(2), 63–79.

Dyer, Jeffrey H., and Harbir Singh (1998), "The relational view: Cooperative strategy and sources of interorganizational competitive advantage," *Academy of Management Review*, 23(4), 660–79.

Eckler, Petya, and Paul Bolls (2011), "Spreading the virus: Emotional tone of viral advertising and its effect on forwarding intentions and attitudes," *Advertising Age*, 11(2), 1–12.

Edelman, David C. (2010), "Branding in the Digital Age: You're Spending All Your Money in All the Wrong Places," *Harvard Business Review*, Spotlight(December), 63–69.

Edwards, Steven M. (2011), "A social media mindset," *Journal of Interactive Advertising*, 12(1), 1–3.

Ehrhart, Christof E. (2010), "Global E-Tailing 2025," *Deutsche Post DHL*, Bonn, Germany.

Eisenhardt, Kathleen M., and Jeffrey A. Martin (2000), "Dynamic capabilities: what are they?," *Strategic Management Journal*, 21(10-11), 1105–21.

Ekelund, Robert, Franklin Mixon, and Rand Ressler (1995), "Advertising and information: an empirical study of search, experience and credence goods," *Journal of Economic Studies*, 22(2), 33–43.

Elias, Peter, Amiel Feinstein, and Claude E. Shannon (1956), "A note on the maximum flow through a network," *IRE Transactions on Information Theory*, 2(4), 117–19.

Ellison, N B, C Steinfield, and C Lampe (2011), "Connection Strategies: Social Capital Implications of Facebook-enabled Communication Practices," *New Media & Society*, (W. E. Learning Through Landscapes Trust, ed.), 13(6), 873–92.

Ellison, Nicole B, Cliff Lampe, Charles Steinfield, and Jessica Vitak (2010), "With a Little Help From My Friends: How Social Network Sites Affect Social Capital Processes," in *A Networked Self Identity Community and Culture on Social Network Sites*, Z. Papacharissi, ed., Routledge, 124–45.

Ellison, Nicole B., Charles Steinfield, and Cliff Lampe (2007), "The Benefits of Facebook Friends: Social Capital and College Students' Use of Online Social Network Sites," *Journal of Computer-Mediated Communication*, 12(4), 1143–68.

Emerson, Richard M. (1976), "Social Exchange Theory," *Annual Review of Sociology*, Handbooks of sociology and social research, (J. Delamater, ed.), 2(1), 335–62.

Enders, Albrecht, Harald Hungenberg, Hans-Peter Denker, and Sebastian Mauch (2008), "The long tail of social networking.," *European Management Journal*, 26(3), 199–211.

Enders, Albrecht, and Tawfik Jelassi (2000), "The converging business models of Internet and bricks-and-mortar retailers," *European Management Journal*, 18(5), 542–50.

Erdem, Tülin, Joffre Swait, and Susan Broniarczyk (1999), "Brand equity, consumer learning and choice," *Marketing Letters*, 10(3), 301–18.

Eroglu, Sevgin A., Karen A. Machleit, and Lenita M. Davis (2001), "Atmospheric qualities of online retailing: a conceptual model and implications," *Journal of Business Research*, 54, 177–84.

Ess, Charles (2008), "Luciano Floridi's philosophy of information and information ethics: Critical reflections and the state of the art," *Ethics and Information Technology*, 10(2-3), 89–96.

Evans, Joel R., and Anil Mathur (2005), "The value of online surveys," *Internet Research*, 15(2), 195–219.

Évrard, Yves (1993), "La satisfaction des consommateurs: état des recherches," *Revue Française du Marketing*, 144, 53–66.

Fahey, L. (1989), "The New Corporate Strategy.," *Academy of Management Review*, 14(3), 459–60.

Fahey, Thomas, Mohammed Hajibashi, Ashish Jandial, and Sundip Naik (2014), "Winning in the Digital Channel."

Fang, Yu-Hui (2012), "Does online interactivity matter? Exploring the role of interactivity

Farquhar, Lee Keenan (2009), "Identity negotiation on Facebook.com," *Theses and Dissertations*, University of Iowa.

Farris, Paul W., Neil T. Bendle, Phillip E. Pfeifer, and David J. Reibstei (2010), *Marketing Metrics: The Definitive Guide to Measuring Marketing Performance*, (Wharton School Publishing, ed.), New Jersey: Pearson Prentice Hall Inc.

Felix, Reto (2012), "Brand communities for mainstream brands: the example of the Yamaha R1 brand community," *Journal of Consumer Marketing*, 29(3), 225–32.

Fernback, Jan, and Brad Thompson (1995), "Virtual Communities: Abort, Retry, Failure?," *Annual Convention of the International Communication Association*, <http://www.rheingold.com/texts/techpolitix/VCcivil.html> (Sep. 19, 2013).

De Figueiredo, John (2000), "Finding Sustainable Profitability in the E-commerce," *MIT Sloan Management Review*, 41(4), 41–52.

Finn, Adam, Luming Wang, and Tema Frank (2009), "Attribute Perceptions, Customer Satisfaction and Intention to Recommend E-Services," *Journal of Interactive Marketing*, 23(3), 209–20.

Fiore-Silfvast, Brittany (2012), "User-Generated Warfare : A Case of Converging Wartime Information Networks and Coproductive Regulation on YouTube," *International Journal of Communication*, 6(24), 1965–88.

Fischer, Marilyn (2008), "Mead and the International Mind," *Transactions of the Charles S. Peirce Society*, 44(3), 508–31.

Fischer, Timo, and Joachim Henkel (2010), "Capturing the Most Value from Innovation - Strategy Choices of R&D and Marketing Managers," in *SSRN Electronic Journal*, 1–39.

Fisher, Tia (2009), "ROI in social media: A look at the arguments," *Journal of Database Marketing & Customer Strategy Management*, 16(3), 189–95.

Floridi, Luciano (2004), "Open Problems in the Philosophy of Information," *Metaphilosophy*, 35(4), 554–82.

——— (2010), "The philosophy of information: Ten years later," *Metaphilosophy*, 41(3), 402–19.

Forrester Inc. (2010), "The ROI Of Social Media Marketing," Cambridge, MA: O'Reilly Media.

——— (2011), "US Online Retail Forecast, 2012 To 2017," Cambridge, MA.

——— (2015), "eCommerce Forecast, 2014 To 2019 (US)," Cambridge, MA.

Fort, Karën, Gilles Adda, and K: Bretonnel Cohen (2011), "Amazon Mechanical Turk: Gold Mine or Coal Mine?," *Computational Linguistics*, 37(2), 413–20.

Francis, Julie E. (2007), "Internet retailing quality: one size does not fit all," *Managing Service Quality*, 17(3), 341–55.

——— (2009), "Category-specific RECIPEs for internet retailing quality," *Journal of Services Marketing*, 23(7), 450–61.

Franke, George R., Bruce A. Huhmann, and David L. Mothersbaugh (2004), "Information Content and Consumer Readership of Print Ads: A Comparison of Search and Experience Products," *Journal of the Academy of Marketing Science*, 32(1), 20–31.

Freelon, Deen G (2010), "ReCal: Intercoder Reliability Calculation as a Web Service," *International Journal of Internet Science*, 5(1), 20–33.

Freeman, L (1979), "Centrality in social networks conceptual clarification," *Social Networks*, 1(3), 215–39.

Frey, Davide, Arnaud Jégou, and Anne-Marie Kermarrec (2011), "Social market: combining explicit and implicit social networks," in *International Symposium on Stabilization, Safety, and Security of Distributed Systems*.

Friedman, Lawrence G., and Timothy R. Furey (1999), *The Channel Advantage*, Linacre House, Jordan Hill, Oxford OX2 8DP: Butterworth-Heinemann.

Füller, Johann, Roland Schroll, and Eric von Hippel (2013), "User generated brands and their contribution to the diffusion of user innovations," *Research Policy*, 42(6-7), 1197–1209.

Funk, Tom (2012), *Advanced Social Media Marketing*, (1st, ed.), Apress.

Gangadharbatla, Harsha (2008), "Facebook me: Collective self-esteem, need to belong, and Internet self-efficacy as predictors of the igeneration's attitudes toward social networking sites," *Journal of Interactive Advertising*, 8(Spring), 5–15.

Gao, Lingling, and Xuesong Bai (2014), "Online consumer behaviour and its relationship to website atmospheric induced flow: Insights into online travel agencies in China," *Journal of Retailing and Consumer Services*, 1–13.

Gao, Xin, Mayer Alvo, Jie Chen, and Gang Li (2008), "Nonparametric multiple comparison procedures for unbalanced one-way factorial designs," *Journal of Statistical Planning and Inference*, 138(8), 2574–91.

Garcia, Rosanna, and Roger Calantone (2002), "A critical look at technological innovation typology and innovativeness terminology: A literature review," *Journal of Product Innovation Management*.

Gardner, Meryl Paula (1985), "Mood states and consumer behavior: a critical review," *Journal of Consumer Research*, 12(3), 281–300.

Garg, R, R Telang, M Smith, D Krackhardt, and R Krishnan (2009), "Peer Influence and Information Diffusion in Online Networks : An Empirical Analysis," *Analysis*, (2009), 1–25.

Garg, Rajiv, Michael D. Smith, and Rahul Telang (2011), "Measuring Information Diffusion in an Online Community," *Journal of Management Information Systems*, 28(2), 11–37.

Gartner Inc. (2013), "Leverage Design Ethnography to Boost Enterprise Social Networking Success," Stamf, CT. United States of America.

——— (2014), "Agenda Overview for Retail, 2014," Stamf, CT. United States of America.

Garvin, David A. (1984), "What does 'product quality' really mean," *MIT Sloan Management Review*, 26(1).

Gelbrich, Katja (2011), "I Have Paid Less Than You! The Emotional and Behavioral Consequences of Advantaged Price Inequality," *Journal of Retailing*, 87(2), 207–24.

Geyskens, Inge, Katrijn Gielens, and Marnik G. Dekimpe (2002), "The market valuation of internet channel additions," *Journal of Marketing*, 66(2), 102–19.

Giamanco, Barbara, and and Kent Gregoire (2012), "Tweet Me, Friend Me, Make Me Buy," *Harvard Business Review*, (July-August), 88–93.

Gibbons, Deborah E. (2004), "Network Structure and Innovation Ambiguity Effects on Diffusion in Dynamic Organizational Fields.," *Academy of Management Journal*, 47(6), 938–51.

Giles, Martin (2010), "A world of connections," *The Economist*, London, UK.

Gillin, Paul (2008), "New media, new influencers and implications for the public relations profession," *Journal of New Communications Research*, II(2), 1–10.

Girard, Tulay, and Paul Dion (2010), "Validating the search, experience, and credence product classification framework," *Journal of Business Research*, 63(9-10), 1079–87.

Gladwell, Malcolm (2000), *The Tipping Point: How Little Things Can Make a Big Difference*, Book.

——— (2008), *Outliers: The story of success*, Hachette UK.

Gladwin, Thomas N., and Geert Hofstede (1981), "Culture's Consequences: International Differences in Work-Related Values," *The Academy of Management Review*.

Gneiser, Martin, Julia Heidemann, Mathias Klier, Andrea Landherr, and Florian Probst (2010), "Valuation of online social networks taking into account users' interconnectedness," *Information Systems and e-Business Management*, 10(1), 61–84.

Godden, Duncan R., and Alan D. Baddeley (1975), "Context-dependent memory in two natural environments: On land and underwate," *British Journal of Psychology*, 66, 325–31.

——— (1980), "When does context influence recognition memory?," *British Journal of Psychology*, 71, 99–104.

Goh, Yi Sheng, Veena Chattaraman, and Sandra Forsythe (2013), "Brand and category design consistency in brand extensions," *Journal of Product & Brand Management*, 22, 272–85.

Granovetter, Mark S. (1973), "The strength of weak ties," *American Journal of Sociology*, 78(6), 1360–80.

——— (1983), "The strength of weak ties: A network theory revisted," in *Sociological Theory*, 201–33.

Gray, Peter O. (2010), *Psychology*, New York, New York, USA: Worth Publishers.

Di Gregorio, Dante (2013), "Value Creation and Value Appropriation: An Integrative, Multi-Level Framework," *Journal of Applied Business and Economics*, 15(1999), 39–54.

Grewal, Dhruv, R Krishnan, Julie Baker, and N Borin (1998), "The effect of store name, brand name and price discounts on consumers' evaluations and purchase intentions," *Journal of Retailing*, 74(3), 331–52.

Gruen, Thomas W., Talai Osmonbekov, and Andrew J. Czaplewski (2006), "eWOM: The impact of customer-to-customer online know-how exchange on customer value and loyalty," *Journal of Business Research*, 59(4), 449–56.

Gulati, Ranjay, Nitin Nohria, and Akbar Zaheer (2000), "Strategic Networks," *Strategic Management Journal*, 21(3), 203–15.

Habibi, MR, Michel Laroche, and MO Richard (2014), "Brand communities based in social media: How unique are they? Evidence from two exemplary brand communities," *International Journal of Information Management*, 34(2), 123–32.

Hagel, John, and Arthur G. Armstrong (1997), "Net gain: expanding markets through virtual communities," in *Net gain: expanding markets through virtual communities*, Boston, Massachusetts: Harvard Business School Press, 41–185.

Hahn, Minhi, Sehoon Park, Lakshman Krishnamurthi, and Andris A. Zoltners (1994), "Analysis of New Product Diffusion Using a Four-Segment Trial-Repeat Model," *Marketing Science*, (P. Internet Encyclopedia Of, ed.), 13(3), 224–47.

Hamel, Gary (2000), *Leading the revolution*, Boston, Massachusetts, United States: Harvard Business School Press.

Hamouda, Manel, and Rym Srarfi Tabbane (2013), "Impact of Electronic Word of Mouth Evaluation on Purchase Intention: The Mediating Role of Attitude toward the Product," *International Journal of Online Marketing*, 3(2), 20–32.

Handbooks in Communication and Media (2015), *The Handbook of the Psychology of Communication Technology*, Wiley-Blackwell.

Handfield, Robert B, Steve V Walton, Lisa K Seegers, and Steven a Melnyk (1997), "'Green' value chain practices in the furniture industry," *Journal of Operations Management*, 15(4), 293–315.

Hanna, Richard, Andrew Rohm, and Victoria L Crittenden (2011), "We're all connected: The power of the social media ecosystem," *Business Horizons*, 54(3), 265–73.

Hanson, Gary, and Paul Haridakis (2008), "YouTube Users Watching and Sharing the News: A Uses and Gratifications Approach," *Journal of Electronic Publishing*, 11(3), 1–17.

Harper, Douglas (2015), "Communication," *Online Etymology Dictionary*.

Hart, Phillip M., and Rick Dale (2014), "With or without you: The positive and negative influence of retail companions," *Journal of Retailing and Consumer Services*, 21(5), 780–87.

Hartley, Ralph Vinton Lyon (1928), "Transmission of information," *Bell System Technical Journal*, 7, 535–63.

Hausman, Angela V., and Jeffrey Sam Siekpe (2009), "The effect of web interface features on consumer online purchase intentions," *Journal of Business Research*, 62(1), 5–13.

Heidemann, Julia, Mathias Klier, and Florian Probst (2010), "Identifying key users in Online Social Networks: A PageRank Based Approach," in *Proceedings of the 31st International Conference on Information Systems*, 1–22.

Heilemann, John Arthur (2008), "Download: The True Story of the Internet," *Science Channel - Discovery Channel*, <http://youtu.be/aa0opnZ00l4?t=12m33>.

Hennig-Thurau, T., E C Malthouse, C Friege, S Gensler, L Lobschat, A Rangaswamy, and B Skiera (2010), "The Impact of New Media on Customer Relationships," *Journal of Service Research*, 13(3), 311–30.

Hennig-Thurau, Thorsten, Kevin P. Gwinner, Gianfranco Walsh, and Dwayne D. Gremler (2004), "Electronic word-of-mouth via consumer-opinion platforms: What motivates consumers to articulate themselves on the Internet?," *Journal of Interactive Marketing*, 18(1), 38–52.

Hennig-Thurau, Thorsten, Mark B Houston, and Shrihari Sridhar (2006), "Can good marketing carry a bad product? Evidence from the motion picture industry," *Marketing Letters*, 17(3), 205–19.

Hennig-Thurau, Thorsten, and Gianfranco Walsh (2003), "Electronic word-of-mouth: motives for and consequences of reading customer articulations on the internet," *International Journal of Electronic Commerce*, 8(2), 51–74.

Hernández, Blanca, Julio Jiménez, and M. José Martín (2009), "Key website factors in e-business strategy," *International Journal of Information Management*, 29(5), 362–71.

Hernández Sampieri, Roberto, Carlos Fernández Collado, and Pilar Baptista Lucio (2014), *Metodología de la investigación*, Mexico City, Mexico: McGraw-Hill Education.

Higgs, Eric, and Sundeep Sahay (2000), "Holding on to Reality: The Nature of Information at the Turn of the Millennium," *The Information Society*.

Hinterhuber, Hans H., and Boris M. Levin (1994), "Strategic networks - The organization of the future," *Long range planning*, 27(3), 43.

Hoffman, Donna L., and Marek Fodor (2010), "Can you measure the ROI of your social media marketing?," *MIT Sloan Management Review*, 52(1), 40–50.

Hoffman, Donna L., and Thomas P. Novak (1997), "A new marketing paradigm for electronic commerce," *The Information Society*.

——— (2012a), "What is the social web?," in *Handbook of Marketing Strategy*, S. Venkatesh and G. S. Carpenter, eds., Cheltenham, UK: Edward Elgar, 202–14.

——— (2012b), "Toward a Deeper Understanding of Social Media," *Journal of Interactive Marketing*, 26(2), 69–70.

Hofstede, Geert (1980), "Motivation, leadership, and organization: Do American theories apply abroad?," *Organizational Dynamics*, 9(1), 42–63.

——— (1983), "National cultures in four dimensions: A research based theory of cultural differences among nations," *International Studies of Management & Organization*, 13(1/2), 46–74.

Holbrook, Allyson L., Jon A. Krosnick, David Moore, and Roger Tourangeau (2007), "Response Order Effects in Dichotomous Categorical Questions Presented Orally The Impact of Question and Respondent Attributes," *Public Opinion Quarterly*, 71(3), 325–48.

Holden, Christopher J., Trevor Dennie, and Adam D. Hicks (2013), "Assessing the reliability of the M5-120 on Amazon's mechanical Turk," *Computers in Human Behavior*, 29(4), 1749–54.

Holey, Pallavi N., and Vishwas T. Gaikwad (2014), "Google Glass Technology," *International Journal of Advance Research in Computer Science and Management Studies*, 2(3), 278–81.

Homans, George C. (1961), *Social behavior: Its elementary forms*, NY Harcourt Brace Javanovich, (R. K. Merton, ed.), Harcourt, Brace & World.

Hosein, Nasim Z. (2012), "Measuring the Purchase Intention of Visitors to the Auto Show," *Journal of Management & Marketing Research*, 9, 1–17.

Hsieh, Tony (2010a), *Delivering Happiness: A Path to Profits, Passion, and Purpose, Source*, New York, New York, USA: Business Plus.

——— (2010b), "How I did it - Zappos's CEO on Going to Extremes for Customers," *Harvard Business Review*, (July-August), 1–5.

Hsieh, Yi-Ching, Jinshyang Roan, Anurag Pant, Jung-Kuei Hsieh, Wen-Ying Chen, Monle Lee, and Hung-Chang Chiu (2012), "All for one but does one strategy work for all? Building consumer loyalty in multi-channel distribution," *Managing Service Quality*, 22(3), 310–35.

Hsu, Chiu-Ping, Yi-Fang Chiang, and Heng-Chiang Huang (2012), "How experience-driven community identification generates trust and engagement," *Online Information Review*, 36(1), 72–88.

Hsu, Meng-Hsiang, Teresa L. Ju, Chia-Hui Yen, and Chun-Ming Chang (2007), "Knowledge sharing behavior in virtual communities: The relationship between trust, self-efficacy, and outcome expectations," *International Journal of Human-Computer Studies*, 65(2), 153–69.

Hu, N, J Zhang, and PA Pavlou (2009), "Overcoming the J-shaped distribution of product reviews," *Communications of the ACM*, 3–6.

Hu, Nan, Ling Liu, and Jie Jennifer Zhang (2008), "Do online reviews affect product sales? The role of reviewer characteristics and temporal effects," *Information Technology and Management*, 9(3), 201–14.

Hu, Nan, Paul A Pavlou, and Jennifer Zhang (2007), "Why do Online Product Reviews have a J-shaped Distribution? Overcoming Biases in Online Word-of-Mouth Communication," *Marketing Science*, 198(February 2007), 7–13.

Huang, JH, and YF Chen (2006), "Herding in online product choice," *Psychology & Marketing*, 23(5), 413–28.

Huang, Peng, Nicholas H. Lurie, and Sabyasachi Mitra (2009), "Searching for Experience on the Web: An Empirical Examination of Consumer Behavior for Search and Experience Goods," *Journal of Marketing*, 73(March), 55–69.

Huberman, Bernardo A, Daniel M Romero, and Fang Wu (2008), "Social networks that matter: Twitter under the microscope," in *arXiv:0812.1045*, 1–9.

Hung, Kineta H., and Stella Yiyan Li (2007), "The Influence of eWOM on Virtual Consumer Communities: Social Capital, Consumer Learning, and Behavioral Outcomes," *Journal of Advertising Research*, 47(4), 485.

Hyllegard, Karen, Molly Eckman, Alejandro Molla Descals, and Miguel Angel Gomez Borja (2005), "Spanish consumers' perceptions of US apparel speciality retailers' products and services," *Journal of Consumer Behaviour*, 4(5), 345–62.

Internet Live Stats (2014), "Internet Users by Country."

Internet Retailer Magazine (2012), "Top 500 Guide, portal to e-commerce data."

Internet World Stats (2013), "Internet Users Worldwide," Bogota, Colombia.

Ipeirotis, Panagiotis G. (2010), "Demographics of mechanical turk," *SSRN Electronic Journal*.

Irshad, Wasseem (2012), "Service Based Brand Equity, Measure of Purchase Intention, Mediating Role of Brand Performance," *Academy of Contemporary Research Journal*, 1(1), 1–10.

Jacoby, Jacob (2002), "Stimulus-organism-response reconsidered: an evolutionary step in modeling (consumer) behavior," *Journal of Consumer Psychology*, 12(1), 51–57.

Jacoby, Jacob, Jerry C. Olson, and Rafael A. Haddock (1971), "Price, brand name, and product composition characteristics as determinants of perceived quality.," *Journal of Applied Psychology*, 55(6), 570–79.

Jacquet, Jennifer (2011), "The Pros & Cons of Amazon Mechanical Turk for Scientific Surveys," *Scientific American*, <http://blogs.scientificamerican.com/guilty-planet/2011/07/07/the-pros-cons-of-amazon-mechanical-turk-for-scientific-surveys/>.

Jang, SooCheong (Shawn), and Young Namkung (2009), "Perceived quality, emotions, and behavioral intentions: Application of an extended Mehrabian–Russell model to restaurants," *Journal of Business Research*, 62(4), 451–60.

Jansen, Bernard J., and Soo Young Rieh (2010), "The seventeen theoretical constructs of information searching and information retrieval," *Journal of the American Society for Information Science and Technology*, 61(8), 1517–34.

Jansen, Bernard J., Mimi Zhang, Kate Sobel, and Abdur Chowdury (2009), "Twitter power: Tweets as electronic word of mouth," *Journal of the American Society for Information Science and Technology*, 60(11), 2169–88.

Jarillo, J. Carlos (1988), "On Strategic Networks," *Strategic Management Journal*, 9(1), 31–41.

Jermier, John M., and Linda C. Forbes (2011), "Metaphor as the Foundation of Organizational Studies: Images of Organization and Beyond," *Organization & Environment*.

Jo, Myung-Soo (2007), "Should a quality sub-brand be located before or after the parent brand? An application of composite concept theory," *Journal of the Academy of Marketing Science*, 35(2), 184–96.

Johnston, Kevin, Maureen Tanner, Nishant Lalla, and Dori Kawalski (2011), "Social capital: the benefit of Facebook 'friends,'" *Behaviour Information Technology*, (May 2012), 1–13.

Jones, Brian, John Temperley, and Anderson Lima (2009), "Corporate reputation in the era of Web 2.0: the case of Primark," *Journal of Marketing Management*, 25(9-10), 927–39.

Kachhi, Dinaz, and Michael W. Link (2009), "Too Much Information: Does the Internet Dig Too Deep?," *Journal of Advertising Research*, 49(1), 74.

Kanter, Rosabeth Moss, and Herbert Blumer (1971), "Symbolic Interactionism: Perspective and Method.," *American Sociological Review*, 36(2), 333.

Kaplan, Andreas M., and Michael Haenlein (2010), "Users of the world, unite! The challenges and opportunities of Social Media," *Business Horizons*, 53(1), 59–68.

——— (2011), "The early bird catches the news: Nine things you should know about micro-blogging," *Business Horizons*, 54(2), 105–13.

Karat, Clare-Marie, Christine Halverson, Daniel Horn, John Karat, and Ann Arbor (1999), "Patterns of Entry and Correction in Large Vocabulary Continuous Speech Recognition Systems," in *Proceedings of the SIGCHI Conference on Human Factors in Computing Systems*, ACM, 568–75.

Kauffman, Robert J., and Bin Wang (2008), "Tuning into the digital channel: evaluating business model characteristics for Internet firm survival," *Information Technology and Management*, 9(3), 215–32.

Kavada, Anastasia (2012), "Engagement, bonding, and identity across multiple platforms: Avaaz on Facebook, YouTube, and MySpace," *Journal of media and communication research*, MedieKultu(52), 28–48.

Kavanaugh, Andrea, Debbie Reese, John Carroll, and Mary Rosson (2005), "Weak Ties in Networked Communities," *The Information Society*, (M. Huysman, E. Wenger, and V. Wulf, eds.), 21(2), 119–31.

Kawaf, Fatema, and Stephen Tagg (2012), "Online shopping environments in fashion shopping: An SOR based review.," *Marketing Review*, 12(2), 161–80.

Kehrwald, Benjamin (2008), "Understanding social presence in text-based online learning environments," *Distance Education*, 29(1), 89–106.

Keller, Kevin Lane (1993), "Conceptualizing, Measuring, and Managing Customer-Based Brand Equity," *Journal of Marketing*, 57(1), 1–22.

——— (2010), "Brand Equity Management in a Multichannel, Multimedia Retail Environment," *Journal of Interactive Marketing*, 24(2), 58–70.

——— (2013), "Chapter 4: Advertising and Brand Equity," in *The SAGE Handbook of Advertising*, 54–71.

Keller, Kevin Lane, and David A. Aaker (1992), "The Effects of Sequential Introduction of Brand Extensions," *Journal of Marketing Research*, 29(1), 35–50.

Kerin, RA, PR Varadarajan, and RA Peterson (1992), "First-mover advantage: A synthesis, conceptual framework, and research propositions," *The Journal of Marketing*, 56(4), 33–52.

Kietzmann, Jan H., Kristopher Hermkens, Ian P. McCarthy, and Bruno S. Silvestre (2011), "Social media? Get serious! Understanding the functional building blocks of social media," *Business Horizons*, 54(3), 241–51.

Kilian, Thomas, Nadine Hennigs, and Sascha Langner (2012), "Do Millennials read books or blogs? Introducing a media usage typology of the internet generation," *Journal of Consumer Marketing*, 29(2), 114–24.

Kim, Jihyun, and Jihye Park (2005), "A consumer shopping channel extension model: attitude shift toward the online store," in *Journal of Fashion Marketing and Management*, 106–21.

Kim, Jiyoung, and Sharron J Lennon (2012), "Effects of reputation and website quality on online consumers' emotion, perceived risk and purchase intention," *Journal of Research in Interactive Marketing*, 7(1), 33–56.

Kim, Jun B, Paulo Albuquerque, and Bart J Bronnenberg (2011), "Mapping Online Consumer Search," *Journal of Marketing Research*, XLVIII(February), 13–27.

Kim, Soyoung, and Leslie Stoel (2004), "Dimensional hierarchy of retail website quality," *Information & Management*, 41(5), 619–33.

Kim, W. Chan (2005), *Blue Ocean Strategy: How to Create Uncontested Market Space and Make Competition Irrelevant*, Harvard Business Review Press.

Kim, Yong-Man, and Kyu-Yeol Shim (2002), "The influence of Internet shopping mall characteristics and user traits on purchase intent," *Irish Marketing Review and Journal of Korean Academy of Marketing Science*, 15(2), 25–34.

Kivran-Swaine, Funda, Priya Govindan, and Mor Naaman (2011), "The Impact of Network Structure on Breaking Ties in Online Social Networks: Unfollowing on Twitter," in *Proceedings of the SIGCHI Conference on Human Factors in Computing Systems*, CHI '11, ACM, 1101–4.

Klein, Heinz K., and Michael D Myers (1999), "A Set of Principles for Conducting and Evaluating Interpretive Field Studies in Information Systems," *MIS Quarterly*, 23(1), 67.

Knight, Dee K., and Eun Young Kim (2007), "Japanese consumers' need for uniqueness: Effects on brand perceptions and purchase intention," *Journal of Fashion Marketing and Management*, 11(2), 270–80.

Korgaonkar, Pradeep, Ronnie Silverblatt, and Tulay Girard (2006), "Online retailing, product classifications, and consumer preferences," *Journal of Internet Research*, 16(3), 267–88.

Kornberger, Martin (2011), "Social media in branding: Fulfilling a need," *Journal of Brand Management*, 18(9), 688–96.

Kotler, Philip (1973), "Atmospherics as a marketing tool," *Journal of Retailing*, 49(4), 48–64.

——— (2008), "The Five Competitive Forces That Shape Strategy," *Harvard Business Review*.

——— (2012), "On Marketing," *Chicago Humanities Festival*, United States of America: Chicago Humanities Festival, <http://youtu.be/sR-qL7QdVZQ?t=17m49s> (Dec. 1, 2013).

Kotler, Philip, Linden Brown, Steward Adam, and Gary Armstrong (2006), *Marketing, (2006) Marketing, 7th Ed. Pearson Education Australia/Prentice Hall.*, Pearson Education Australia.

Kotler, Philip, and Kevin Lane Keller (2012), *Marketing Management 14e. Pearson Education Limited*, (P. Kotler, ed.), Prentice Hall.

Kozinets, Robert V., Kristine De Valck, Andrea C. Wojnicki, and Sarah J.S. Wilner (2010), "Networked Narratives: Understanding Word-of-Mouth," *Journal of Marketing*, 74(March), 71–89.

Krackhardt, David (1992), "The strength of strong ties: The importance of philos in organizations," in *Networks and organizations: Structure, form, and action*, 216–39.

Krosnick, Jon a., and Duane F. Alwin (1987), "An Evaluation of a Cognitive Theory of Response-Order Effects in Survey Measurement," *Public Opinion Quarterly*, 51(2), 201.

Kumar, V., and Rohan Mirchandani (2012), "Marketing, Increasing the ROI of Social Media Marketing," *MIT Sloan Management Review*, 54(1).

Kurts, D. L. (1993), "The 22 immutable laws of marketing: Violate Them at Your Own Risk!," *The Journal of Consumer Marketing*, 10(4), 2–70.

Kwak, Haewoon, Changhyun Lee, Hosung Park, and Sue Moon (2010), "What is Twitter, a Social Network or a News Media?," in *Proceedings of the 19th International World Wide Web Conference Committee*, WWW '10, ACM Press, 591–600.

Kwek, Choon Ling, Hoi Piew Tan, and Teck-Chai Lau (2010), "Investigating the Shopping Orientations on Online Purchase Intention in the e-Commerce Environment: A Malaysian Study.," *Journal of Internet Banking & Commerce*, 15(2), 1–22.

Kwon, Joseph, and Ingoo Han (2013), "Information Diffusion with Content Crossover in Online Social Media: An Empirical Analysis of the Social Transmission Process in Twitter," in *46th Hawaii International Conference on System Sciences*, Ieee, 3292–3301.

Lafferty, Barbara, Ronald Goldsmith, and Stephen Newell (2002), "The dual credibility model: The influence of corporate and endorser credibility on attitudes and purchase intentions," *Journal of Marketing Theory and Practice*, 10(3), 1–12.

Laroche, Michel, Mohammad Reza Habibi, and Marie-Odile Richard (2013), "To be or not to be in social media: How brand loyalty is affected by social media?," *International Journal of Information Management*, 33(1), 76–82.

Laroche, Michel, Mohammad Reza Habibi, Marie-Odile Richard, and Ramesh Sankaranarayanan (2012), "The effects of social media based brand communities on brand community markers, value creation practices, brand trust and brand loyalty," *Computers in Human Behavior*, 28(5), 1755–67.

Laroche, Michel, Chankon Kim, and Lianxi Zhou (1996), "Brand familiarity and confidence as determinants of purchase intention: an empirical test in a multiple brand context," *Journal of Business Research*, 37, 115–20.

Lee, Hyun-Hwa, and Jihyun Kim (2008), "The effects of shopping orientations on consumers' satisfaction with product search and purchases in a multi-channel environment," *Journal of Fashion Marketing and Management*, 12(2), 193–216.

Lee, Mira, and Seounmi Youn (2009), "Electronic word of mouth (eWOM): How eWOM platforms influence consumer product judgement," *International Journal of Advertising*, 28(3), 473.

Lee, Seunghyun, Sejin Ha, and Richard Widdows (2011), "Consumer responses to high-technology products: Product attributes, cognition, and emotions," *Journal of Business Research*, 64(11), 1195–1200.

Lee, Younghwa, and Kenneth A. Kozar (2006), "Investigating the effect of website quality on e-business success: An analytic hierarchy process (AHP) approach," *Decision Support Systems*, 42(3), 1383–1401.

Leech, Nancy L., and Anthony J. Onwuegbuzie (2011), "Beyond constant comparison qualitative data analysis: Using NVivo," *School Psychology Quarterly*, 26(1), 70–84.

Lengel, Robert H., and Richard L. Daft (1988), "The selection of communication media as an executive skill," *The Academy of Management Executive*, II(3), 225–32.

Levin, Daniel Z., and Rob Cross (2004), "The Strength of Weak Ties You Can Trust: The Mediating Role of Trust in Effective Knowledge Transfer," *Management Science*, 50(11), 1477–90.

Li, Min, Z.Y. Dong, and Xi Chen (2012), "Factors influencing consumption experience of mobile commerce: A study from experiential view," *Internet Research*, 22(2), 120–41.

Liaw, Gou-Fong, Zong-Wei Zhu, and Yao-Hsien Lee (2005), "The Effects of Risk Reduction Strategies on Consumers' Perceptions and Online Purchase Intention," *Pan-Pacific Management Review*, 8(1), 1–37.

Liebendorfer, Robert (1960), "Mind, self and society," *Today's Speech*.

Lieberman, Marvin B., and David B. Montgomery (1988), "First-mover advantages," *Strategic Management Journal*, 9(Summer Special), 41–58.

——— (1998), "First-mover (dis) advantages: Retrospective and link with the resource-based view," *Strategic Management Journal*, 19(June), 1111–25.

Lim, Jeen-Su, and Richard W. Olshavsky (1988), "Impacts of consumers' familiarity and product class on price-quality inference and product evaluations," *Quarterly Journal of Business and Economics*, 27(3), 130–46.

Limbu, Yam B, Marco Wolf, and Dale Lunsford (2012), "Perceived ethics of online retailers and consumer behavioral intentions The mediating roles of trust and attitude," *Journal of Research in Interactive Marketing*, 6(2), 133–54.

Lin, Jhih-syuan, and Jorge Peña (2011), "Are you Following Me? A Content Analysis Of TV Networks' Brand Communication On Twitter," *Journal of Interactive Advertising*, 12(1), 17–29.

Lin, Kuan-Yu, and Hsi-Peng Lu (2011), "Why people use social networking sites: An empirical study integrating network externalities and motivation theory," *Computers in Human Behavior*, 27(3), 1152–61.

Lipsman, Andrew, Graham Mudd, Mike Rich, and Sean Bruich (2012), "The Power of 'Like': How Brands Reach (and Influence) Fans through Social-Media Marketing," *Journal of Advertising Research*, 52(1), 40.

Litvin, Stephen, Ronald Goldsmith, and Bing Pan (2008), "Electronic word-of-mouth in hospitality and tourism management," *Tourism Management*, 29, 458–68.

Liu, Xia, Alvin C. Burns, and Yingjian Hou (2013), "Comparing online and in-store shopping behavior towards luxury goods," *International Journal of Retail & Distribution Management*, 41(11), 885–900.

Lumpkin, G.T., and Gregory Dess (2004), "E-Business Strategies and Internet Business Models:

Lumpkin, G.T., Scott B. Droege, and Gregory G. Dess (2002), "Achieving Sustainable Competitive Advantage and Avoiding Pitfalls," *Organizational Dynamics*, 30(4), 325–40.

M.E., Par (2015), "Spartoo ouvre son premier magasin," *Le Dauphiné Libéré*, Grenoble, France.

MacKenzie, Scott, Richard Lutz, and George Belch (1986), "The role of attitude toward the ad as a mediator of advertising effectiveness: A test of competing explanations," *Journal of Marketing Research*, 23(2), 130–43.

Maclaran, Pauline, Michael Saren, Barbara Stern, and Mark Tadajewski (2011), "Theorizing Advertising: Managerial, Scientific and Cultural Approaches," in *The SAGE Handbook of Marketing Theory*.

Madureira, António, Frank den Hartog, Harry Bouwman, and Nico Baken (2013), "Empirical validation of metcalfe's law: How Internet usage patterns have changed over time," *Information Economics and Policy*, 25(4), 246–56.

De Maeyer, Peter (2012), "Impact of online consumer reviews on sales and price strategies: a review and directions for future research," *Journal of Product & Brand Management*.

Magretta, Joan (2002), "Why business models matter," *Harvard Business Review*.

Malhotra, Naresh K., and David F. Birks (2007), *Marketing Research*, New Jersey, US: Pearson Education.

Malhotra, Neil (2008), "Completion Time and Response Order Effects in Web Surveys," *Public Opinion Quarterly*, 72(5), 914–34.

Marsden, Peter V. (1990), "Network data and measurement," *Annual Review of Sociology*, 16(1990), 435–63.

Martins, Luis L., Violina P. Rindova, and Bruce E. Greenbaum (2015), "Unlocking the Hidden Value of Concepts: A Cognitive Approach to Business Model Innovation," *Strategic Entrepreneurship Journal*, 9(1), 99–117.

Mata, Francisco J., William L. Fuerst, and Jay B. Barney (1995), "Information technology and sustained competitive advantage: a resource-based analysis," *MIS quarterly*, 19(4), 487–505.

Matei, Sorin, and Sandra J. Ball-Rokeach (2001), "Real and Virtual Social Ties: Connections in the Everyday Lives of Seven Ethnic Neighborhoods," *American Behavioral Scientist*, 45(3), 550–64.

Matzler, Kurt, Viktoria Veider, and Wolfgang Kathan (2015), "Adapting to the Sharing Economy," *MIT Sloan Management Review*, 1–11.

Mayo, Micahel C., and Gordon S. Brown (1999), "Building a competitive business model.," *Ivey Business Journal*, 63(3), 18–23.

Mazaheri, Ebrahim, Marie Odile Richard, Michel Laroche, and Linda C. Ueltschy (2014), "The influence of culture, emotions, intangibility, and atmospheric cues on online behavior," *Journal of Business Research*, 67(3), 253–59.

McCarthy, E. Jerome (1960), "Basic Marketing: A Managerial Approach," Homewood, IL: Irwin.

McClave, James T., P. George Benson, and Terry Sincich (2008), *Statistics for Business and Economics*, Pearson Education.

McDonald, Colin, and Jane Scott (2007), "2. A Brief History of Advertising," in *The SAGE Handbook of Advertising*, 17–35.

McFadyen, M A, M Semadeni, and A A Cannella (2008), "Value of Strong Ties to Disconnected Others: Examining Knowledge Creation in Biomedicine," *Organization Science*, 20(3), 552–64.

McFedries, P. (2007), "All A-Twitter," *Institute of Electrical and Electronics Engineers*, 84.

McKinsey (2013), *Chief Marketing & Sales Officer Forum: Big Data, Analytics, and the Future of Marketing & Sales*, New York, New York, USA: McKinsey & Company.

Mennecke, Brian E., Janea L. Triplett, Lesya M. Hassall, Zayira Jordán Conde, and Rex Heer (2011), "An Examination of a Theory of Embodied Social Presence in Virtual Worlds*," *Decision Sciences*, 42(2), 413–50.

Merikle, Philip, Daniel Smilek, and John Eastwood (2001), "Perception without awareness: perspectives from cognitive psychology," *Cognition*, 79(1-2), 115–34.

Metcalfe, Robert (1995), "Metcalfe's law: A network becomes more valuable as it reaches more users," *InfoWorld*, 17(40), 53–54.

Meyers, Lawrence S., Glenn Gamst, and Anthony J. Guarino (2013), *Applied Multivariate Research. Design and Interpretation*, London, UK: Sage Publications, Inc.

Michon, Richard, Jean-Charles Chebat, and L.W. Turley (2005), "Mall atmospherics: the interaction effects of the mall environment on shopping behavior," *Journal of Business Research*, 58(5), 576–83.

Mikusz, M., C. Jud, and T. Schäfer (2015), "Business Model Patterns for the Connected Car and the Example of Data Orchestrator," in *Lecture Notes in Business Information Processing*, Springer International Publishing, 167–73.

Mills, Donald L. (1983), "Organizations: Rational, Natural and Open Systems," *Canadian Journal of Sociology*.

Minniti, Antonio (2011), "Knowledge appropriability, firm size, and growth," *Journal of Macroeconomics*, 33(3), 438–54.

Mislove, Alan, and Massimiliano Marcon (2007), "Measurement and analysis of online social networks," in *Proceedings of the Internet Measurement Conference*.

Mitchell, Gareth (2013), "Privacy is the currency of online retail, and it's too high a price to pay for what we're getting," *Debate Digital Privacy*, (August), 26–27.

Mizik, Natalie, and R Jacobson (2003), "Trading off between value creation and value appropriation: The financial implications of shifts in strategic emphasis," *Journal of Marketing*, 67(1), 63–76.

Molyneaux, Heather, Susan O'Donnell, Kerri Gibson, and Janice Singer (2008), "Exploring the Gender Divide on YouTube: An Analysis of the Creation and Reception of Vlogs," *American Communication Journal*, 10(2), 721–26.

Montgomery, Jacob M., and Josh Cutler (2013), "Computerized Adaptive Testing for Public Opinion Surveys," *Political Analysis*, 21(2), 172–92.

Montoya-Weiss, Mitzi M., Glenn B. Voss, and Dhruv Grewal (2003), "Determinants of online channel use and overall satisfaction with a relational, multichannel service provider," *Journal of the Academy of Marketing Science*, 31(4), 448–58.

Moore, Marguerite (2012), "Interactive media usage among millennial consumers," *Journal of Consumer Marketing*, 29(6), 436–44.

Morris, Michael, Minet Schindehutte, and Jeffrey Allen (2005), "The entrepreneur's business model: Toward a unified perspective," *Journal of Business Research*, 58(6), 726–35.

Morwitz, Vicki G., Joel H. Steckel, and Alok Gupta (2007), "When do purchase intentions predict sales?," *International Journal of Forecasting*, 23(3), 347–64.

Mousavi, Seyedreza, and Haluk Demirkan (2013), "The Key to Social Media Implementation: Bridging Customer Relationship Management to Social Media," in *46th Hawaii International Conference on System Sciences*, Ieee, 718–27.

Moussetis, Robert (2011), "Ansoff revisited: How Ansoff interfaces with both the planning and learning schools of thought in strategy," *Journal of Management History*, 17(1), 102–25.

Mullet, Gary M., and Marvin J. Karson (1985), "Analysis of purchase intent scales weighted by probability of actual purchase," *Journal of Marketing Research*, 22(1), 93–96.

Muñiz, Albert M, and Hope Jensen Schau (2011), "How to inspire value-laden collaborative consumer-generated content," *Business Horizons*, 54, 209–17.

Muniz Jr, Albert M, and Thomas C O'Guinn (2001), "Brand Community," *Journal of Consumer Research*, 27(4), 412–32.

Murdough, Chris (2009), "Social media measurement: It's not impossible," *Journal of Interactive Advertising*, 10(1), 94–100.

Murthy, Dhiraj (2013), *Twitter: Social Communication in the Twitter Age*, Cambridge, UK: Polity Press.

Myers, Seth A., Chenguang Zhu, and Jure Leskovec (2012), "Information Diffusion and External Influence in Networks," in *Proceedings of the 18th ACM SIGKDD International Conference on Knowledge Discovery and Data Mining*, ACM Press, 33.

Naik, Prasad A., and Kay Peters (2009), "A Hierarchical Marketing Communications Model of Online and Offline Media Synergies," *Journal of Interactive Marketing*, 23(4), 288–99.

Nair, Anil, Joseph Trendowski, and William Judge (2008), "The theory of the growth of the firm, by Edith T. Penrose: A review.," *Academy of Management Review*, (Books reviews), 1026–29.

Nakayama, Makoto, Norma Sutcliffe, and Yun Wan (2010), "Has the web transformed experience goods into search goods?," *Electronic Markets*, 20(3-4), 251–62.

National Transportation Safety Board (1990), "Aircraft accident report: Avianca, the airline of columbia Boeing 707-321B, HK 2016 Fuel Exhaustion," Washington, D.C.

Naylor, Rebecca Walker, Cait Poynor Lamberton, and Patricia M. West (2012), "Beyond the 'like' button: the impact of mere virtual presence on brand evaluations and purchase intentions in social media settings," *Journal of Marketing*, 76(November), 105–20.

Neisser, Ulric (1976), *Cognition and reality: Principles and implications of cognitive psychology*, New York, United States: W. H. Freeman and Company.

Nelson, Philip (1970), "Information and consumer behavior," *The Journal of Political Economy*, 78(2), 311–29.

Nelson, Richard R. (1991), "Why do firms differ, and how does it matter?," *Strategic Management Journal*, 12(S2), 61–74.

Netemeyer, Richard G., and Kelly L. Haws (2011), "Involvement, Information Processing, and Affect," in *Handbook of Marketing Scales: Multi-Item Measures for Marketing and Consumer Behavior Research*.

Newman, Mark E. J. (2003), "The structure and function of complex networks," *Society of Industrial and Applied Mathematics Review*, (S. N. Dorogovstev and J. F. F. Mendes, eds.), 45(2), 58.

Nichols, Wes (2013), "Advertising Analytics 2.0," *Harvard Business Review*, (March), 60–68.

Nielsen (2012), "How Digital Influences How We Shop Around the World," *Nielsen Global Survey*, New York, New York, USA.

——— (2014a), "E-commerce: Evolution or revolution in the fast-moving consumer goods world?," New York, NY.

——— (2014b), "The U.S. Digital Consumer Report," New York, NY.

Noble, Andrew, James Anderson, and Sam Thakarar (2015), "Three rules for building the modern retail organization," Boston, Massachusetts, United States.

Noble, Charles H., Stephanie M. Noble, and Mavis T. Adjei (2012), "Let them talk! Managing primary and extended online brand communities for success," *Business Horizons*, 55(5), 475–83.

Nonaka, Ikujiro (2007), "The knowledge-creating company," *Harvard Business Review*.

Novak, Thomas P., and Donna L. Hoffman (1996), "Marketing in Hypermedia Computer-Mediated Environments: Conceptual Foundations," *Journal of Marketing*, 60(3), 50–68.

Noyes, Jan M, and Kate J Garland (2008), "Computer- vs. paper-based tasks: are they equivalent?," *Ergonomics*, 51(9), 1352–75.

Nunally, Jum C., and Ira H. Bernstein (1967), *Psychometric theory*, New York, New York, USA: McGraw-Hill.

O'Reilly, K, and Sherry Marx (2011), "How young, technical consumers assess online WOM credibility," *Qualitative Market Research: An ….*

Obal, Michael, Gordon Burtch, and Werner Kunz (2011), "How Can Social Networking Sites Help Us? The Role of Online Weak Ties in the IMC Mix," *International Journal of Integrated Marketing Communications*, 3(2), 33–47.

Obal, Michael, and Werner Kunz (2013), "Cross-Cultural Differences in the Usage of Online Experts: The Influence of Power Distance and Individualism," *Social Science Research Network (SSRN)*, April(2253630), 1–26.

OECD (2007), "Participative web: User-Created Content."

Oestreicher-Singer, Gal, and Arun Sundararajan (2012), "Recommendation networks and the long tail of electronic commerce," *MIS Quarterly*, 36(1), 65–83.

Oh, Onook, Manish Agrawal, and H. Raghav Rao (2013), "Community Intelligence and Social Media Services: A Rumor Theoretic Analysis of Tweets During Social Crises," *MIS Quarterly*, 37(2), 407–26.

Olshavsky, Richard, and Anand Kumar (2001), "Revealing the actual roles of expectations in consumer satisfaction with experience and credence goods," *Journal of Consumer Satisfaction, Dissatisfaction and Complaining Behaviour*.

Olson, Jerry C. (1978), "Inferential Belief Formation in the Cue Utilization Process," in *Advances in Consumer Research*, K. Hunt, ed., Ann Abor, MI: Association for Consumer Research, 706–13.

Osterwalder, Alexander (2004), "The Business Model Ontology - A Proposition in a Design Science Approach," Ecole des Hautes Etudes Commerciales de l'Université de Lausanne.

Osterwalder, Alexander, Yves Pigneur, and Christopher L. Tucci (2005), "Clarifying business models: Origins, present, and future of the concept," *Communications of the Association for Information Systems*, 15(1), 1–43.

Oude Ophuis, Peter A. M., and Hans C. M. Van Trijp (1995), "Perceived quality: a market driven and consumer oriented approach," *Food quality and Preference*, 3293(94).

Pace, Stefano (2008), "YouTube: an opportunity for consumer narrative analysis?," *Qualitative Market Research: An International Journal*, 11(2), 213–26.

Paek, Hye-Jin, Thomas Hove, Hyun Ju Jeong, and Mikyoung Kim (2011), "Peer or expert? The persuasive impact of YouTube public service announcements producers," *International Journal of Advertising*, 30(1), 161.

Pan, Ming-Chuan, Chih-Ying Kuo, Ching-Ti Pan, and Wei Tu (2013), "Antecedent of purchase intention: online seller reputation, product category and surcharge," *Internet Research*, 23(4), 507–22.

Paolacci, Gabriele, and Jesse Chandler (2014), "Inside the Turk: Understanding Mechanical Turk as a Participant Pool," *Current Directions in Psychological Science*, 23(3), 184–88.

Paolacci, Gabriele, Jesse Chandler, and Panagiotis G. Ipeirotis (2010), "Running experiments on amazon mechanical turk," *Judgment and Decision Making*, 5(5), 411–19.

Parasuraman, A., and Dhruv Grewal (2000), "The Impact of Technology on the Quality-Value-Loyalty Chain: A Research Agenda," *Journal of the Academy of Marketing Science*, 28(1), 168–74.

Park, Do-Hyung, and Jumin Lee (2008), "eWOM overload and its effect on consumer behavioral intention depending on consumer involvement," *Electronic Commerce Research and Applications*, 7(4), 386–98.

Park, JungKun, Frances Gunn, and Sang-Lin Han (2012), "Multidimensional trust building in e-retailing: Cross-cultural differences in trust formation and implications for perceived risk," *Journal of Retailing and Consumer Services*, 19(3), 304–12.

Parker, Sean (2009), "Network effects," *Web 2.0 Summit*, <http://youtu.be/GZautIZJu2Y>.

Patel, Chirag (2013), "Successful service retail channel expansions: The roles of technical and brand integration," *Industrial Marketing Management*.

Patterson, Anthony (2012), "Social-networkers of the world, unite and take over: A meta-introspective perspective on the Facebook brand," *Journal of Business Research*, 65(4), 527–34.

Pavlick, Ellie, Matt Post, Ann Irvine, Dmitry Kachaev, and Chris Callison-Burch (2014), "The Language Demographics of Amazon Mechanical Turk," *Transactions of the Association for Computational Linguistics*, 2, 79–92.

Peer, Eyal, and Gabriele Paolacci (2012), "Selectively recruiting participants from Amazon Mechanical Turk using qualtrics," *SSRN Electronic Journal*.

Pénard, Thierry, and Nicolas Poussing (2010), "Internet Use and Social Capital: The Strength of Virtual Ties," *Journal of Economic Issues*, 44(3), 569–95.

Peng, Mike W., Canan C. Mutlu, Steve Sauerwald, Kevin Y. Au, and Denis Y. L. Wang (2015), "Board interlocks and corporate performance among firms listed abroad," *Journal of Management History*, 21(2), 257–82.

Penrose, Edith (1959), *The theory of the growth of the firm*, London, UK: Basil Blackwell and Mott Ltd.

Perea y Monsuwé, Toñita, Benedict G.C. Dellaert, and Ko de Ruyter (2004), "What drives consumers to shop online? A literature review," *International Journal of Service Industry Management*, 15(1), 102–21.

Peterson, Robert A. (1994), "Meta-analysis of Alpha Cronbach's Coefficient," *Journal of Consumer Research*, 21(2), 381–91.

Phillips, Jean M. (1998), "Effects of Realistic Job Previews on Multiple Organizational Outcomes: a Meta-Analysis," *Academy of Management Journal*, 41(6), 673–90.

Phillips, Lynn W., and Brian Sternthal (1977), "Age differences in information processing: A perspective on the aged consumer," *Journal of Marketing Research*, 14(4), 444–57.

Pitelis, Christos N. (2004), "Edith Penrose and the resource-based view of (international) business strategy," *International Business Review*, 13(4), 523–32.

Poddar, Amit, Naveen Donthu, and Yujie Wei (2009), "Web site customer orientations, Web site quality, and purchase intentions: The role of Web site personality," *Journal of Business Research*, 62(4), 441–50.

Popescu, Manoela (2012), "Psychology of Communication – Between Myth and Reality," *International Journal of Academic Research in Accounting, Finance and Management Sciences*, 2(1), 321–25.

Porter, Michael E. (1985), *Competitive Advantage, Strategic Management*, New York, New York, USA: Free Press.

——— (1991), "A conversation with Michael Porter: International competitive strategy from a European perspective," *European Management Journal*.

——— (1996), "Operational effectiveness is not strategy," *Harvard Business Review*, (December), 61–78.

——— (2001), "Strategy and the Internet," *Harvard Business Review*, 79(1), 63–78.

Porter, Michael E., and Victor E. Millar (1985), "How information gives you competitive advantage," *Harvard Business Review*, 63(4), 149–60.

Portes, Alejandro (1998), "Social Capital: Its Origins and Applications in Modern Sociology," *Annual Review of Sociology*, 24(1), 1–24.

Poster, Mark (1990), *The mode of information: Poststructuralism and social context*.

Potts, Jason, Stuart Cunningham, John Hartley, and Paul Ormerod (2008), "Social network markets: a new definition of the creative industries," *Journal of Cultural Economics*, 32(3), 167–85.

Prabhu, Jaideep C., Rajesh K. Chandy, and Mark E. Ellis (2005), "The impact of acquisitions on innovation: poison pill, placebo, or tonic?," *Journal of Marketing*, 69(January), 114–30.

Preston, CC, and AM Colman (2000), "Optimal number of response categories in rating scales: reliability, validity, discriminating power, and respondent preferences," *Acta psychologica*, 104(1), 1–15.

Procter, Joanne, and Martyn Richards (2002), "Word-of-mouth marketing: beyond pester power," *Young Consumers Insight and Ideas for Responsible Marketers*, 3(3), 3–11.

Qian, Dajun, and Osman Ya (2012), "Diffusion of Real-Time Information in Social-Physical Networks," in *Global Communications Conference (GLOBECOM)*, IEEE, 2072–77.

Qin, Li (2011), "Word-of-Blog for Movies: A Predictor and an Outcome of Box Office Revenue?," *Journal of Electronic Commerce Research*, 12(3), 187–98.

Qu, Zhe, Youwei Wang, Shan Wang, and Yanhui Zhang (2013), "Implications of online social activities for e-tailers' business performance," *European Journal of Marketing*, 47(8), 1190–1212.

Rahtz, Don R., and David L. Moore (1989), "Product class involvement and purchase intent," *Psychology and Marketing*, 6(2), 113–27.

Ramcharran, Harri (2013), "E-Commerce Growth and the Changing Structure of the Retail Sales Industry," *International Journal of E-Business Research*, 9(2), 46–60.

Rawal, Priyanka (2013), "AIDA Marketing Communication Model: Stimulating a purchase decision in the minds of the consumers through a linear progression of steps," *International Journal of Multidisciplinary Research in Social & Management Sciences*, 1(1), 37–44.

Rayburn, Steven W., and Kevin E. Voss (2013), "A model of consumer's retail atmosphere perceptions," *Journal of Retailing and Consumer Services*, 20(4), 400–407.

Rayport, Jeffrey F., and John J. Sviokla (1995), "Exploiting the Virtual Value Chain," *Harvard Business Review*, 73(6), 75–85.

Reagans, Ray (2005), "Preferences, Identity, and Competition: Predicting Tie Strength from Demographic Data," *Management Science*, 51(9), 1374–83.

Reay, I., S. Dick, and J. Miller (2009), "An analysis of privacy signals on the World Wide Web: Past, present and future," *Information Sciences*, 179(8), 1102–15.

Rheingold, Howard (2000), *The Virtual Community: Homesteading on the Electronic Frontier*, The MIT Press.

Rice, Ronald E. (1993), "Media Appropriateness," *Human Communication Research*, 19(4), 451–84.

Richard, Marie-Odile (2005), "Modeling the impact of internet atmospherics on surfer behavior," *Journal of Business Research*, 58(12), 1632–42.

Rigby, Darrell K. (2011), "The future of shopping," *Harvard Business Review*, (December), 65–76.

Rigby, Darrell K., and Suzanne Tager (2014), "Leading a Digical transformation," *Bain & Company*, Boston, Massachusetts, United States.

Rikakis, Thanassis, Aisling Kelliher, and Nicole Lehrer (2013), "Experiential Media and Digital Culture," *IEEE Computer Society*, 46(1), 46–54.

Roest, Henk, and Aric Rindfleisch (2010), "The influence of quality cues and typicality cues on restaurant purchase intention," *Journal of Retailing and Consumer Services*, 17(1), 10–18.

Rose, Daniel E. (2008), "The Information-Seeking Funnel," *National Science Foundation on*

Rose, Susan, Moira Clark, Phillip Samouel, and Neil Hair (2012), "Online Customer Experience in e-Retailing: An empirical model of Antecedents and Outcomes," *Journal of Retailing*, 88(2), 308–22.

Rose, Susan, Neil Hair, and Moira Clark (2011), "Online Customer Experience: A Review of the Business-to-Consumer Online Purchase Context," *International Journal of Management Reviews*, 13, 24–39.

Rosen, Deborah E., and Elizabeth Purinton (2004), "Website design," *Journal of Business Research*, 57(7), 787–94.

Ross, Joel, Lilly Irani, M. Six Silberman, Andrew Zaldivar, and Bill Tomlinson (2010), "Who are the crowdworkers?: shifting demographics in mechanical turk," in *Conference on Human Factors in Computing Systems CHI*, ACM.

Rosvall, Martin, and Carl T Bergstrom (2008), "Maps of random walks on complex networks reveal community structure.," *Proceedings of the National Academy of Sciences of the United States of America*, 105(4), 1118–23.

Rozwell, Carol, and Rita L Sallam (2013), "Hype Cycle for Content and Social Analytics," Gartner Inc. Stamford, CT USA.

Rumelt, Richard P. (1979), "Evaluation of strategy: Theory and models," *Strategic management: A new view of business policy and planning*, 196–212.

Rumelt, Richard P., Dan E. Schendel, and David J. Teece (1994), "Fundamental Issues in Strategy," in *Fundamental Issues in Strategy A Research Agenda*, R. P. Rumelt, D. E. Schendel, and D. J. Teece, eds., Harvard Business School Press, 9–47.

——— (1995), *Fundamental Issues in Strategy: A Research Agenda for the 1990s*, Harvard Business School Press Books.

Sallnäs, Eva-lotta, Kirsten Rassmus-Gröhn, and Calle Sjöström (2001), "Supporting Presence in Collaborative Environments by Haptic Force Feedback," *ACM Transactions on Computer-Human Interaction*, 7(4), 461–76.

Sam, Mohd Fazli Mohd, and Md Nor Hayati Tahir (2009), "Web site quality and consumer online purchase intention of air ticket," *International Journal of Basic & Applied Sciences*, 9(10), 4–9.

San José-Cabezudo, Rebeca, and Carmen Camarero-Izquierdo (2012), "Determinants of opening-forwarding e-mail messages," *Journal of Advertising*, 41(2), 97–112.

Sarvary, M, PM Parker, and MG Dekimpe (2000), "Global diffusion of technological innovations: A coupled-hazard approach," *Journal of Marketing Research*, 37(1), 47–59.

Sashi, C.M. (2012), "Customer engagement, buyer-seller relationships, and social media," *Management Decision*, 50(2), 253–72.

Sautter, Pookie, Michael R. Hyman, and Vaidotas Lukošius (2004), "E-Tail Atmospherics: A Critique of the Literature and Model Extension.," *Journal of Electronic Commerce Research*, 5(1), 14–24.

Schau, Hope Jensen, Albert M Muñiz, and Eric J Arnould (2009), "How Brand Community Practices Create Value," *Journal of Marketing*, 73(5), 30–51.

Schenk, Eric, and Claude Guittard (2009), "Crowdsourcing: What can be Outsourced to the Crowd, and Why?," *Workshop on Open Source Innovation, Strasbourg, France*, 1–29.

Schramm, Wilbur (1954), "How communication works," in *The process and effects of mass communication*, Urbana, Illinois: University of Illinois Press, 3–26.

Schultz, Don E (2010), "Distance Is Measure In More Than Miles," *Marketing News*, 44(9), 11.

Schumpeter, Joseph A. (1934), *The Theory of Economic Development: An Inquiry into Profits, Capital, Credit, Interest, and the Business Cycle*, Harvard University Press, Cambridge, MA. United States.

——— (1942), "Creative destruction," in *Capitalism, socialism and democracy*, New York: Harper, 82–85.

Schwarz, Norbert, Hans-J. Hipper, and Elisabeth Noëlle-Neumann (1992), "Retrospective reports: The impact of response alternatives," in *Autobiographical memory and the validity of retrospective reports*, New York, USA: Springer-Verlag, 187–202.

Scott, William R., and F. Gerald (2007), *Organizations and Organizing: Rational, Natural, and Open System Perspectives*, *Organizations and Organizing*.

Seddon, Peter B., Geoffrey P. Lewis, Phil Freeman, and Graeme Shanks (2004), "The Case for Viewing Business Models as Abstractions of Strategy," *Communications of the Association for Information Systems*, 13(1), 427–42.

Seiders, Kathleen, Glenn B. Voss, Dhruv Grewal, and Andrea L. Godfrey (2005), "Do Satisfied Customers Buy More? Examining Moderating Influences in a Retailing Context," *Journal of Marketing*, 69(4), 26–43.

Seraj, Mina (2012), "We Create, We Connect, We Respect, Therefore We Are: Intellectual, Social, and Cultural Value in Online Communities," *Journal of Interactive Marketing*, 26(4), 209–22.

Shafer, Scott M., H. Jeff Smith, and Jane C. Linder (2005), "The power of business models," *Business Horizons*, 48(3), 199–207.

Shannon, Claude E. (1949), "Communication in the presence of noise," *Proceedings Institute of Radio Engineers*, 37(1), 10–21.

——— (1950), "Memory requirements in a telephone exchange," *Bell System Tech. J.*

——— (1993), *Collected Papers*, (N. J. A. Sloane and A. D. Wyner, eds.), New York, New York, USA: IEEE Press.

Shannon, Claude E., and Warren Weaver (1949), *The Mathematical Theory of Communication*, Urbana,

Shapiro, Carl, and Hal R. Varian (1999), "The Information Economy," in *Information Rules A strategic guide to the Network Economy*, 1–18.

Shaw, Eric H., D.G. Brian Jones, and Paula A. Mclean (2011), "Chapter 2: The Early Schools of Marketing Thought," in *The SAGE Handbook of Marketing Theory*, P. Maclaran, M. Saren, B. Stern, and M. Tadajewski, eds., London, UK: SAGE Publications Ltd, 27–42.

Shaw, R. S., Charlie C. Chen, Albert L. Harris, and Hui-Jou Huang (2009), "The impact of information richness on information security awareness training effectiveness," *Computers & Education*.

Shin, Namchul (2001), "Strategies for Competitive Advantage in Electronic Commerce," *Journal of Electronic Commerce Research*, 2(4), 164–71.

Short, John, Ederyn Williams, and Bruce Christie (1976), *The social psychology of telecommunications*, Hoboken, NJ: John Wiley & Sons, Ltd.

Shriver, Scott K., Harikesh S. Nair, and Reto Hofstetter (2013), "Social Ties and User-Generated Content: Evidence from an Online Social Network," *Management Science*, 59(6), 1425–43.

Silver, C. (2014), "QDA Miner (With WordStat and Simstat)," *Journal of Mixed Methods Research*, 1–2.

Singh, J., and D. Sirdeshmukh (2000), "Agency and Trust Mechanisms in Consumer Satisfaction and Loyalty Judgments," *Journal of the Academy of Marketing Science*, 28(1), 150–67.

Slama, Mark E., and Armen Tashchian (1985), "Selected socioeconomic and demographic characteristics associated with purchasing involvement," *Journal of Marketing*, 49(1), 72–82.

——— (1987), "Validating the SOR paradigm for consumer involvement with a convenience good," *Journal of the Academy of Marketing Science*, 15(1), 36–45.

Smith, Andrew N., Eileen Fischer, and Chen Yongjian (2012), "How Does Brand-related User-generated Content Differ across YouTube, Facebook, and Twitter?," *Journal of Interactive Marketing*, 26(2), 102–13.

Smith, Ted, James R. Coyle, Elizabeth Lightfoot, and Amy Scott (2007), "Reconsidering Models of Influence: The Relationship between Consumer Social Networks and Word-of-Mouth Effectiveness," *Journal of Advertising Research*, 47(4), 387–97.

Snelson, Chareen (2011), "YouTube across the Disciplines: A Review of the Literature," *MERLOT Journal of Online Learning and Teaching*, 7(1), 159–69.

Sonnier, Garrett P., Leigh McAlister, and Oliver J. Rutz (2011), "A Dynamic Model of the Effect of Online Communications on Firm Sales," *Marketing Science*, 30(4), 702–16.

Sood, A, and GJ Tellis (2005), "Technological evolution and radical innovation," *Journal of Marketing*, 69(3), 152–68.

Sorescu, Alina, Ruud T. Frambach, Jagdip Singh, Arvind Rangaswamy, and Cheryl Bridges (2011), "Innovations in Retail Business Models," *Journal of Retailing*, 87(1), S3–16.

Spink, Amanda, and Charles Cole (2004), "A Human Information Behavior Approach to a Philosophy of Information," *Library Trends*, 52(3), 373–80.

Steenkamp, Jan-Benedict E.M. (1990), "Conceptual model of the quality perception process," *Journal of Business Research*, 21(4), 309–33.

Steiman, Melissa Landau, and Mikhia Hawkings (2010), "When Marketing Through Social Media, Legal Risks Can Go Viral," *Intellectual Property & Technology Law Journal*, 22(8), 1–10.

Steinfield, Charles (2002), "Understanding click and mortar e-commerce approaches: A conceptual framework and research agenda," *Journal of Interactive Advertising*, 2(2), 1–10.

Stephen, Andrew T., and Jeff Galak (2012), "The Effects of Traditional and Social Earned Media on Sales: A Study of a Microlending Marketplace," *Journal of Marketing Research*, 49(October).

Steyn, Peter, Åsa Wallström, and Leyland Pitt (2010), "Consumer-generated content and source effects in financial services advertising: An experimental study," *Journal of Financial Services Marketing*, 15(1), 49–61.

Stieglitz, Stefan, and Linh Dang-Xuan (2013), "Emotions and Information Diffusion in Social Media—Sentiment of Microblogs and Sharing Behavior," *Journal of Management Information Systems*, 29(4), 217–48.

Stoeckl, Ralph, Patrick Rohrmeier, and Thomas Hess (2007), "Motivations to produce user generated content: Differences between webloggers and videobloggers," in *20th eConference: Merging and Emerging Technologies, Processes, and Institutions. Bled, Slovenia*, 398–413.

Stone-Romero, Eugene F., Dianna L. Stone, and Dhruv Grewal (1997), "Development of a multidimensional measure of perceived product quality," *Journal of Quality Management*, 2(1), 87–111.

Strutton, David, David G. Taylor, and Kenneth Thompson (2011), "Investigating generational differences in e-WOM behaviours: for advertising purposes, does X = Y?," *International Journal of Advertising*, 30(4), 559.

Sujan, Mita (1985), "Consumer knowledge: Effects on evaluation strategies mediating consumer judgments," *Journal of Consumer Research*, 12(1), 31–46.

Sun, Baohong, and Vicki G. Morwitz (2010), "Stated intentions and purchase behavior: A unified model," *International Journal of Research in Marketing*, 27(4), 356–66.

Sung, Yongjun, Yoojung Kim, Ohyoon Kwon, and Jangho Moon (2010), "An Explorative Study of Korean Consumer Participation in Virtual Brand Communities in Social Network Sites," *Journal of Global Marketing*, 23(5), 430–45.

Sylvester, Chad M., Gordon L. Shulman, Anthony I. Jack, and Maurizio Corbetta (2007), "Asymmetry of anticipatory activity in visual cortex predicts the locus of attention and perception," *The Journal of Neuroscience*, 27(52), 14424–33.

Szybillo, George J., and Jacob Jacoby (1974), "Intrinsic versus extrinsic cues as determinants of perceived product quality.," *Journal of Applied Psychology*, 59(1), 74–78.

Takeuchi', Hirotaka (2013), "Knowledge-Based View of Strategy," *Universia Business Review*, (40), 68–79.

Tan, Gek Woo, and Kwok Kee Wei (2006), "An empirical study of Web browsing behaviour: Towards an effective Website design," *Electronic Commerce Research and Applications*, 5(4), 261–71.

Taylor, David G., Jeffrey E. Lewin, and David Strutton (2011), "Friends, Fans, and Followers: Do Ads Work on Social Networks? How Gender and Age Shape Receptivity," *Journal of Advertising Research*, 51(1), 258.

Teece, David J. (2010), "Business Models, Business Strategy and Innovation," *Long Range Planning*, 43(2-3), 172–94.

Teece, David J., Gary Pisano, and Amy Shuen (1997), "Dynamic capabilities and strategic management," *Strategic Management Journal*, 18(7), 509–33.

Teixeira, Thales (2012), "The new science of viral ads," *Harvard Business Review*, 90(March), 25–28.

Teltzrow, Maximilian, Bertolt Meyer, and Hans-Joachim Lenz (2007), "Multi-channel consumer perceptions," *Journal of Electronic Commerce Research*, 8(1), 18–31.

The Economic Intelligence Unit (2012), "Agent of change," London, UK.

Thomas Aichner, and Frank Jacob (2015), "Measuring the Degree of Corporate Social Media Use," *International Journal of Market Research*, 57(2), 257–75.

Timmerman, C. Erik, and S. Naga Madhavapeddi (2008), "Perceptions of Organizational Media Richness: Channel Expansion Effects for Electronic and Traditional Media Across Richness Dimensions," *IEEE Transactions on Professional Communication*, 51(1), 18–32.

Timmers, Paul (1998), "Business Models for Electronic Markets," *Electronic-Markets*, 8, 3–8.

Tiryakioglu, Filiz, and Funda Erzurum (2011), "Use of Social Networks as an Education Tool," *Contemporary Educational Technology*, 2(2), 135–50.

Todd, Jick D. (1979), "Mixing qualitative and quantitative methods: Triangulation in action," *Administrative Science Quarterly*, 24(4), 602–11.

Tongia, Rahul, and Ernest J. Wilson III (2011), "The flip side of Metcalfe's law: Multiple and growing costs of network exclusion," *International Journal of Communication*, 5(1), 665–81.

Trusov, Michael, A Bodapati, and RE Bucklin (2009), "Determining influential users in internet social networks," *Journal of Marketing Research*, XLVII(August), 643–58.

Trusov, Michael, Randolph E Bucklin, and Koen Pauwels (2009), "Effects of Word-of-Mouth Versus Traditional Marketing: Findings from an Internet Social Networking Site," *Journal of Marketing*, 73(September), 90–102.

Tu, Chih-Hsiung, and Marina McIsaac (2002), "The relationship of social presence and interaction in online classes," *The American Journal of Distance Education*, 16(3), 131–50.

Tulving, Endel, and Donald M. Thomson (1973), "Encoding specificity and retrieval processes in episodic memory.," *Psychological Review*, 80(5), 352–73.

Tumasjan, Andranik, Timm O. Sprenger, Philipp G. Sandner, and Isabell M. Welpe (2010), "Predicting Elections with Twitter: What 140 Characters Reveal about Political Sentiment," in *Proceedings of the Fourth International AAAI Conference on Weblogs and Social Media*, 178–85.

Turley, L. W., and Ronald E. Milliman (2000), "Atmospheric effects on shopping behavior: a review of the experimental evidence," *Journal of Business Research*, 49, 193–211.

Tushman, Michael L., and David a. Nadler (1978), "Information Processing as an Integrating Concept in Organizational Design," *The Academy of Management Review*, 3(3), 613.

United Kingdom National Archives (2012), "Education System in the United Kingdom," *GOB.UK*, <https://www.gov.uk/government/uploads/system/uploads/attachment_data/file/219167/v01-2012ukes.pdf>.

United Kingdom Office for National Statistics (2013a), "The Effects of Taxes and Benefits on Household Income," London, UK.

——— (2013b), "Key Statistics and Quick Statistics for local authorities in the United Kingdom," London, UK.

United States Census Bureau (2012), "Current Population Survey," Washington, D.C.

——— (2013), "Educational Attainment of the Population 18 Years and Over, by Age, Sex, Race, and Hispanic Origin: 2013," Washington, D.C.

——— (2014a), "Income and Poverty in the United States: 2013," Washington, D.C.

——— (2014b), "Computer and Internet Use in the United States: 2013 American Community Survey Reports," Washington, D.C.

United States Census Bureau News (2014), "Quarterly Retail E-Commerce Sales," Washington, D.C.

De Valck, Kristine, Gerrit H. Van Bruggen, and Berend Wierenga (2009), "Virtual communities: A marketing perspective," *Decision Support Systems*, 47(3), 185–203.

De Vaus, David (2011), *Research Design in Social Research*, Research Design in Social Research, London, UK: SAGE Publications.

Vázquez-Casielles, Rodolfo, Leticia Suarez-Alvarez, and Ana-Belén del Río-Lanza (2013), "The Word of Mouth Dynamic: How Positive (and Negative) WOM Drives Purchase Probability: An Analysis of Interpersonal and Non-Interpersonal Factors," *Journal of Advertising Research*, 53(1), 43.

Vessey, Iris, and Dennis Galletta (1991), "Cognitive Fit: An Empirical Study of Information Acquisition," *Information Systems Research*, 2(1), 63–84.

Villanueva, Julian (2008), "The impact of marketing-induced versus word-of-mouth customer acquisition on customer equity growth," *Journal of Marketing Research*, XLV(February), 48–59.

Visser, Penny S., Jon A. Krosnick, and Paul J. Lavrakas (2000), "Chapter 9: Survey research," in *Handbook of research methods in social and personality psychology*, 223–52.

Wakefield, Jane (2015), "Amazon opens physical bookshop in Seattle," *BBC News*, London, UK.

Walker, Gordon, Bruce Kogut, and Weijian Shan (1997), "Social Capital, Structural Holes and the Formation of an Industry Network," *Organization Science*, 8(2), 109–25.

Walters, David (2004), "A business model for the new economy," *International Journal of Physical Distribution & Logistics Management*.

Wang, Fang, Milena Head, and Norm Archer (2002), "E-tailing: An analysis of web impacts on the retail market," *Journal of Business Strategies*.

Wang, Yong Jian, Michael S. Minor, and Jie Wei (2011), "Aesthetics and the online shopping environment: Understanding consumer responses," *Journal of Retailing*, 87(1), 46–58.

Wasserman, Stanley, and Katherine Faust (1994), *Social Network Analysis: Methods and Applications*, *Social Networks*, Structural analysis in the social sciences, 8, (M. Granovetter, ed.), Cambridge University Press.

Waters, Richard D., and Paul M. Jones (2011), "Using Video to Build an Organization's Identity and Brand: A Content Analysis of Nonprofit Organizations' YouTube Videos," *Journal of Nonprofit Public Sector Marketing*, 23(3), 248–68.

Watts, Duncan J. (2004), "The' new' science of networks," *Annual review of sociology*, 30, 243–70.

Watts, Duncan J., Peter Sheridan Dodds, and Mark E. J. Newman (2002), "Identity and Search in Social Networks," *Science*, 296(5571), 4.

Watts, Duncan J., and Steven H. Strogatz (1998), "Collective dynamics of 'small-world' networks.," *Nature*, (M. Newman, A.-L. Barabási, and D. J. Watts, eds.), 393(6684), 440–42.

Wei, Chun-Wang, Nian-Shing Chen, and Kinshuk (2012), "A model for social presence in online classrooms," *EducationTechnology Research and Development*, 60(3), 529–45.

Weill, Peter, and Stephanie L. Woerner (2013), "Business Model Optimizing Your Digital Business Model," *MIT Sloan Management Review*, 54(3), 70–78.

Weisberg, Jacob, Dov Te'eni, and Limor Arman (2011), "Past purchase and intention to purchase in e-commerce: The mediation of social presence and trust," *Internet Research*, 21(1), 82–96.

Wen, Chen, Bernard C.Y. Tan, and Klarissa Ting-Ting Chang (2009), "Advertising effectiveness on social network sites: An investigation of tie strength, endorser expertise and product type on consumer purchase intention," in *International Conference on Information Systems*, 1–19.

West, Richard L., and Lynn H. Turner (2003), *Introducing communication theory: analysis and application*, New York, New York, USA: McGraw-Hill Humanities/Social Sciences/Languages.

——— (2010), *Introducing communication theory: analysis and application*, New York, New York, USA: McGraw-Hill Humanities/Social Sciences/Languages.

Wiener, Morton, and Albert Mehrabian (1968), *Language within language: Immediacy, a channel in verbal communication*, Ardent Media.

Wijaya, Bambang Sukma (2012), "The development of hierarchy of effects model in advertising," *International Research Journal of Business Studies*, 5(1), 1–7.

Wind, Jerry, and Vijay Mahajan (2002), *Digital Marketing: Global Strategies from the World's Leading Experts*, Wiley.

De Winter, Joost (2013), "Using the Student's t -test with extremely small sample sizes," *Practcial Assessment, Research & Evalutaion*, 18(10), 1–12.

Wirtz, Bernd W., Oliver Schilke, and Sebastian Ullrich (2010), "Strategic Development of Business Models," *Long Range Planning*, 43(2-3), 272–90.

Wolfram Alpha (2014), "Average English Word Length," *Computational Knowledge Engine*.

Wood, Andrew F., and Matthew J. Smith (2001), *Online communication: Linking technology, identity, & culture*, Mahwah, NJ. United States: Lawrence Erlbaum Associates.

Wood, Charles M., and Lisa K. Scheer (1996), "Incorporating Perceived Risk into Models of Consumer Deal Assessment and Purchase Intent.," *Advances in Consumer research*, (1985), 399–405.

Wrench, Jason S., and Narissra M. Punyanunt-Carter (2007), "The Relationship between Computer-Mediated-Communication Competence, Apprehension, Self-Efficacy, Perceived Confidence, and Social Presence," *Southern Communication Journal*, 72(4), 355–78.

Wright, Kevin B. (2005), "Researching Internet-Based Populations: Advantages and Disadvantages of Online Survey Research, Online Questionnaire Authoring Software Packages, and Web Survey Services," *Journal of Computer-Mediated Communication*, 10(3).

Wu, Juanjuan, Hae Won Ju, Jieun Kim, Cara Damminga, Hye-Young Kim, and Kim K.P. Johnson (2013), "Fashion product display: An experiment with Mockshop investigating colour, visual texture, and style coordination," *International Journal of Retail & Distribution Management*, 41(10), 765–89.

Xiang, Zheng, and Ulrike Gretzel (2010), "Role of social media in online travel information search," *Tourism Management*, 31(2), 179–88.

Xiu-he, Yu, Guo Xi-tong, and Yao Qi-yan (2011), *The effect of online word-of-mouth in electronic markets: An investigation of the culture differences in the Chinese and U.S. contexts*, 2011 International Conference on Management Science Engineering 18th Annual Conference Proceedings, IEEE, 34–40.

Xu, Bo Xu Bo, and Lu Liu Lu Liu (2010), *Information diffusion through online social networks*, Emergency Management and Management Sciences ICEMMS 2010 IEEE International Conference on, IEEE, 53–56.

Yagan, Osman, Dajun Qian, Junshan Zhang, and Douglas Cochran (2013), "Conjoining Speeds up Information Diffusion in Overlaying Social-Physical Networks," in *IEEE Journal on Selected Areas in Communications*, 1038–48.

Yang, Chyan, Yi-Chun Hsu, and Suyanti Tan (2010), "Predicting the determinants of users' intentions for using YouTube to share video: moderating gender effects.," *Cyberpsychology behavior and social networking*, 13(2), 141–52.

Yang, Jun, Enping (Shirley) Mai, and Joseph Ben-Ur (2012), "Did you tell me the truth? The influence of online community on eWOM," *International Journal of Market Research*, 54(3), 369–90.

Yang, Taining (2012), "The decision behavior of Facebook users," *Journal of Computer Information Systems*, (Spring), 50–59.

Yao, Song, and Carl F. Mela (2011), "A Dynamic Model of Sponsored Search Advertising," *Marketing Science*, 30(3), 447–68.

Ye, Qiang, Rob Law, Bin Gu, and Wei Chen (2011), "The influence of user-generated content on traveler behavior: An empirical investigation on the effects of e-word-of-mouth to hotel online bookings," *Computers in Human Behavior*, 27(2), 634–39.

Yeasmin, Sabina, and Khan Ferdousour Rahman (2012), "'Triangulation' Research Method as the Tool of Social Science Research," *Bup Journal*, 1(1), 154–63.

Yen, Benjamin, and Yihong Yao (2015), *The Internet of things (IoT): Shaping the future of e-commerce*, Harvard Business Review, 1–15.

Yip, George S. (2004), "Using Strategy to Change Your Business Model," *Business Strategy Review*, 15(2), 17–24.

Yoo, Y, and M Alavi (2001), "Media and group cohesion: Relative influences on social presence, task participation, and group consensus," *MIS Quarterly*, 25(3), 371–90.

Yudelson, Julian (1999), "Adapting McCarthy's Four P's for the Twenty-First Century," *Journal of Marketing Education*, 21(1), 60–67.

Zailskaite-Jakste, Ligita, and Rita Kuvykaite (2012), "Implementation of Communication in Social Media by Promoting Studies at Higher Education Institutions," *Journal of Engineering Economics*, 23(2), 174–88.

Zeithaml, Valerie A. (1988), "Consumer Perceptions of Price, Quality, and Value: A Means-End Model and Synthesis of Evidence," *Journal of Marketing*, 52(July), 2–22.

Zemanek, H. (1990), "Philosophy of information processing," *Fresenius' Journal of Analytical Chemistry*, 337(2), 176–85.

Zhou, Lianxi, Zhiyong Yang, and Michael K. Hui (2009), "Non-local or local brands? A multi-level investigation into confidence in brand origin identification and its strategic implications," *Journal of the Academy of Marketing Science*, 38(2), 202–18.

Zhou, Zhimin, Qiyuan Zhang, Chenting Su, and Nan Zhou (2012), "How do brand communities generate brand relationships? Intermediate mechanisms," *Journal of Business Research*, 65(7), 890–95.

Ziefle, M (1998), "Effects of display resolution on visual performance," *Human factors*, 40(4), 554–68.

Zikmund, William A., Barry J. Babin, Jon C. Carr, and Mitch Griffin (2012), *Business Research Methods*, Cengage Learning.

Zimmermann, Christian (2000), "Information Rules: A Strategic Guide to the Network Economy by Carl Shapiro and Hal R. Varian. Review," *Journal of Economic Literature*, 38(2), 425–26.

Zott, Christoph, and Raphael Amit (2007), "Business Model Design and the Performance of Entrepreneurial Firms," *Organization Science*, 18(2), 181–99.

——— (2008), "The fit between product market strategy and business model: Implications for firm performance," *Strategic Management Journal*, 29(1), 1–26.

——— (2010), "Business Model Design: An Activity System Perspective," *Long Range Planning*, 43(2-3), 216–26.

Zott, Christoph, Raphael Amit, and Jon Donlevy (2000), "Strategies for value creation in e-commerce: Best practice in Europe," *European Management Journal*, 18(5), 463–75.

Zott, Christoph, Raphael Amit, and Lorenzo Massa (2011), "The Business Model: Recent Developments and Future Research," *Journal of Management*, 37(4), 1019–42.

Made in the USA
Middletown, DE
28 February 2018